T0270562

Hack to the Future

How World Governments Relentlessly Pursue and Domesticate Hackers

Emily Crose

WILEY

Library of Congress Cataloging in Publication data available on request.

Cover images: Laptop: © SynchR/Getty Images,
                Skull: © Aleksei Elkin/Getty Images,
                Type: © revel.stockart/Getty Images,
                Stamp: © reservoir dots/Shutterstock
Cover design: Wiley

SKY10087502_101124

Dedicated to my wife, who supports my hair-brained schemes, and the community of hackers who brought me here.

Contents at a Glance

Contents

Introduction

O ver the course of the last 50 years, a subculture of technical geeks have gone from a small regionally separated group to one of the most powerful and mysterious forces in world politics. The public's perception of hackers has been heavily influenced through three main sources: how the media portrays them, how the government interacts with them, and how hackers represent themselves through their actions and the culture they create.

Amateur hackers of the 1970s were proceeded by engineers at elite universities and military organizations who developed the technologies of the future behind locked doors. When these advanced-for-their-time computer technologies escaped the walls of highly funded laboratories, they fell into the hands of a preexisting coterie of proto-hackers called *phone phreakers*. How these early hackers went from a barely noticeable nuisance to sitting in the back rooms with modern political hatchet-men in roughly 40 years is the subject of this book.

Technology has taken such a major part of everyday life that nearly everyone has some understanding of what cybersecurity is and why it's important. Although hacking as we think of it today exists as a fairly mainstream activity, it took several decades to achieve the respect it has today. The growth of modern consumer technology, and the industry of security that has been built up around it, has been forged by a dedicated cohort of nerds with the time, financial resources, and passion to create it. (I use the term *nerd* lovingly and apply it to myself.)

Writing a book about something as esoteric as *hacker culture* and how it came became prevalent is a challenge. Defining such a diverse group that has been around in one form or another for at least a century in its modern form is a difficult answer to give. Over the years, even the term *hacking* has been seen as controversial, especially among hackers themselves. Depending on who hears the term, it might inspire a range of emotional responses from unearned pride to stomach-turning cringe.

Some in the hacking community may recoil at the use of this term due to how wildly overgeneralized it is. At different times, the term *hacker* has been used as a way to demonize us or create guilt by association, unfairly implying that all of those who find ways of subverting technology are somehow definitionally criminal. At other times, the term has been overused to the point of being cliché. Admittedly, the words *hacker* and *hacking* are easy cultural touchpoints for people both inside and outside of the global community of hackers.

In spite of their controversial nature, I have chosen to use terms like *hacker*, *hacking*, and *hacking community* because they are a middle ground between outsiders, aspirational observers, and the wide spectrum of experts who these terms have described over the decades. Readers of this book should therefore understand that, in many cases, there are more accurate terms for practitioners of specific types of modern security.

The relationship between hackers and their governments is a mixed bag. Modern hackers are a product of the mistrustful Cold War era, which explains a lot about why their relationship with law enforcement was so fraught. Cold War fears of communism created a broader tribalistic fear of outsiders. During the Cold

War, fear of people who were considered "weird" became synonymous with America's fear of communism.

The same sort of skepticism hackers faced in the 1970s and 1980s was a milder version of previous moral panics, such as the Lavender Scare of the 1950s in which members of the latent LGBT community were seen as a threat to American stability. During this period, hundreds of queer government employees lost their jobs as a result of McCarthy-like purges. Although McCarthy's ultimate disgrace and public censure in 1954 were a firm rebuke of the sort of "witch hunt" politics he championed, fear of outsiders never went out of style.

As institutions of authority, governments have a natural skepticism of any person or group threatening to undermine that authority. This is true throughout the world. When I began writing this book, I didn't want to retread well-worn paths, examining specific individuals or groups in painstaking detail. For the individuals who I cover in this book, I mention their stories only as milestones in a long and complicated history. Many of them have written autobiographies that I encourage my audience to read. They are talented professional writers who will tell their stories with higher fidelity than I would ever be able to.

Instead, the goal of this book is to examine the contours of the history of hacking as seen primarily through three different perspectives: art, government, and from the viewpoint of hackers themselves. I have also tried to take a global approach to the material in this book in recognition that hacking has never been the exclusive dominion of one nationality. In fact, some of the most talented hackers in the world come from places you may least expect.

No matter where in the world hackers come from, a government somewhere has relentlessly pursued them, be it the American government and the legendary hackers of Melbourne,

Australia, or the Chilean government's pursuit of cybernetics genius Stafford Beer. Hacking is a team sport, and to apply a nationalistic bias, especially in today's interconnected world, would be both outdated and naïve.

What Does This Book Cover?

This book covers the following topics:

Chapter 1: A Subculture Explained   A re-telling of the 1903 story of magician Nevil Maskelyne and how his live disruption of a demonstration of Guglielmo Marconi's radio system illustrates the early roots of hacker culture, defined by curiosity, mischief, defiance, and perseverance. It also explores the evolution of the hacker community, its diverse nature, common values, and the shifting perceptions surrounding hackers.

Chapter 2: Uncle Sam and Technology   An examination of U.S. government history and the pre-internet employment of hackers and engineers in various agencies, including NASA, the military, and three-letter intelligence agencies such as the FBI, NSA, and CIA.

Chapter 3: Commercializing Technology   This chapter covers the development of modern consumer technology, specifically the Plain Old Telephone System (POTS), and the foundations of the modern hacking community within the phone phreaking community.

Chapter 4: Digital Disruption   In the 1970s, researchers in American tech labs began researching and theorizing ways to break the very same computer systems they were busy building.

Chapter 5: Hacker Rehabilitation   An analysis of some of the earliest hacks against the American government and how hackers got a second chance at redemption.

Chapter 6: On the Other Side of The Wall Why exactly did hacking develop in the way it did in the United States? What were some of the conditions that led to computer hacking being so prevalent inside America's Cold War borders?

Chapter 7: Hackers of the World, Unite! How early attempts to create computer networks developed outside of the context of North America, including a look at how some of the earliest European hacking groups got started.

Chapter 8: Electronic Delinquents American spy agencies begin to take an interest in computer networks, using emerging research into ARPANET as a model for their own classified computer systems. Law enforcement also takes an interest in the activities of hackers, testing legal efforts to crack down on them.

Chapter 9: Hackers Go Mainstream Two of the most prolific hackers of the 1980s and 1990s are apprehended, both marking the end of an era and the beginning of a new life for the global hacking community at large.

Chapter 10: The DEF CON Effect The acceptance of hackers continues to grow, resulting in the birth of an entire industry of computer security.

Chapter 11: In from the Cold The American government recognizes the potential value of embracing hackers and changes their approach to both prosecute *and* recruit them.

Chapter 12: Anonymous A new strain of hacktivism surprises governments and powerful private organizations throughout the world. New approaches are developed to respond to hackers in this new age.

Chapter 13: Spy vs. Spy American law enforcement finds an effective way of recruiting hacktivists to become informants against their own. The FBI finally finds a way to partner with hackers to achieve its national defense goals.

Chapter 14: Cybernetting Society An analysis of the effect broadband Internet and mobile Internet-connected devices had on voting populations in the early 2010s. Hackers show their stripes in various global revolutions, becoming active participants in conflict of their own volition.

Chapter 15: Hackers Unleashed Governments around the world begin to integrate hackers into their ranks, using their talents to influence geopolitics through military and intelligence operations.

Chapter 16: Cyberwar Hackers find themselves in life-and-death geopolitical conflict, the implications of which threaten global stability.

Chapter 17: Politics As Usual The world of politics finds uses for hackers, although the intentions of those hackers are unclear. Boundaries are redrawn as hacking becomes a legitimate pathway to political power.

Epilogue A final look at the current state of hacking, including the aftermath of the mid-2010s elections, and how national governments plan to forge new policies and relationships with hackers.

The Pre-Broadband Era

The pre-broadband era was to hackers what the Seven Seas was for age-of-sail explorers: a place of boundless possibility and few guardrails to protect innocent computer users. Being online during the pre-broadband age took a great deal of interest and technical competence. These two factors effectively acted as gatekeepers, promising entry to the hidden online world. Before broadband Internet, there were two distinct worlds: the online world and the real world. Entering one of these worlds meant that a user needed to leave the other, but the necessity to disconnect kept visitors to the online world tethered to the reality outside their window.

1

A Subculture Explained

A storm was brewing in the United Kingdom in June a, 1903. It wasn't the historic rain storm that fell over the United Kingdom that same year, but a very different kind of storm that would mark the beginning of an age of technology-fueled communication. This communication age would act as a cultural touchstone stretching over 100 years into the future with ripples that have reached our current day.

Arthur Blok, a young assistant to a scientist named Sir John Ambrose Fleming, was sitting in a lecture hall at London's Royal Institute, working on a demonstration of wireless radio technology. Ambrose was present as an "unimpeachable witness" to the operation of Guglielmo Marconi's wireless "syntonic" technology. Ambrose himself was an accomplished inventor with 20 years of experience in electrical engineering and physics. He had been following Marconi's innovations in radio for years and had even staked his own reputation on Marconi's technology.

This demonstration was a proof of concept of Marconi's radio technology, showing the public the viability of long-distance wireless transmissions sent from a site in Cornwall, in the southwest of the United Kingdom. The messages were then to be received at a listening post in Chelmsford, located in the southeast. Once there, the messages would be rebroadcast to the Royal Institute in London, which had constructed a 60 foot tower on the roof of the demonstration hall especially for this occasion. In the months before the Royal Institute demonstration, Marconi had made public claims about the security of his technology. In an article published on February 9, 1903, in the *St. James Gazette*, the following exchange was had between the reporter and Marconi[1]:

Reporter: "Do you admit the possibility of tapping?

Marconi: "Theoretically, the messages may be tapped. During the experiments on the Carlo Alberto, an installation was set up close to our station and tapping did take place, but then no attempt was made at secrecy. . . ."

The reporter then asked Mr. Marconi, "Do you say then, Mr. Marconi, that you can confine the currents?"

To which Marconi replied, "Not exactly confine them, but I can tune my instruments so that no other instrument that is not similarly tuned can tap my messages. . . ."

Radio signal interception was a hot topic in 1903, with many advanced nations not only beginning to adopt radio technology in their overseas communications (including diplomatic and wartime transmissions) but also dabbling in early efforts to intercept radio communications.

---

[1] St. James Gazette Feb 9, 1903

Inside the Royal Institute, Blok was busy tending to the radio equipment that would be used in the demonstration. Unexpectedly, Blok heard an incoming message. The demonstration wasn't supposed to officially start for a few more minutes, but the rhythmic flashing of an arc lamp attached to the radio equipment confirmed that a message was indeed coming through. In a 1958 interview, Blok remembers what happened in the Royal Institute that day vividly,

> *But when I plainly heard the astounding word "rats" spelt out in Morse, the matter took on a new aspect. And when this irrelevant word was repeated, suspicion gave place to fear.*

Not only was this unusual, but it was also alarming. Had something inside the system malfunctioned? His worst fears would be confirmed a moment later with a message that was a coherent series of words. They were rude but poetic, and began,

> *There was a young fellow of Italy*
> *Who diddled the public quite prettily. . .*

The poem was aimed at Marconi, who was an Italian immigrant. This crass poem confirmed that some form of sabotage was at play. When Marconi was notified of the interference, he had an idea of who could've sent such a message.

Nevil Maskelyne, a stage magician by trade, was supposed to be in attendance in the lecture hall that day. Instead, he had decided to construct his own antenna. Sitting in a room nearby the Royal Institute, Maskelyne timed his attack perfectly. He was a known competitor of Marconi. In the weeks before the public Royal Institute demonstration, Maskelyne had challenged Marconi's monopoly of wireless technology, which had prohibited other scientists like Maskelyne from doing their own experiments and patenting similar radio technologies.

After losing a contract to Marconi to provide wireless services to Lloyd's of London, Maskelyne abandoned commercially competing with Marconi and set his focus on sabotaging Marconi personally. The hijacking of the Marconi-Fleming demonstration had proven to the public that Marconi's claims of syntonic transmission weren't entirely accurate and had completely ruined the professional reputation of Mr. Fleming. The hijacking also stained Marconi's reputation as well, although Marconi would go on to be recognized for his achievements in radio technology regardless.

This event was an important milestone in the development of at least one cornerstone of what we might now refer to as *hacker culture*. Maskelyne not only gave us an early example of *spamming* (i.e., repeating the word *rats* in an attempt to jam the legitimate transmission sent to the Royal Institute), he also pioneered what we would later call *trolling*. A direct result of the incident was a "flame war" between Maskelyne and Marconi, with each publicly condemning the other over their activities both in business and technology.

Although Maskelyne came from a wealthy family, he possessed what we might now consider to be a "hacker" ethos. He was a self-educated electrician who had been working with wireless technology for a few years before he hijacked Marconi's demonstration. By 1900, he had already managed to get the public's attention through high-profile demonstrations of his own wireless experiments and had established himself as an expert in wireless technology among his peers.

In one such demonstration, Maskelyne sent a radio message from a ground station up to a flying hot-air balloon, an almost-recognizable version of *stunt hacking* today. In another demonstration, he used a radio transmitter to remotely ignite gunpowder. Always the showman, he made a spectacle of his technological ideas.

In the Maskelyne affair, we can see how the threads of a culture form seemingly out of nowhere. Even though there were no terms at the time that could be used to specifically describe Maskelyne's activities, he was using techniques that made the most sense for him at the time. For example, crowding out a single channel communication system with nonsense messages is a problem that persists today.

Today, the Maskelyne affair has become obscure even among members of this hacking community who can trace its lineage back to this event. Modern hackers don't interact with the Maskelyne affair for its cultural value. In fact, it isn't thought of much at all.

Defining a Community

Popular media has created a certain hacker stereotype that has been reinforced in television and movies for decades. In the 1980s and 1990s, the stereotype was a smart and carefree teenager who used their knowledge and access to create disruptions, either intentionally or unintentionally. They're often shown wearing hoodies (with the hood up, while alone inside the house) and sometimes wearing sunglasses to cover their eyes. You might even see them wearing gloves to keep their fingerprints off their keyboards (to minimize evidence, of course) as they commit esoteric acts of cybercrime.

During the 2016 election, candidate Donald Trump even referenced a well-known trope of the "400-pound guy on his bed" as the likely culprit for a hack of the Democratic National Committee (DNC), which is thought to have had an impact on that election. Popular depictions also tend to show hackers as white men, which isn't an all-around accurate depiction either.

The global community of hackers has been as diverse and vibrant as the general population. What has changed from decade to decade within the hacker community has been the treatment of this group by outside influence. This outside influence has had a major impact on the development of new generations of hackers coming up within the community. One major influence has been world governments trying to figure out the best way to govern this population.

Despite the ever-changing public understanding of exactly what a hacker is, there are some true commonalities that tend to define this notoriously mercurial group.

Common Hacking Virtues

One place we can look for broad definitions and commonalities about hackers is in a common system of values. It's important to remember that not all hackers will maintain the same value system in the same way as any other member of the same community. Many hackers choose to associate themselves with some common qualities that they may feel improve their work. The following is a discussion of values that many hackers feel applies to them.

Curiosity

Despite being a cliché, *curiosity* is a common trait of the hacker personality. When presented with a locked box, the average hacker will want to use every tool in their arsenal to open it just to find out what's inside. Unsurprisingly, puzzles are popular with hackers. It's common to find puzzle-based games at hacker conferences throughout the world hosted in rooms full of people all tinkering and finagling data and exploits to break into computers specially designed to be breached by these hackers.

It's common for hackers to be unsatisfied by being told they can't do something. Regardless of how big a technical challenge may be, hackers are often willing to spend hundreds of hours of their personal time focused on solving a niche problem. Even when no financial gain is offered, the reward is simply the feeling of accomplishment.

What happens if I push this button in just this way? What if I offer this prompt too much information? What if I offer it not enough? What if I give it something that it doesn't expect entirely? Hackers are excited by the prospect of discovering something that nobody even knew was there, possibly even discovering something that wasn't intended to exist at all. This is the power of curiosity that hackers feel, and when they finally find it, the feeling of discovery can be intoxicating.

Mischief

Just as strong as the drive of satisfied curiosity among hackers is the motivation to do pranks. Most hackers have a wonderful sense of humor that they reflect in the outcomes of their hacks, and often in the code they write. After all, who needs money when you can have a good laugh?

Sometimes, it's difficult for the average person to know why some hackers do the things that they do. As we'll see in future chapters, sometimes *mischief* is the point. In the hacker community, pranks come in many forms—sometimes appearing as pranks "just for the lulz" and sometimes appearing as mean-spirited "flame wars" that end with personal attacks and private information being published. Whatever form mischief takes, these pranks are forms of self-expression that can be worth more than just money.

After all, the only thing more satisfying than defeating the unbreakable security of a friend's web server is defacing his web page with a message declaring your own superiority. Gaining unauthorized access to a system thought to be secure is a recipe for mischief and chaos, and it is often done in good humor. . .but not always.

Defiance

Hackers don't like to be told something can't be done. Whether something can't be done for legal or technical reasons, hackers thrive on the chase of proving their naysayers wrong. There's a famous hacker trope about "voiding warranties." Because product warranties typically require that users don't modify the product's hardware or software for a warranty to remain effective, *defying* the terms of a warranty and purposefully voiding the terms of service is a hacker's rite of passage.

In the same way that the *Titanic* was considered unsinkable, some products are marketed as "unhackable." The fastest way to prove that a product is indeed "hackable" is to declare it is perfectly secure, yet even marketers continue to tempt fate by inviting hackers to prove their claims wrong. We see this level of hubris in modern marketing, as we can clearly see as far back as the Maskelyne Affair.

Perseverance

One of the most recognizable keys to success for modern tech startups is the concept of "fail fast." Fail fast dictates that solutions should be developed quickly and prove their value or "fail fast" so that a new attempt can be made. This approach to discovery relies on an attitude of *perseverance* to be successful. Hackers have also come to adopt the same attitude whether they're building something that has never been built before, coding something new and complex, or finding a way to get into a secure system.

Most hackers are willing to spend days (or even weeks) on a single problem, single-mindedly focused on finding a solution before they can move onto a new challenge. It's common to hear this focus attributed by hackers themselves to a diagnosis of attention deficit hyperactive disorder (ADHD). Whatever may be the cause of this uncanny focus and dedication, the effect on problem-solving is undeniable.

Terms

One of the first things to deal with when talking about hackers and their community is their relationship with the term *hacker* itself. Not everyone in the community likes to be referred to as a hacker. Some in the community feel that the term is dated, is inaccurate, or has a generally negative connotation. The Oxford dictionary defines a hacker as "A person who uses computers to gain unauthorized access to data." A second definition of the term is "An enthusiastic and skillful computer programmer or user." Both definitions do not acknowledge entire segments of the community of tinkerers to whom the modern use of the term typically applies.

For example, neither definition includes members of the community who participate in *hardware hacking*. Hardware hackers can be found sitting at a workbench carefully soldering contacts onto printed circuit boards or rigging components together to create unique devices for other purposes, such as long-range communications or Wi-Fi hacking. Their creations can be highly functional, beautiful pieces of art, or both at the same time! Despite not being explicitly mentioned by the dictionary definition of hacking, they are no less important to the culture of the community.

One may wonder, if the term is so controversial and inaccurate, why bother using the term at all? Despite being inexact, the terms *hacker* and *hacking* are the most convenient terms we currently have to describe members of this broad community and their activities.

The truth is the malicious connotation of the term *hacker* was placed on the community by the news media over decades of covering the actions of those who rightly or wrongly attracted the attention of law enforcement.

In fact, law enforcement attention hasn't always been deserved. The legal system notoriously lags significantly far behind the development of new technologies to the point that hackers have become comfortable occasionally operating in a legal gray area. As one example, some security researchers examine products to assess their security value. Doing this can come with certain risks that may include legal liability. In the past, security researchers working in good faith intending to improve the security for all the users of a given system, have faced lawsuits from the same corporations who rejected taking actions on their findings.

The concept of *responsible disclosure* was born from the need of security researchers who had just found a security vulnerability and shared that vulnerability with the vendor of the product containing the vulnerability. Hackers who stay within legal, ethical, and moral boundaries with their activities may refer to themselves as *white hat*.

The term *white hat* comes from the Western genre, where the virtuous hero always dons a white-colored hat. The white-hat cowboy fights for good against the forces of evil using a superior set of values—truth, justice, and, of course, the American way. We tend to see the white hat as a one-dimensional avatar of goodness rather than a quality that can be shaped by the complicated decisions the cowboy might make.

The existence of a white hat then must necessitate the existence of a *black hat*. Predictably, black-hat activity doesn't adhere to legal, ethical, and moral boundaries. However, many black hats work day jobs as legitimate security professionals with their client's best interests at heart. In this case, that individual may consider themselves a *gray hat*—someone who subscribes to a moral and/or ethical framework but has comfort with legal ambiguity.

The language hackers use is so important to us that it has become part of our culture. Knowing the difference between an intrusion detection system (IDS) and intrusion prevention system (IPS) could mean the difference between keeping an attacker out of a sensitive network and only identifying when one might have already gained access. It's for this reason that our language is constantly being reworked.

The changing nature and social implications of the greater culture that the hacker subculture is a part of means that we might stop using one set of terms and start using another. Terms like *master* and *slave* have become outdated, often being replaced by other, more specific words. The same is true of terms like *white hat* and *black hat*. Regardless of what color a hacker's hat is, they're all citizens of the same ecosystem.

It's also important to remember that hats are removable and aren't a permanent fixture of a hacker's personality as much as it is a replaceable feature of a person's daily attire. It's more helpful to think of the *white hat* and *black hat* as terms that are applied to activities, not necessarily a person in general. For example, a person who makes money on the side performing cybercrime (i.e., black-hat activities) may work a perfectly legal and ethical day job as a penetration tester. We should not confuse a hacker's activity one day with their overall personal ethics on another.

There is also a distinction between the concepts of hacking professionally and the idea of hacking recreationally. Not all work in this field is paid work, and many security-related projects start as unofficial research projects that hackers might do when they aren't working their day job. These side projects are no less impactful and, in some cases, can be considered even more consequential as they tend to be passion projects rather than mundane security operations.

There's a close relationship between hackers and the more formal, professional "information security" community. The differences between these two communities are subtle but important. While all information security professionals might consider themselves hackers, not all hackers consider themselves to be information security professionals.

The field of information or cybersecurity sprung from the recognition by mainstream industries that their most important systems, which are all now connected to the Internet, are prone to being attacked. The reasoning, therefore, is that it's better to pay someone to breach your network and report their findings so that they can be addressed so that they can be addressed before an uncontrolled breach occurs.

The field of cybersecurity has created an environment for legitimizing activities that would be frowned on in any other context. As such, it has become a popular career field for individuals with an interest in subverting computer systems without being at risk legally. The activity most associated with hackers is, of course, getting unauthorized access to systems. This is usually referred to as *exploitation*, or the act of taking advantage of "vulnerabilities" that a hacker may find in a system. Exploiting a computer and getting it to operate in the way the hacker intends is the typical context where this term is applied and understood by the public.

Computer exploitation is a complex topic that has changed with the advent of security measures designed to make exploitation more difficult. On the other hand, the basic concept and approach to exploitation hasn't changed much at all. Although the techniques may change, the methodology is the same—make the machine do something it is not supposed to do. Hackers can, and often do, apply this same concept to other nontechnical areas as well.

Some hackers who are skilled in the field of *social engineering* (or "people hacking") take advantage of social expectations and standard operating procedures (SOPs) to exploit their way into positions of trust with others. The hacker may find a vulnerability in the form of a helpful office employee holding a door for someone they think is a co-worker struggling with a stack of boxes or a handyperson who has their hands full carrying a ladder inside. The hacker may then exploit that vulnerability to gain access to an area in which they do not have permission to be.

Vulnerabilities are like unlocked doors all around us. Hackers are merely the ones turning the handle and then walking through them.

Hackers and Secrecy

In his 2003 book *Hacker Culture*, author Douglas Thomas noted that any history of the hacking community should be recognized as a convergence of technology and secrecy. Critically, secrecy as a cultural thread is sewn through the fabric of the hacker community and is visible in their habits and interactions.

To my wife's frustration, when I talk about other members of the hacking community, I sometimes refer to friends and colleagues with the name they use online. These self-given names (or *handles*) can be used as an individual's persona both on and offline. In recent years, the practice of being recognized offline by a name used online has made its way out of hacker spaces. To most members of the hacking community, names and identities are treated as flexible pieces of information that are not only open to revision but expected to change as we grow and reinvent ourselves.

This fluidity in names is reflective of a culture that regularly deals in secrecy. Whether they're working under a nondisclosure agreement (NDA) or for a top-secret government program, secrecy, privacy, and anonymity are native ground for hackers. This secrecy can even be seen in the unwritten rules hackers use to interact with one another. Like communicating in public, etiquette dictates that there are some questions that are appropriate to ask a hacker and some questions that aren't. This principle applies to information that may be considered sensitive, which may include knowledge of vulnerabilities (weaknesses that may allow unauthorized access to a computer or network).

Like magicians, tricks of the trade are important to those who possess vulnerability information. Offensive security practitioners (sometimes called *red teamers*) tend to keep their best techniques private, sharing them only with a tight-knit group of collaborators. On more than one occasion, I've seen my coworkers react angrily upon learning that someone who they entrusted a special technique had used their technique and "burned" it by allowing it to be caught by an antivirus program. This renders techniques useless at worst or may increase the risk of identification at best.

Even practitioners in "blue team" or defensive activities have realized their own need for secrecy in recent years, as Fortune 500 companies that have hired teams of experts to clean up a severe breach take ethically questionable steps to ensure that the breach is kept out of the public eye. Secrecy is a long-running tradition in the hacker community and applies to professional life as much as it does personal life.

Summary

The hacking community is a difficult-to-define collection of clever tinkerers who work in a wide array of areas of interest. While we're generally introverted, there are situations where we can and do enjoy the company of others. How the media and government define who we are and our actions over the years have created misunderstandings that have kept our subculture cryptic to outsiders.

Armed with this broad understanding of how the hacking community exists and operates today, we can begin to understand the cultural contours of each successive generation of hackers. We can also start to see how misconceptions from outside groups shape the public's changing perception of who and what hackers are.

Even from the beginning, hackers have had a rebellious streak that can be seen throughout each ensuing decade. That rebelliousness has often been misunderstood by government, media, and industry leaders. These misunderstandings have led to life-changing decisions that include legal action aimed at financially curtailing hackers' activity and at times even arrest.

When government leaders began to understand the power that hackers represented in the oncoming high-tech future, these leaders began to see that power as a weapon that could be wielded rather than feared. Over the 40 years since hacking became mainstream, world governments came to believe they could domesticate hackers for geopolitical gain. However, the truth about the relationship between hackers and their governments is a story that is still being written.

CHAPTER

2

Uncle Sam and Technology

In early September 1947, a computer system housed at a Naval base in Virginia began acting erratically. This computer was notoriously bulky, taking up an entire room, and consuming incredible amounts of electricity because of its use of vacuum tubes. The Harvard Mark II was controlled by a single dedicated console built into a nearby desk and could only be operated by highly skilled users.

Built at Harvard University, this computer was purpose-built for the U.S. Navy by a man named Howard Aiken. Its job was to perform the difficult math required to calculate ballistic missile trajectories. Their lumbering size made these early computers prone to difficult-to-diagnose problems. Finding the source of a malfunction could take an afternoon worth of searching.

To solve the problem the Mark II was having that September, a member of the maintenance team reached into the oversized apparatus and pulled an insect out of the complex twist of wires and circuitry. It was then taped to a page of the daily maintenance journal with a note beneath, "First actual case of a bug being found." It is thought by many that the woman who found the bug was the legendary computer scientist Grace Hopper. However, while it's true that Hopper was on the team that found the bug, it likely wasn't Hopper herself who made the note in the maintenance journal.

This story of the first computer bug has been retold so many times it has created its own legend. As with any good myth, there are plenty of misunderstandings and misinterpretations. One such misinterpretation is that this incident coined the term *computer bug*. It's a believable enough story, but this wasn't the first time the term had been used in this context.

At the time that Hopper's infamous bug was found, engineers had already been calling electronic defects *bugs* for decades. Some trace the original use of the term *bug* in the context of engineering back to Thomas Edison, who noted that he'd found a "bug in my apparatus" in one of his prototype telephones in a letter to a colleague dated March 3, 1878.

Despite the myth of the term's origin in Hopper's Naval research lab, it's still one of the many anecdotes about early computing history that has been told thousands of times by hackers. It illustrates one of the challenges with telling any cultural origin story: not all anecdotes are verifiable. On the other hand, not all stories *need* to be verifiable for them to have an important cultural impact.

Today, we remember Hopper as a quiet and dedicated scientist. Hopper's long list of contributions to computer science can't be denied, along with her work breaking glass ceilings before most people knew there was a ceiling that needed to be broken.

Ask anyone in the field of computer science to name a female programmer, and Hopper's name is sure to be the among the first names mentioned. Often pictured in her Navy uniform, her stoic gaze behind her trademark brow-frame glasses, Hopper is a genuine, well-earned legend in the history of hacking. Hopper's story follows a short lineage of electronics and computer experts forged in early twentieth century conflict that was nurtured by world governments' global struggle for power. In the twentieth century, the nation that conquered technology often conquered the world.

World War I

The U.S. government's adoption of technology goes back to the turn of the century. As we've seen in the example of Maskelyne's radio interception, the importance and impact of radio technology on the First and Second World Wars cannot be understated. In fact, the involvement of the United States in WWI hinged on the wireless interception of the historic Zimmermann telegram.

The Zimmerman telegram was a secret message sent by Germany from a radio facility located in the United States known as the "Telefunken plant" to Mexico 14 years after Maskelyne hijacked Marconi's wireless demonstration. (The Telefunken plant was operating secretly under a "cutout" or "front" company called the Atlantic Communication Company located in West Sayville, New York.) The interception of the Zimmermann telegram draws a direct line between technology and the geopolitical events that shape our world. As the First World War developed, the U.S. military began treating radio and telephone communications as one in the same.

First established during the American Civil War, the U.S. Army Signal Corps became responsible for managing wartime communications. By WWI, the Army Signal Corps became known as a hub of technological innovation both in communications and interception technology. Although many of these technologies are taken for granted today, they had the power to change the outcomes of war in the early 1900s. Innovations such as the tactical FM radio, radio telephones, and even early radar prototypes were at the bleeding edge of technology under Colonel William Blair, who directed Signal Corps research from Ft. Monmouth, Virginia.

Codebreaking

After WWI, most modern world governments had accepted that control of electronic communications technology was essential for national defense. Many of these same governments established government bureaucracies for managing intelligence collected by signals interception. In the immediate wake of WWI, the United States tasked cryptologist Herbert O. Yardley with the transformation of the U.S. Army Cryptographic Section (tasked with decrypting encoded messages sent by world rivals) into a joint operation between the U.S. Army and the U.S. State Department.

This new department was referred to as either the Cipher Bureau or The American Black Chamber, as it is more popularly known. This bureau operated under the auspices of a private business communication company called the New York City Commercial Code Company. This organization lasted until Secretary of State Henry L. Stimson disbanded the organization famously saying, "Gentlemen do not read each other's mail." The defunding of this service was a historic blow to the development of America's intelligence capability, but it wouldn't be long before the United States was back in the market for skilled communication hackers.

The need for American communication experts become obvious with the outbreak of the Second World War with the major intelligence failure at Pearl Harbor. The failure of the United States to decrypt Japan's plan to attack Pearl Harbor cost

2,400 American servicemen their lives and drew America into WWII. The attack was devastating, and it highlighted the need for greater allied effort to decrypt Axis communications used by both Japan and Germany.

As the war raged on, the United Kingdom directed its effort toward breaking the Nazi cipher system known as *Enigma*. For this work, the United Kingdom established a codebreaking unit in an English countryside manor called Bletchley Park. It was here that famed computer scientist and codebreaker Alan Turing managed to finish the work started by his Polish counterparts. This was no small accomplishment in computer engineering, and when Enigma was finally broken, it produced some of the most valuable intelligence of the war.

Enigma itself was a feat of computer engineering. Complex webs of electrical wires encased in special rotors would reconfigure their electronic arrangement whenever a key on the keyboard was pressed.

However, computers and programmers weren't working only on codebreaking problems for the war effort. In the United States, analog computers, such as the predecessor to Hopper's computer, the Harvard Mark I, were used to complete calculations for the highly classified Manhattan Project.

As WWII ended, a new world power conflict could be seen on the horizon between the United States and the Soviet Union. This conflict would be defined by technological and economic rivalry. The environment this conflict created became the perfect cultural backdrop for a young community of hackers.

The Cold War

The Second World War had been won, but it would be only a few short years before the world would be cast back into conflict among the victors. In many ways, the Cold War was a continuation of a conflict that began before WWII. In the post-WWI period, Soviet Bolsheviks overthrew Russian Tsarist forces and reorganized Russia into a nation modeled after Marxist theory.

The communist economic system stood in stark contrast to American capitalism. Before the outbreak of hostilities in Europe, the American government had deemed communism a fundamental threat to American values of capital extraction and sought to eradicate communist ideology from their shores.

Hitler's rise to power in Europe before WWII had diverted attention from both capitalist and communist nations but only temporarily. This forced the American agenda of anticommunism to go dormant during the war. When WWII ended, the United States and the Soviet Union picked up right where they left off before the war.

At the heart of the Cold War was a paranoia that America's communist enemies were already within our borders. This paranoia pervaded American life and was regularly exacerbated by U.S. political leadership, who stoked fears of communism. During this time, which would come to be called the *second red scare*, fear of "the other" was synonymous with fear of communism. It was common for derogatory terms like *pinko* or *commie* to be used against anyone whose behavior or appearance went against the grain.

Union laborers arguing for better pay and working conditions were often on the receiving end of cruel mistreatment by anti-communist cold warriors. During the worst days of the second red scare, scores of innocent Americans were blackballed from work opportunities and even faced harsh government-led investigations.

Government organizations such as the House Un-American Activities Committee (HUAC) led by Joseph McCarthy were convened under the banner of rooting out communism. HUAC terrorized everyday Americans and encouraged neighbors to turn each other in for suspicion of communist activities. *McCarthyism*, as it would come to be called, would harken back to America's puritanical past during the witch hunts of the 1600s and would be compared quite literally in Arthur Miller's timeless play *The Crucible*.

The most sinister aspect of McCarthyism was the effect it had on both the powerful and the meek. This fact was clearly demonstrated by the famous Hollywood "blacklists" on one hand for powerful, high-visibility actors and actresses and by the "lavender scare" persecutions of queer government officials in the 1950s and 1960s.

The weight of social paranoia directed at "others" successfully suppressed any form of counterculture in the United States, with its many members fearing that they would be next to be accused of and investigated for communist activities. After all, if they could come after Lucille Ball, they could come after any average computer engineer. It was within this setting of extreme prejudice and fear that many young hackers were born into, and it would prove to be a formative time for many of them.

Foreign Intelligence

Up until the post-war period, the capacity of the U.S. government to conduct intelligence-related activities was limited by a noninterventionist attitude among Americans in the early twentieth century. It wasn't until the late-1940s and early-1950s that the U.S. Intelligence Community (USIC) was given a mandate to continue their operations permanently. One of the biggest changes that the intelligence community would go through during the post-war period was a change from intelligence activities exclusively conducted by the military to include civilian targets who had economic intelligence value.

During WWII, intelligence collection and sabotage organizations shared the same organizations. Units like the Office of Strategic Services (OSS) in the United States and the Special Operations Executive (SOE) in the United Kingdom were responsible for disrupting Axis plans and targeting their leadership. After the war, these organizations would be reconstituted, and their activities continued into the Cold War.

Not only would their activities be continued, but they would also be expanded and formalized. Groups like OSS and SOE were given tremendous latitude to conduct their operations and with very little oversight. This lack of oversight would also continue after the war as OSS morphed into the Central Intelligence Agency (CIA). The CIA's post-war mandate expanded to include all regions on the planet. CIA collected intelligence and planned operations globally to counter the growing influence of pro-worker communism.

The INTs

As post-war intelligence became formalized, so did the language used to describe and organize intelligence activities. Intelligence collection was organized by the source it came from. Broadly referred to as "the INTs," these terms simplified intelligence collection sources. Words such as HUMINT, COMINT, and SIGINT described sources of intelligence such as human, communication, and signals-sourced intelligence, respectively.

SIGINT SIGINT, or "SIGnals INTelligence" has changed immensely over time. Originally used during the Boer War, the British used Marconi wireless sets on their naval ships and in army units in the late 1800s for long-range communication.

The Boers managed to capture a few British radio sets. Seeing the value of being able to both listen into British transmissions and produce their own, the Boers put these radios to their own use. The British noticed the use of the rogue radio transmissions and began their own program of interception on their own stolen radio transmissions. This became the beginning of SIGINT for the United Kingdom.[1]

As the concept of SIGINT developed and methods of radio transmissions evolved, SIGINT would come to incorporate computer communications. This has been the common understanding of SIGINT in the U.S. intelligence community for many decades. Even now, many of the offensive-focused hackers hired by the U.S. government work for America's SIGINT agency, the National Security Agency (NSA), although some may also be hired by other intelligence agencies to support their missions as well.

COMINT   The appearance of "COMmunications INTelligence" at first may sound similar in nature to SIGINT, but in fact, COMINT is a spin-off of SIGINT. While SIGINT deals broadly with the collection of signals such as radio and Internet transmissions, COMINT deals strictly with the collection and analysis of voice information transmitted by telephones.

HUMINT   When most people think of spies, they're thinking of HUMINT, or "HUMan INTelligence." HUMINT is considered the oldest form of intelligence collection and involves extracting intelligence directly from talking to people. HUMINT may be enabled by technology to improve its effectiveness and secrecy

---

[1] Chapman, J. W. M. (2002). British Use of "Dirty Tricks" in External Policy Prior to 1914. *War in History, 9*(1), 60–81. http://www.jstor.org/stable/26014122

(often referred to as "OPerational SECurity," or OPSEC), but the core competency of HUMINT is still human-focused.

It may seem at first glance that HUMINT wouldn't have any relevance to the hacking community based on what most people know about hackers. In fact, hackers are also capable of using HUMINT to accomplish their goals. Hackers have adopted techniques to extract sensitive information from individuals. They may not call it "HUMINT," but the hacker concept of *social engineering* is certainly an extension of the same principles.

Central Intelligence Agency

The Central Intelligence Agency was established immediately after WWII, evolving out of the wartime role that its predecessor organization, the OSS, played. Created in 1947 and championed by the boisterous personality of "Wild" Bill Donovan, the CIA was imagined as the main decision-making authority for all matters of overseas intelligence gathering. CIA's notoriety has been well established with Americans over its decades in operation and presence in American pop culture.

Computer Scientists of Operation Paperclip   One of the first roles that the CIA took on in the immediate aftermath of WWII was to track down Third Reich scientists and import their knowledge into the United States. This was done through a government-wide project called Operation Paperclip. Operation Paperclip controversially included assisting card-carrying Nazis in obtaining U.S. citizenship. The most famous of which was Werhner von Braun, the rocket scientist who helped the United States win the space race. Von Braun once famously collaborated in a documentary program about space exploration and rocket science alongside Walt Disney himself. Von Braun was also the subject of a song by Tom Lehrer that highlighted the controversy of his Nazi past, "Once ze rockets are up, who cares where zey come down? 'That's not my department,' says Werhner von Braun."

The scientists that the U.S. government was interested in importing from the Third Reich covered the gamut of cutting-edge science from rocketry to chemical engineering. Under Operation Paperclip, the United States targeted electrical engineers and computer scientists with the intent to use their skills for America's post-war empire. One such scientist was a man named Konrade Zuse.

Alongside the use of analog computers, engineers were developing the first digital computers. In 1941, Zuse released the Z3, which was credited as one of the earliest digital computers. In 1947, an article appeared in an American Mathematical Society journal discussing Zuse's work in digital computing. This article caught the interest of intelligence officers working on Operation Paperclip who began investigating Zuse as a potential target of the program.

An August 1949 memorandum from the newly established Department of the Air Force titled "Procurement of Paperclip Specialists" references Zuse as a target of Operation Paperclip.

Although the U.S. efforts ultimately failed in recruiting Zuse to work in America, the project was considered a broad success. One recruitment that did succeed was Fritz Karl Preikschat. Preikschat's list of accomplishments include contributions to modern digital communications, such as the phased array satellite system, blind landing systems for airplanes, and even the dot matrix teletypewriter.

National Security Agency

The National Security Agency can trace its origins back to any number of predecessor organizations, many of which were historically focused on the interception and decryption of enemy signals. In 1957, President Truman issued a memorandum concurring with an earlier memo, which called for the creation of a new organization tasked with protecting the nation's critical communications. This memorandum officially reorganized the Armed Forces Security Agency into what we now know as the NSA. The NSA would eventually come to be responsible not only for protecting U.S. government electronic communications but also for intercepting and decrypting the communications of other nations.

Because Truman's 1957 memo was considered classified information, the public wasn't aware of the NSA's official creation. This led to the agency's unofficial, tongue-in-cheek designation as "No Such Agency." It wasn't until the Vietnam War era that the NSA would show off its communication interception capability.

The NSA earned a negative reputation through the exposure of programs aimed to collect the communications of Americans, including Project Minaret and Project Shamrock. These highly classified projects were designed to surveil and suppress so-called dissident activity and were used to silence critics of U.S. government activity such as the Vietnam War. These projects were active at a time where there was very little oversight into the U.S. intelligence community's activities both at home and abroad.

In the late 1980s, the NSA received a presidential mandate to both collect intelligence from foreign computer systems, and maintain America's own computer defense. NSA still held a charter for clandestine COMINT collection, and under President Ronald Reagan, that charter would be expanded to include the responsibility of setting cyber defense policy.

The NSA has maintained a focus on SIGINT since the 1970s. As computer technology emerged, NSA began to collaborate more with private companies. The NSA is the home of the true nerds in the intelligence community. The NSA employs a spectrum of technical experts to carry out its mission and has been a known recognized player in the hacking scene since the 1980s. Its reputation for hiring and collaborating with hackers over the years is well documented and continues today.

Federal Bureau of Investigation

The Federal Bureau of Investigation (FBI) is one of the oldest intelligence community agencies in the United States, forged from the growing culture of fear centered on anarchists and communists during the first period of anti-communist hysteria. The "first red scare" became a mandate for the FBI to counter what was seen as a rising tide of communism inside the borders of the United States.

Bringing together cross-agency efforts that included the Department of Justice (DoJ), Department of Labor (DoL), and the Treasury, the FBI was the successor of the Bureau of Investigation created in 1908. However, it would be another 30 years before the FBI would officially be created as an independent service in 1935, serving the needs of the Department of Justice (DoJ).

Although the FBI always maintained a presence outside the United States, the purview of the FBI is strictly focused on the domestic security of the United States. Led throughout its early years by its notoriously paranoid founding director, J. Edgar Hoover, the FBI's reputation among many Americans for being involved in crime almost as much as it prosecuted is well earned.

The FBI's role in law enforcement after WWII had retracted somewhat, ceding ground to the newly created CIA on matters of foreign intelligence. But their presence inside the United

States was set to widen dramatically in comparison to what it had been before the war.

Advanced Research Projects Agency

The Advanced Research Projects Agency (ARPA) has gone by many different names since it was founded in 1958. Known today as the Defense Advanced Research Projects Agency (DARPA), its mission is to undertake advanced technological research projects with military value, many of which later become consumer products. Founded as a response to the launch of Sputnik in 1957, ARPA initially poured its budget into the investment of research into space-based command-and-control systems. Among ARPA's earliest contributions to military research and development were projects into how to connect computer systems to one another.

The Development of ARPANET The predecessor for our modern understanding of the Internet began with an ARPA project researching how to connect computer systems to one another. The result of this work was a proof-of-concept system called ARPANET. Short for Advanced Research Projects Agency NETwork, the project to develop this interconnected network of computers began in 1966. The need for ARPANET was obvious, as computers began to be used more extensively throughout the military. Around the time that ARPANET was in development, the most advanced computer systems in the world were working on incredibly complex calculations with military applications, such as calculating nuclear yields and ballistic missile trajectories.

In 1962, ARPA found a trailblazer of early interconnected computing in Dr. Joseph "Lick" Licklider. During his time building the agency's computer research division, Licklider pursued policies that pushed the boundaries of computer technology.

Under his leadership, the idea of time-sharing computer resources would democratize computer-based applications in the earliest decades of the technology.

Many of those in the hacker community today are subjected to stories from elder community members about how long it would take for them to get their computerized punch cards in order and to the computer lab on time so that they could run their program during their assigned time slot. This was a direct result of Licklider's impact on computer technology and the culture surrounding it. Of course, Licklider's resounding contribution was the humanitarian guidance that he lent to the direction of interconnected computing.

In the mid-1960s, Licklider's work often crossed into the realm of science fiction. Not only was the basic concept of computers out of reach for most Americans, the thought of connecting them together would have been like something out of *Star Trek*. Being at the bleeding edge of technology has many benefits, including creating an ideological context for that technology to exist within. Licklider didn't imagine interconnected computers for the sake of military conquest. Optimistically, Licklider imagined computer networks for the benefit of mankind.

In Licklider's essay "The Intergalactic Computer Network" published in 1963, he describes a community of people working together to complete projects in technology, academics, and even art:

> *In the first place, it is evident that we have among us a collection of individual (personal and/or organizational) aspirations, efforts, activities, and projects. These have in common, I think, the characteristics that they are in some way connected with advancement of the art or technology of information processing, the advancement of intellectual capability (man, man-machine, or machine), and the approach to a theory of science. The individual parts are, at least to some extent,*

mutually interdependent. To make progress, each of the active research
needs a software base and a hardware facility more complex and more
extensive than he, himself, can create in reasonable time.[2]

Putting the users first emphasized that the invention of
interconnected computer systems was meant to enrich human
interaction, particularly among collaborating groups of creators.
This humanitarian imagination of our high-tech future wasn't
understood in Licklider's terms. For U.S. government leaders in
both the military and intelligence community, the prospect of
interconnected computers held a very different value.

ARPANET in Practice   Licklider had a vision, but it would take
more research and new technologies to make his vision a reality.
This research would take place in the high-tension context of the
Cold War where the specter of nuclear war colored. In this context, the United States needed a military communications network that would be resistant to interruptions caused by a nuclear
war. It was this question specifically that Paul Baran of the Rand
Corporation was pondering when he proposed the concept of
packet switching.

Packet Switching

The fundamental concept that made ARPANET successful was
packet switching technology. *Packet switching* organizes and formats information before it is sent across a computer network.
The inventor of packet switching, Paul Baran, was working to
meet the needs of nuclear-survivable command-and-control for
America's nuclear arsenal. Packet switching was originally

---

[2] The Intergalactic Computer Network - 1963

intended to be used in AM radios. Instead, Baran adapted his idea to work with computers and tested his technology with miniaturized computers in the 1960s.

Packet switching was further improved by University of California – Los Angeles (UCLA) professor Leonard Kleinrock and his team of graduate students. At the time, formalized teams of researchers like these were common and wouldn't have defined themselves as hackers, but their relevance to the invention of networked computer technology was clear. It was Kleinrock and his graduates who successfully tested the first remote system login and established the first permanent ARPANET connection in 1969 between the research institutes at UCLA and Stanford. In a matter of weeks, the network doubled in size. See Figure 2.1.

National Aeronautics and Space Administration

Another organization created in the wake of the Sputnik launch was, of course, the National Aeronautics and Space Administration (NASA). Officially created the year after the ARPA, NASA's mission was the scientific research of avionics, space, and the physics that makes them work. Because of the nature of this work, NASA required significant amounts of mathematical calculations. At first, this work was done by hand. These manual computations were being done by "human computers" who painstakingly crunched numbers for rocket trajectories.

NASA Hackers   NASA would become an early adopter not only of women in the workforce but also of racially integrated workspaces, famously employing African-American women, which was recently memorialized in the film *Hidden Figures*. Margot Lee Shetterly, author of *Hidden Figures*, names 80 African-American women who were on staff at NASA and helped

ARPANET LOGICAL MAP, MARCH 1977

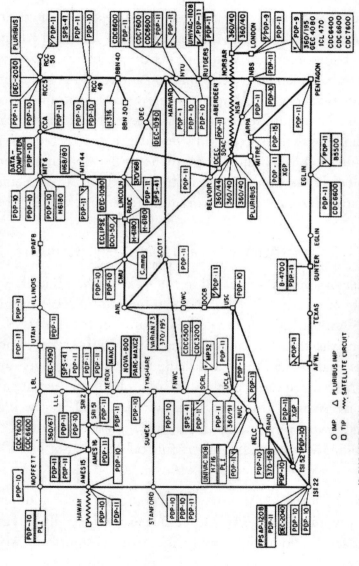

(PLEASE NOTE THAT WHILE THIS MAP SHOWS THE HOST POPULATION OF THE NETWORK ACCORDING TO THE BEST
INFORMATION OBTAINABLE, NO CLAIM CAN BE MADE FOR ITS ACCURACY)

NAMES SHOWN ARE IMP NAMES, NOT NECESSARILY HOST NAMES

○ IMP   △ PLURIBUS IMP
□ TIP   ∿ SATELLITE CIRCUIT

FIGURE 2.1 A map of ARPANET hosts in March, 1977

build NASA's renowned computational legacy. These women were so valued for their computing abilities that the first American in space, John Glenn, personally asked Katherine Johnson to verify his flight path in 1962. Because of the volume and difficulty of these calculations, it wasn't long before the work of human computing was transferred to computers via computer programming. This change swept many of the women who were previously employed as human computers directly into the field of computer programming.

When electronic computers were commodified for aeronautic calculation, these human computers became the foremost programmers in the world. While programmers like Dorothy Vaughan, Mary Jackson, and Katherine Johnson were using FORTRAN to calculate flight paths into their computers, programmers in other divisions like Margaret Hamilton were using *assembly language* to build onboard instrumentation for the Apollo command module.

Instead of using punch cards, Hamilton's assembly programming was literally hardwired into systems that were then built directly into the Apollo space capsules. These programming instructions were added to magnetic fibers, which were then sent to textile mills, where they would be woven together into ropes of computer memory. The women working with this rope memory for the instrument panels were called "LOL," short for little old ladies. Hamilton herself was called the "rope mother."

These women were among the earliest hackers of the modern age and were regularly challenged to make their electronic systems function in unique ways and to solve difficult problems not just in space travel but also those in the field of computer engineering. These women stand as proof that the global hacker community was always much more diverse than it has been given credit for, even from the beginning.

A Leak in the Walled Garden

By the early 1960s, it was becoming clear that the future of computers wasn't meant to be confined to a laboratory. Engineers were already working on making computers smaller and more portable, which was needed before computers could truly break out of their lab walls. Miniature computer systems such as the Simon 1 (also referred to as Simple Simon) became available as early as 1950 but were capable of only simple calculations for educational purposes. With an interface consisting of only lights and toggle switches, Simon 1 contained just two bits of memory.

Simon 1's value was in proving that digital computing could be miniaturized. Simon 1 was a purpose-built computer. It cost $600, and it wasn't widely released to the public. However, the novelty of the Simon 1 was enough to intrigue future computer engineers. With miniaturization, computing was poised to make the leap from the enclosed halls of research and military labs into the public marketplace within the next decade.

Seven years later, the IBM 610 was produced for commercial applications. The IBM 610 featured a somewhat recognizable keyboard interface but still had a similar light and switch interface like the Simon 1. IBM produced 180 units of the 610 model, which cost buyers $55,000. IBM then followed their 610 model with the 1620 in 1959, this time shifting the interface toward the more familiar typewriter or teletype-based experience with an interface that was physically printed to paper for the user.

The earliest recognizable modern hackers were more akin to institutionalized engineers than the rebellious hacker image we are more familiar with today. Despite being more buttoned-up than their 1970s counterparts, these hackers were the unwitting foundation of future generations.

3

Commercializing Technology

The Plain Old Telephone System (POTS) voice telephone network was a logical evolution of the Morse telegraph. It quickly became a commodity not only for businesses but also for average American citizens. Anyone born before the 1990s likely remembers using this system to call family and friends. The POTS was so ubiquitous it's easy to take for granted the size and scale of the system, as many Americans did.

Telephony

Before modern telephone equipment revolutionized telephone switchboards, human operators were employed to connect callers to their intended recipients. These operators busily connected phone line to phone line by hand for hours every day and were expected to know every complexity of the phone system.

This highly technical job required workers who could both understand the interconnections of the telephone system *and* be able to communicate clearly with telephone users. Women, as it turns out, were great for this type of work. Even before women gained the right to vote in the United States, America's switchboards were one of the first technical fields to be dominated by women.

Telephone operators would eventually be phased out in favor of automated phone–switching systems. Little did the phone companies know, but their automated switching systems came with a fundamental design flaw. The automated system understood the telephone number the user intended to reach via an audible tone, representing each number the user pressed. In the 1970s, an unsuspecting group of hackers would take advantage of this feature and exploit it to their benefit.

The Phone Phreakers

Attacks on the phone system started slowly. Individual explorers, calling themselves "phone phreakers" first began by learning the inner workings of the commercial telephone system. The telephone system was like a sprawling city—an interactive space spanning throughout the whole world with mysteries and hidden corners at every switching station. These explorers learned what backdoors the phone companies had created for themselves to service the telephone network, and devised ways of using them for their own gain. Like service entrances or secretive back alleys, these hidden methods could give a person with the right knowledge access to areas and resources within the system that the average user would never even know existed.

The telephone system was indeed expansive. Commercial telephone service had been in service since the late 1870s. By the late 1960s, the telephone system had grown to a byzantine network of interconnected devices managed by a combination of humans and machines. To understand just how arcane this system had become, we must remember that the telephone system worked very differently in the 1960s than it does today.

Placing a telephone call to your local area was easy to do in the 1960s. You could simply rotary (or, starting in 1963, by using a fancy new "touch-tone" phone) dial the local number of the person you wanted to call, and the local network would connect you directly to the recipient. The major telephone companies had invested in improving interconnected infrastructure in municipalities, which made these local calls a mostly painless experience for their customers. These systems were typically well-utilized and worth the maintenance cost for the phone companies as well. Placing a long-distance call was a whole other matter, however.

Long-distance calls were expensive and often required operator assistance. Telephone connections between major cities in the 1960s required main (or *trunk*) lines that a telephone user would need to be connected through to place a call. Trunk lines were like telecommunications highways, directly connecting major cities to one another. Trunk lines would carry high volumes of telephone traffic between two different major cities but could also be used to connect customers outside of major cities to other distant areas serviced by a main trunk line. The use of trunk lines was relatively simple for major cities that were geographically situated near one another but for longer distances (perhaps between a caller in Boston and a receiver in Houston) the call required multiple operators working together to complete the connection. Once the connection was complete, the caller could expect to pay a high fee for this feat of technological engineering.

Figure 3.1 is an example of a March 1960 long-distance telephone map that shows the system's complexity at the time. The space for phone phreakers to explore was seemingly infinite.

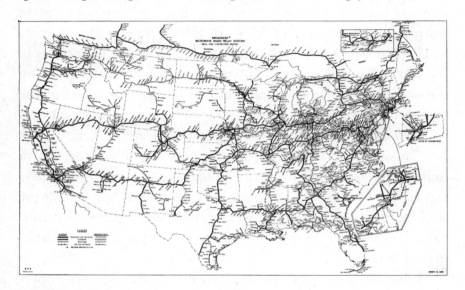

FIGURE 3.1 A 1960 long-distance telephone map

These explorers learned about inward operators and how, by simply asking them confidently enough, these operators could connect them to any telephone in the world for free. When the telephone system switched from analog to digital and, therefore required fewer operator interactions, they also learned that they could exploit these digital systems through a complex set of tuned frequencies. These frequencies would signal the acoustic phone system that a certain number on the handset was being pressed. For instance, pressing the button labeled "1" on a telephone handset plays a 1209 Hz or 697 Hz tone that would be interpreted as the number 1 by the telephone system. When a series of numeric tones matching a standard telephone number pattern included the correct timing between the numbers received by the phone system; it would be interpreted as a recognizable telephone number, and the caller's connection would be made.

These tones were part of a wide range of standardized tone-based codes, which could be presented to a telephone system that would illicit a certain response from the telephone network. Most users would only ever interact with the standard set of dialing instructions (e.g., dialing the telephone number, possibly including an area code of a friend or neighbor), but there were many other special tone-based codes that could make the telephone system react in different ways. Some codes would send test signals to the receiver end, while others would connect a caller to the line operator. Others, still, would do more interesting things like connect the user to the coin refund operator or even indicate that a certain value of coin had just been put into the payphone.

Many of these explorers didn't even know there were people out there like them. It would take the public arrest of one of their own to realize just how wide this community really was.

On June 4, 1971, a news headline buried deep beneath the leading story of a drunk passenger hijacking United Airlines flight 796 read, "Police Apprehend Phone-Addicted USF Whistler." Josef Carl Engressia had been arrested on his second charge of defrauding the South Central Bell Telephone Company. Engressia, who was born blind, adapted to his disability by learning that he could emulate the tones generated by the telephone system simply by whistling them into his telephone handset. Engressia initially used this talent for his own entertainment, harmlessly making free international calls and talking to receivers throughout the world.

Engressia, who took the name "Joybubbles," had been warned about this behavior on a previous occasion but continued whistling his way into free telephone calls anyway. With his innocent demeanor, Joybubbles was a sympathetic character. He would become one of the first hackers arrested and became something of a folk hero due to his treatment by law enforcement. His arrest became a rallying point for other telephone system explorers like him.

Calling themselves *phone phreakers*, this band of misfits shared tricks of the trade with one another. In the same way that the Wild West attracted scoundrels to explore and exploit the far reaches of westward expansion, so, too, did the telephone system call out to this new generation of scruffy digital rapscallions. Untamed in its own way, the telephone system had its own rules that could be bent or even broken by phreakers using the right combination of skill, determination, and charisma.

The phone phreakers took the art of persuading people to a whole new level. The act of convincing a person with access to something valuable, be it information or control, is known to modern hackers as *social engineering*. As opposed to technical engineering, social engineering emphasizes verbal skills—exactly the kind that come in handy when using a telephone. For phone phreakers, being able to con a mark at the phone company was crucial knowledge.

One Whistle to Rule Them All

It wasn't long before phreakers began building their own tools to aid in their exploration of the phone system. One such tool could be found in a box of still-produced Cap'n Crunch cereal. In the shape of a musical note with a small rectangular resonating chamber attached at the side, the Bo'sun Whistle was a common addition to any phreaker's toolkit.

The Bo'sun whistle produced a 2600 Hz tone that, when whistled into a telephone receiver, would indicate to the phone system that the line was "idle" or ready to make a call. Once the phone system heard this tone, it reacted by treating any number dialed as if it were a new call being placed. This would, in turn, allow a phreaker to place a new call without requesting more money from the dialer. The 2600 Hz tone cast a wide shadow across the whole hacking community. The number "2600" would become a magical one, referenced by hackers even today. It has become so popular over time that the 2600 Hz tone may be the oldest operating meme still used by the hacking community. However, the Bo'sun whistle was merely a low-cost way for phreakers without the talent of Joybubbles to generate the tones needed to explore the telephone system.

Of course, phreakers weren't the only technical operators inside the phone system. They were intermingled in telephone networks with legitimate phone company lineworkers who had their own reasons to bypass paying for every call they needed to make. To interact or service a telephone line, a lineworker would need a *lineman's handset*. Similar in appearance to a typical telephone handset, the *lineman's handset* was modified to include a rotary or touch-tone numeric input that a lineman could use to place test calls. Using the lineman's handset as a template, phreakers produced their own devices to simulate phone system tones in a compact, convenient device.

Blue and Red Boxes

Because many of the service tones used by the telephone system could be heard audibly over a payphone when it was legitimately used, phreakers could hold a recording device's microphone to the handset's earpiece and record the sounds generated when a certain denomination of money was placed into the coin slot. These tones could then be replayed into another phone at a later time, tricking the system into believing it had received money when it had not. Phreakers called their recording devices containing these tones *red boxes*. While no one is sure exactly why red boxes were given this name, the popular belief is that the first devices of each to be made matched the color for which they were named.

In the late 1960s, industrious hackers constructed *blue boxes* to help them more easily interact with the phone system. Each blue box featured a touch-tone keyset and contained all the necessary tones required to subvert the digital telephone system. Phreakers could use an attached speaker to generate the same phone system tones as a lineman's handset. A good blue box could imitate a wider range of tones that weren't included in the lineman's handset. Blue boxes were seen as the Ferrari of phone phreaking and became a treasured tool for phreakers.

Blue boxes enabled phreakers to do things they had never been able to do before. Not only could they make free phone calls, but they could traverse the phone system in more unique ways. By being able to disguise their transmissions as legitimate phone traffic, they could more convincingly persuade a telephone operator that they were genuinely a phone company employee, giving them access to new tools and pathways that they didn't have access to prior to the innovation of the blue box.

The blue box also allowed phreakers to indulge their mischievous side by allowing them to contact people by phone who were traditionally inaccessible to the average person, including the rich and famous. Some phreakers even claimed to have prank called President Nixon using advanced phone phreaking techniques.

As the price of technical components dropped and cheap integrated circuits became more ubiquitous, two intrepid young phone phreakers by the names of Steve Wozniak and Steve Jobs realized a great business opportunity in producing blue boxes. They began assembling and selling blue boxes to an increasing audience of phone phreakers in the early 1970s. Cutting their teeth in the world of business by finding a niche market excited to buy a specialized product, Wozniak built the blue boxes by hand, while Jobs did the work of marketing them.

Rock Stars Are Born

As phone phreaking gained more publicity, so did the practitioners. In 1971, *Esquire Magazine* published a first-of-its-kind article titled "Secrets of the Little Blue Box" on phone phreakers and the blue boxes they used. Before this, the public hadn't yet been widely exposed to the concept of phone phreaking. Before the *Esquire* article, phreaking was an underground culture. If an average person at the time had seen a phreaker on the street, they may have been dismissed simply as a Beatnik of some sort, but certainly not the keepers of privileged knowledge.

For many who read the *Esquire* article, this was the first time they were learning that a young community of awkward telephone hackers even existed. *Esquire* didn't just report on phreakers from the outside, they also spoke directly to some hackers of the time. A phreaker by the name of Fraser Lucey demonstrated to the article's author how to call a payphone at Waterloo station in London and then proceeded to have a chat with an unsuspecting passerby who'd happened to pick up the phone. All free of charge.

Lucey was *stunt hacking*, or hacking without a driving purpose. In front of the *Esquire* writer, Lucey hacked the phone system, placing free international telephone calls for nothing more than the attention he would receive. Despite the dubious legality of his activities, Lucey would take his blue box out in public to show off his seemingly superhuman powers to mildly surprised observers. On its own, phreaking was a gentle amusement, but not particularly impressive to the average person. The full realization of the importance of this ability would not be seen for decades.

Another phreaker who was mentioned in the *Esquire* article was a man by the name of Captain Crunch. Although the article never gave his true name, another phreaker using the alias 'Al Gilbertson' described Captain Crunch as the "most legendary phone phreak" at least as capable of stunt hacking as Lucey. *Esquire* portrayed Captain Crunch as a man of mystery. He used a false name and was rumored to tour the United States in a Volkswagen van full of esoteric telephone engineering devices that he used exclusively for phreaking. To the layperson, Captain Crunch sounded like an elusive and powerful renegade. Was he a Soviet spy? The wayward heir of a millionaire family? Nobody knew for sure. Readers believed that Captain Crunch could make the sprawling telephone system bend to his will and was so transient that it's unimaginable if he could ever be captured.

In reality, Captain Crunch was nothing but a man with a complicated legacy named John Draper. Draper's legend began in the U.S. Air Force, where he was known for making long-distance calls to his friends. Draper would blow his magic Bo'sun whistle into the phone, and poof! Their costly phone charges would disappear, letting them talk longer free of charge. Over time, Draper's legend outgrew him. While other phreakers went on to achieve greater degrees of personal success both in phreaking and later in the business of hacking, Draper's notoriety as a legendary phone phreaker plateaued.

For much of his life, Draper enjoyed a "rock star" existence within the phreaking and later the hacking communities. Being recognized as a champion for individual security-related accomplishments carried over into the modern information security community, despite Draper's lack of recent contributions. Even so, most modern hackers can trace their own interest in security topics back to a single individual—a hero who introduced them to the possibilities the hacker community has to offer. For many of them, that person was Draper himself.

Despite Draper's status as a beacon of inspiration for the hacking community over the decades, he's since found himself banned for misconduct from many of the same conferences that once welcomed him as a sage elder. In recent years, Draper's reputation has been tarnished by credible accusations of sexual assault, abuse, and stalking by the very community of which he is a part. Draper's rise and fall is, unfortunately, a story that has been all too familiar in recent years.

The Missing Stair

The accusations against Draper have come with allegations that he is a *missing stair* in the community. A missing stair describes someone with social standing who is untrustworthy and potentially abusive. The term has been credibly used many times in recent years to reference a member of the hacking community with power and influence. It's someone who's looked to as a role model as they climb the social and professional "staircase." Younger community members who look up to these individuals as implicitly trustworthy find themselves surprised to find that instead of being dependable, these individuals have a dark and abusive side.

Missing stair accusations are often spoken softly between hackers and have only increased in the #metoo era. Credible accusations of abuse have been on the rise in many close-knit communities and are not unique to hacking. Like many other groups, hackers are finding ways of digesting challenges with abuse, which has contributed to the culture of hacking in recent years in its own unique ways.

The Personal Computer

In the early 1970s, computational resources were still impractical. Computers were large, prohibitively expensive to the average American, and far too simplistic. Hidden behind the high walls of technical research organizations, this lack of availability led to a walled garden of sorts. Highly funded research organizations capable of operating cutting-edge computers were hard at work on high-minded goals to unlock the possibilities of computer technology.

In the U.S. Department of Defense (DoD), the Advanced Research Projects Agency Network (ARPANET) was just beginning to imagine how computers could be remotely connected, but the people it was connecting still were members of the same narrow community. It would take a fantastic innovation in miniaturization and a whole new sales pitch to bring these devices into the average American's home.

Altair 8800

The first *microcomputer* available to the public was released in January 1975 by a company called Micro Instrumentation and Telemetry Systems. The Altair 8800 was a mail-order personal computer (PC) oddly marketed to both "industrial" applications and hobbyists. The Altair 8800 came with three manuals and required assembly by the user. Those tasked with the burden of marketing the Altair 8800 relied heavily on its potential as a fun technical project for hardware hackers looking for a new challenge, rather than for its potential to solve any practical problems.

Even so, the Altair 8800 did leave an important footprint as the first commercially successful PC. The Altair 8800 managed to break computer technology out of the sacred lab spaces that had confined them for 20 years. The legacy of the Altair 8800 was that it introduced the novelty of microcomputing to the public. It didn't kick-start a home computer revolution, but it was a message to entrepreneurs that the market was developing.

Apple I and II

It's hard to make a case that any other single home computer was as influential as the Apple II. Although PCs were becoming more available through the early half of the 1970s, the Apple II altered that trend. Competitors like IBM and Commodore were busy producing home computing platforms, and although they had some success, neither company seemed to have cracked the code of how to produce a computer for the new user.

Following Apple's first computer (aptly named the Apple I), the Apple II was released on June 10, 1977. The Apple II was the first consumer-market home computer that struck the right balance between design and functionality. This balance became a hallmark of Apple products later in the life of the company. What Apple was selling in the Apple II was not *just* a computer. It was a computer *system*, fully assembled and complete with a monitor and keyboard.

As a fully-fledged computer system, the Apple II gave the consumer market its first look at a practical computer setup. This was one of the main differences between the Apple I and Apple II. The practicality of computers as an everyday tool proved that an appetite for the PC did exist, as long as it was marketed in the right way.

Instead of using the strategy of the Altair 8800 targeting high-tech hobbyists, Apple pitched the Apple II as "the *most* personal computer." It wasn't just a piece of technology—it was a piece of the average person's life. The success of Apple II made the entire concept of consumer technology approachable to a mainstream audience. Designed and built by Steve Wozniak himself, what made the Apple II special is that it was designed, built, and marketed by hackers who could trace their lineage directly back to the phreaking community.

The Apple II represented a bridge between the phone phreakers, the hackers of the past, and computer hackers, the hackers of the future. Many hackers who had been active in the phreaking community would cross over the bridge of affordable personal computers like the Apple II or the Commodore 64 (1982) into the world of computer hacking. In their transit, the phreakers brought the culture they built with them.

Communities

Just as the telephone system was ripe for exploration, computers were a new arena of discovery. They were a frontier promising new adventures for the same demographic that was attracted to phreaking in the first place. Most of them hadn't been involved in building the phone system, but they now had an opportunity to build the future of computer systems.

Community Memory

The Community Memory Project, developed in Berkeley, California, was an early information archival and bulletin board system. Starting in 1973, Community Memory was among the first hybridized "online" communities. It was imagined as a hub for local community information, a sort of bulletin board that was publicly accessible using cutting-edge technology. The project started with three teletype model 33 terminals set up in record shops in the San Francisco Bay Area (see Figure 3.2). These terminals were connected to a 24-bit mainframe, which saved all of the information that users input during the lifetime of the project.

FIGURE 3.2 Community Memory terminal at Leopold's Records in Berkeley, California (1973)

Mark Szpakowski / Wikimedia Commons / CC BY-SA 2.5

Community Memory was born from the libertine belief system of the 1960s that idealized harmonious communities of people working together. Users who found the terminals put them to good use, searching for other community members who needed something. Some in the local community were searching for musicians who could join their band; others looked to buy and sell items. For these individuals, Community Memory was their go-to source for community information.

Community Memory had given hackers a look at what online communities could be. Despite being highly localized, Community Memory was a success. The concept of an online community spanning beyond the boundaries of the Bay Area didn't yet exist, but there was clearly a future for online communities. For hackers and phreakers, Community Memory provided the blueprint for the future of interconnecting people and machines.

Jude Milhon

Another prominent member of the Community Memory Project was a woman named Jude "St. Jude" Milhon. Milhon was a lifelong activist, making a name for herself in her early years protesting America's foreign military interventions. This anti-war ethos that Milhon brought to Community Memory reflected a duality of how the Internet was being imagined. Milhon imagined the online space as a place for organizing activism in addition to providing for people's needs.

This was in stark contrast to the purposes imagined by America's military industrial complex, which was hard at work developing ARPANET. The U.S. government's vision of interconnected computers was based on militarization. Up to that point, the charter for ARPANET was connecting computers for the purpose of military research.

Milhon's contribution to the culture of the Community Memory Project was pronounced and laid the foundation for the rebellious spirit present in the modern hacker ethos. She was a technologist and activist who, in her younger years, was arrested many times for civil disobedience. It was only natural for her to bring her anti-war passions with her to Community Memory.

Another signifier of the hacker ethos Milhon possessed was that she was an autodidact. Milhon began her journey in programing by reading a Fortran manual. After learning programming fundamentals, Milhon applied for a job as a programmer for a vending machine company called Horn and Hardart. At the time, Horn and Hardart sold a popular line of automat machines that served up food to customers behind small, locked doors that would open when a customer paid the machine. Horn and Hardart was in the process of computerizing these machines, and Milhon's understanding of programming fit their needs. Her position at Horn and Hardart put her in a valuable data processing position, which would come in handy for her later participation in Community Memory.

After divorcing her husband and moving to Berkeley, California, Milhon took a job working at the Berkeley Computer Company (BCC), where she made friends with one of the other two founders of Community Memory, Lee Felenstein. Felenstein himself was a programmer and activist, much like Milhon, and the two of them, along with another friend, Efrem Lipkin, joined together through a Bay Area high-tech community called Project One.

Inside the walls of an abandoned candy company warehouse, Project One forged the foundations of the bleeding-edge "move fast and break things" culture that would come to define Silicon Valley. Project One was a first-of-its-kind art and culture commune that promoted the same sort of bohemian culture that gave rise to later art warehouse projects that would come after it. One such project was the ill-fated "Ghost Ship" collective in Oakland, which burned down in a deadly fire in December 2016, killing 36 people.

Age of the Bulletin Board System

Community Memory's small-scale, localized project was only the beginning. In 1978, two men would take the same basic concept of a public note board and port it to computers via the phone system. Ward Christensen and Randy Suess, two friends from the Chicago area, worked together to build the first Computer Bulletin Board System (CBBS). The two named their first program Ward & Randy's CBBS. It wasn't the most creatively named project, but what it lacked in colorful naming, it made up for in longevity. Ward & Randy's BBS operated for more than 20 years until it was finally taken offline in the early 1990s.

Ward and Randy's software lived on, however, and kicked off a revolution in online communication through Bulletin Board System (BBS) technology. The most important aspects BBSs introduced to online communities was the ease by which users could connect with one another. It lowered the latency of communication (i.e., making posts nearly instantly visible to other users, rather than having to wait for the mail) and allowed users to connect and communicate on their own schedules through newly popular home PCs.

BBSs took the speed of telephone connections and combined it with the convenience of a written language. Where Community Memory connected only a few locations around the city of Berkeley, BBSs produced a gathering place for people in a region around a common online location that could be accessed from anywhere.

Despite its novel improvements, BBSs still had to work around the constraints of the telephone phone system. Because of this reliance on the phone system, the mix of phone phreakers and so-called computer phreakers began to merge somewhat. Long-distance calls were still expensive to make, which meant that a localized BBS was necessary to make the idea of a BBS financially feasible.

This gathering around localized BBSs based on area code led to organized groups of "crews" like the New York 212s and the Boston 617s. This dynamic of the BBS rebalanced the bias of Community Memory's hybrid online community from a physical location toward a more online model. Due to not needing to visit a public terminal physically, anonymity became a common aspect of life for BBS users.

Thousands of BBSs hosted across the United States popped up serving all sorts of different niche interest content. With names like Amiga Shareware HQ and LAN Solutions BBS, if you had a specific interest, there was likely a BBS somewhere in the world serving up that content.

BBS users of the time likened the experience of logging on to visiting a friend's house. This made sense, since the computer hosting the BBS was likely being run out of the house of someone in a nearby area code. In many cases, the BBS was hosted on a computer by someone the users knew personally. It's easy to imagine how this form of an online community would've been much more personal than other similar online communities today.

Although some phreakers enjoyed the anonymity that BBSs offered, these systems also offered a pathway to exposure for phreakers looking to increase their public profile. Three phreakers would choose this path and usher in a new level of attention to hackers that had seldom been seen until this time. In the early 1980s, a BBS user in the phreaking scene using the name Roscoe formed a small group of phreakers called Roscoe Gang. Roscoe was the alias of Lewis DePayne, who was joined by fellow phreakers Kevin Mitnick (who went by the name Condor) and Susan Headley (aka Susy Thunder).

Despite the area code limitations of 1980s BBSs, Roscoe Gang managed to cultivate a level of national notoriety that reached beyond these isolated forums. One of the ways they grew this notoriety was by creating controversies on different BBSs. In long-winded BBS records of conversations involving different Roscoe Gang members and their cohorts, they can be seen squabbling about all sorts of irrelevant matters. It wasn't unusual for them to sling accusations about who was sleeping with whom or even who might be secretly working with the Federal Bureau of Investigation (FBI).

We might recognize this type of behavior to be similar in many ways to the modern practice of "cyberbullying" or "trolling." These online attacks were often mean-spirited and fueled by an ongoing series of vendettas that could be satisfied only when one participant in the "flame war" gave up.

Wherever Roscoe Gang went, trouble followed, and so did their reputation. The computer-phreaking community had a love-hate relationship with the controversial characters of Roscoe Gang. The cultural reaction within the broader BBS community was to dismiss these individuals as creating "drama," but Roscoe Gang only continued to gain notoriety as the years progressed.

Their relationship with drama would become another foundational element of the hacking community. Particularly in the 2010s, vicious personal attacks could be posted to outlets like Encyclopedia Dramatica, which still operates today. At times, Roscoe Gang's drama would spill over into larger conflicts between individuals and groups. These feuds often resulted in "pranks" or tit-for-tat acts of reprisal that captivated and annoyed everyone paying attention.

Party Lines

In the late 1800s, telephone companies offered service through *party lines*, connecting all of the customers in a region on the same phone circuit. This meant that callers on a party line could pick up the line and hear a telephone call from another nearby customer underway. This catch was a boon for the nosy neighbor who could pick up the phone and clandestinely catch up on all the neighbor's gossip. Party lines earned a reputation for this unpredictable quality and became a nuisance to average customers. Party lines of this sort were decommissioned in the 1980. Still, the term 'party line' continued to be used for other services, such as group calls or conference bridges, which connected customers from distant regions onto the same call.

This new type of party line allowed more privacy than the traditional party lines did and gave phreakers a long-distance gathering place. Party lines gave new phreakers a chance to schmooze with phreaker royalty. If they could find out when and where a call was being held, party lines offered a chance to rub elbows with some of the biggest names on the phone-phreaking scene, hear about recent phreaker drama, and exchange detailed technical information.

In the 1940s and 1950s, party lines were a nuisance for most users. Depending on what part of the country you were in and where you were, picking up the telephone and talking to a friend came with the risk of someone else picking up a different phone and listening to your private conversation. For the phreaker community, party lines were a cultural boon.

Party lines could support up to nine callers at a time. Phreakers who'd proven themselves trustworthy would be given the telephone numbers for open party lines that could be joined at any time. If the line was full, it just meant you'd have to keep trying until a spot on the party line opened, at which point you could drop into the call and freely talk to anyone else on the line.

Party lines became another location for phreakers and early hackers to share tips and tricks of the trade or to further harass and publicly embarrass your rivals. Combined with BBSs, party lines were a popular way of quickly communicating with other members of the small, isolated communities of phreakers.

CHAPTER

4

Digital Disruption

Vatican City, 1972

A call reached a clerk working inside the Vatican, at the time the home of Pope Paul VI. After a short greeting, the clerk heard a man with a heavy accent. "This is Henry Kissinger calling on behalf of President Nixon. . . ." Calls from world leaders to the Vatican weren't at all unusual, but something stood out about this call. The caller continued in the bombastic accent, "We are at the summit meeting in Moscow, and we need to talk to the Pope."

The clerk notified the caller that the pope was sleeping, but they would send someone to wake him. An hour later, Kissinger called back. Once again, he asked to speak with the pope, but the Vatican clerk was ready this time. They had called the direct number on file for Secretary of State Kissinger and confirmed that the real Henry Kissinger had not called the Vatican earlier that day. The jig was up. The clerk from the Vatican hung up to

61

the great amusement of the imposter. Little did the Vatican clerk know that the caller was the future millionaire cofounder and technical mind behind the Apple Computer company.

In the 2013 book titled *Exploding the Phone: The Untold Story of the Teenage Outlaws Who Hacked Ma Bell*, Steve Wozniak described his call to the Vatican as the biggest prank of his phreaking career. Wozniak's attempt to call the pope had been a light-hearted adventure for a mischievous young phreaker. After all, it wasn't every day that an unknown American teenager got this close to a major spiritual leader, even if it was only through a phone connection. Despite being an innocent tall tale, Wozniak's call to the Vatican hinted at the damage that could be caused by less pure intentions.

Culturally, phone phreakers of the 1960s were a reaction to the democratization of technology driven by the same spirit that inspired mountain climber George Mallory in 1924 to declare why he wanted to climb Mt. Everest: "because it is there." The freedom the telephone system offered served as the perfect playground for a new subgenre of young, working-class Americans. The phone system was an equalizer, not only to the richest Americans; it could connect anyone anywhere in the world.

Through telephone lines, phreakers could go anywhere and con just about anyone, and not all of their exploits were as innocent as Wozniak's. Two years after Wozniak was rebuffed by Vatican staff, another California phreaker made history in an event that has come to be known as "The Santa Barbara Nuclear Scare." Phreakers exploited a flaw in the telephone system that allowed them to reroute incoming calls to Santa Barbara, California, instead of the intended recipient. For about 30 minutes, anyone trying to call family and friends in Santa Barbara from outside the city was redirected to a voice who claimed to be an emergency operator. The callers were then told that their call couldn't be completed due to a nuclear explosion inside the city.

The prank predictably caused panic and concern that World War III had begun, but the phreakers responsible were never caught.

The line between an innocent prank and an alarming incident was often thin with phone phreakers. In most cases, the effect of these pranks was limited to funny stories told between friends rather than serious international incidents. In the 1970s, phreakers were regarded by the U.S. government as a public nuisance more than a serious threat. The result of their activities caused more embarrassment for the phone companies than real damage, but phreakers' high-tech antics and methods improved as digital systems became more ubiquitous. As phreakers became hackers, the list of technologies they could manipulate grew.

The evening hours of November 26, 1977, were unremarkable for residents of Southern England. Residents of the Berkshire and Hampshire areas were likely having supper and watching a local evening news broadcast coverage discussing developments in the Bush War in Rhodesia in which the UK government backed pro-apartheid security forces. Suddenly, the screen became wavy, and the voice of the news anchor began to fade. The anchor's words gave way to static before being replaced by a mysterious, droning, otherworldly voice.

> *"This is the voice of Asteron. I am an authorized representative of the Intergalactic Mission, and I have a message for the planet Earth. . . ."*

The faceless speaker's tone was ominous and went on to urge humanity to disarm and seek a peaceful coexistence. The unsuspecting viewers of Andrew Gardner's evening news broadcast had just witnessed a signal hijacking. In much the same way that Nevil Maskelyne's interruption had happened more than 70 years before, an unknown hijacker had overpowered the local frequency of the ITN's news broadcast and used it to send an anti-war message to the public.

This hijacking made international news and would come to be known as the Southern Television broadcast interruption. The interruption caused panic in the surrounding communities, leading to calls from the surrounding area to the television studio's telephone switchboards. This phreaking event left many questions in its wake, and the person responsible for the interruption has still not been identified.

The same week a decade later, a more famous signal hijacking hit the United States. An unknown individual wearing a mask, recognizable to viewers as the face of oddball, futuristic TV personality Max Headroom, took over the broadcast of a pair of Chicago-area TV stations. During the disruption, the signal hijacker communicated in a droning, high-pitched voice in front of a corrugated metal background. This unauthorized broadcast was clearly improvised, and at one point, the mask-wearing hijacker even bent over and was spanked with a riding crop by a partially visible participant. The Max Headroom incident became a digital-age mystery in its own right, inspiring laughs from some and somehow fear from others.

Both of these events were blueprints for future hackers on how their exploits could be used to mass communicate to the public. In the case of the Southern Television broadcast interruption, it also wouldn't be the last time that weapons of war were a central motivator in what would come to be called *hacktivism* in later decades.

Viral Genesis

While phreakers were experimenting with ways of manipulating signals to disrupt public communications, the academic class of hackers was hard at work in the lab, testing theories of computerized disruption. In the early 1970s, researchers in the private sector developed tools and techniques that would become the foundation of the future industry of computer security. At the same time, independent computer hobbyists amassed their own knowledge and tools, which they used and shared among themselves.

The concept of free information sharing, though popular among hackers today, did not originally include tools such as the Unix operating system developed by AT&T in 1969. At first, projects like Unix stayed behind the same high walls of academia and proprietary research and development as intellectual property assets. This included many of the first attempts at what we now call *malware*.

Computer viruses have always been the go-to tool hackers use in television and movies for decades. Despite this notoriety, most average people don't recognize the differences between categories of malware, such as viruses, worms, and ransomware. The National Institute of Standards and Technology (NIST) defines a computer virus as follows[1]:

> *A computer program that can copy itself and infect a computer without permission or knowledge of the user. A virus might corrupt or delete data on a computer, use e-mail programs to spread itself to other computers, or even erase everything on a hard disk.*

A major question of security researchers in the early 1970s was if a computer program could replicate itself from computer to computer, without needing a human to manually copy it. This is the question Bob Thomas had in mind when he invented the first computer virus in history.

Creeper and Reaper

In zombie movies, a world-changing virus often comes at the hands of scientists hidden deep in a mysterious laboratory. The

---

[1] https://csrc.nist.gov/glossary/term/virus

first computer viruses were no different. In 1971, researcher Bob Thomas created the first recorded computer virus, known as Creeper.

Although it's often credited with being the first computer virus ever written, Creeper doesn't exactly fit into the modern layperson's definition of a virus. Its work didn't cause any damage but was merely proof of concept. Thomas's goal was to prove the hypothesis that a computer program could self-replicate. More importantly, this transfer happened through the code directing the program alone. During testing, Creeper successfully moved itself from one computer to another. It didn't leave a trail of Creeper copies behind and proved Thomas's goal.

His work on Creeper was inspired by a concept presented in a white paper titled "Theory of Self-Reproducing Automata," written by the legendary computer scientist John von Neumann and published in 1966.[2] In his piece, von Neumann compares computer code to the human body. In this imagined context, von Neumann questions if the role of human reproduction has a corollary in the world of computer programming. Could a program be made to reproduce itself? And if so, why would someone want a program to do this? Less than a decade later, Bob Thomas would answer von Neumann's question.

Thomas programmed Creeper in assembly to run on PDP-10 mainframes. As it moved from one connected host to another across the Advanced Research Projects Agency Network (ARPANET), it printed the message:

I'M THE CREEPER, CATCH ME IF YOU CAN!

It would then find another computer on the network and spread itself, leaving no damage behind apart from a few wasted cycles and teletype ink. Creeper was playfully programmed,

---

[2] https://cba.mit.edu/events/03.11.ASE/docs/VonNeumann.pdf

challenging system administrators to a digital game of hide-and-seek. This same fun-loving spirit could be found in future research, both public and private.

Shortly after the first version of Creeper was released, a second version was written and tested on ARPANET by another researcher named Ray Tomlinson. Instead of the file simply moving itself as the first version of Creeper did, the second version would copy itself—meaning that a Creeper file would be present on every host that was infected by Creeper's code. This second version of Creeper was closer to a modern-day virus than the original. If this second version of Creeper can be considered the first true demonstration of a computer virus, then Tomlinson's Reaper program was the first antivirus program. Reaper's purpose was just as simple as Creeper's. Reaper was made to find and remove Creeper wherever it went, using the same methods of self-replication that Creeper did.

Creeper and Reaper set the stage for an entire market built around malware and antivirus programs as digital commodities. In fact, apart from self-replication, the basic concept of modern virus scanners hasn't changed much since the days of Creeper and Reaper. Creeper also gave researchers a preview of the kind of damage that could be done by future viruses with more destructive aims.

Wabbits

Many malware histories reference a curious virus variably called *Rabbit*, *Rabbits*, the *rabbit virus*, or even *Wabbit*. This reference usually came with an attached erroneous claim that it was one of the first, if not the first, virus ever written. The trouble with such histories is that they are incomplete. Rabbit successfully made it into the cultural hacker zeitgeist, but its documented existence leaves much to be desired.

With some sources claiming the origin of Wabbit was in Dallas, others say it was in Washington state, but all sources lack one important component: evidence. Wabbit's true origin seems to have been lost to time. The best available documentation on it is archived in a 1988 forum post. In the post, someone named Bill Kennedy discusses his memory of a virus he called Rabbit and mentions that he came across it in 1974. But he doesn't provide great detail about Rabbit apart from its supposed function.

Were this the end of the story of Wabbit, there would not be much more to tell. At some point, the concept of Wabbit had a greater impact than the original code on which it may have been based. Regardless of its exact origin, Wabbit was a *resource exhaustion attack*. Specifically, Wabbit was believed to use a *fork bomb technique* (i.e., a denial-of-service [DoS] attack) to exhaust the resources of the system on which it was run. When run, it would continuously create two copies of itself until the system's resources had been completely used up. The result of Wabbit running was that the victim computer would crash if proper resource restrictions weren't put in place.

At the time, the fork bomb's consequences were relatively limited. It had high prank potential, but the core concept of a resource exhaustion attack wasn't very practical, given the high bar needed to deliver the attack. The true power of resource exhaustion was in the attacker's ability to launch attacks at will. The fork bomb concept simply had too many requisite conditions for it to be effective in a real-world attack at the time. Despite being impractical at the time of its creation, resource exhaustion attacks would find utility in later years as computer technology became more ubiquitous. They were simply ahead of their time.

Ultimately, Wabbits served an important cultural role in the history of hacking. It was inspirational more than functional and helped lay the concept for attacks that could one day be used in attacks, which proves that even without code, viruses could still have influence.

Virus or Not?

It wasn't long before the idea of the prankster ethos was present throughout the documented history of hacking. Even at its roots, we can see the evidence of the inherently mischievous spirit that early virus programmers had, as shown in one of the best pieces of evidence, the Animal Virus.

All sources agree that Animal didn't begin life as a virus in the classic sense. Its first version was written by a programmer named John Walker in 1975, and began as a 20-question game that ran on Univac 1100 mainframe computers. These popular business machines were run by early system administrators who were responsible for ensuring that the systems remained functional. Like their programmer brethren, system administrators also enjoyed having fun in their work.

Users were prompted to think of an animal, and the game would take the user's input to help determine what animal the user was thinking of. This version of Animal was, by all accounts, not a virus. In fact, it was the oppositive of malicious. In the mid-1970s, software distribution wasn't as simplified as it is today. When a user wanted a copy of a program, they needed to ask for it from the programmer who would then provide the requester with a copy of the program on some form of physical media like magnetic tape. For Walker in 1975, it meant that he had to mail physical copies of Animal to those who requested it. Walker was being asked for copies of Animal so often that the requests became burdensome. It was a time-consuming process, which is why he began to design an easier way to transmit Animal's files.

Walker remembered how he came up with the idea for copying Animal's files in an interview with ZDNET[3]: "I started getting calls from people at other UNIVAC installations asking for tapes of the game. It was really annoying and got me thinking on how best to distribute the game. That's when I thought about making it self-reproducing." Walker called his self-replicating version of Animal "Pervade Animal." Walker would then mail a copy of the software to a requester, who would gleefully load it onto their system. Once Pervade Animal was loaded, it would inspect all accessible directory pathways and copy itself to them without the knowledge of the system administrator. Before the unsuspecting user knew it, they would have a filesystem full of copies of Pervade Animal throughout their system. Although it was annoying, Pervade Animal wasn't as widely destructive as viruses in future decades would be known for.

In addition to being the first example of a Trojan horse, Pervade Animal also has the distinction of being the first true "in-the-wild" virus, meaning that it didn't exist only in the safety of a lab setting.

Despite its typical classification as a virus, Pervade Animal fits better into the category of a *Trojan horse*. Like the Trojan horse of Greek legend, a desirable software product could come packaged with a set of unexpectedly malicious features. In Pervade Animal's case, the hottest game that every Univac 1100 user wanted to get their hands on came with the unfriendly feature of copying itself throughout the system without permission, which could cause unintended consequences.

XERPARC

The cases of Creeper and Pervade Animal proved that von Neumann's concept of self-replicating code wasn't only possible but

---

[3] https://www.zdnet.com/article/the-computer-virus-no-cures-to-be-found

also practical. Seeing the Creeper's success, two researchers at the Xerox company in Palo Alto named John Hupp and John Shoch put their own spin on Creeper's proof of concept.

The pair didn't set out to prove a flaw in network security; rather, their original goal was to research possibilities in the world of distributed computing. Distributed computing brought together a collection of computers on an Ethernet-connected network (i.e. those being given tasks by a central authority) and the "workers" (the programs created to utilize the computing power of those computers) doing the work and sending it back to the central authority.

Both Creeper and Pervade Animal had one major functionality drawback: they both required *user interaction* to continue infecting new computers. In other words, victims needed to trigger their own infection in some way. This challenge was solved by Hupp and Shoch. Their program didn't need a user to do anything for their code to spread from one host to another. Instead, their program searched for idle processors within the company's network. The program would then execute itself on inactive computers and run using the idle computer processing unit (CPU) cycles.

Inspired by science fiction, Hupp and Shoch called their program a *worm* after a story titled "The Shockwave Rider" reflecting the influence that science fiction had on the early hacking community. It was a preview of the tangled relationship that intertwined computer security and media in later years. This fledgling influence would eventually become a cyclic relationship. At this time, however, the hacking community was drawing more of its inspiration from the media, but this wouldn't always be the case.

The first worm Shoch and Hupp created was called the Existential Worm, whose only purpose was to maintain its own existence by running, like a parasite, on victim computers. The pair released their worm onto the Xerox research network and let it run overnight. Despite supposedly taking precautions to ensure that the worm didn't spread beyond their control, the worm broke containment and not only infected new unintended victims but also crashed more than 100 hosts within the Xerox research network. The next morning, Shoch and Hupp found unresponsive computers littering the Xerox Palo Alto Research Center (XERPARC).

Much like the case of Creeper and Reaper, Shoch and Hupp hacked in a failsafe. The two researchers created an *antibody packet* that could be sent to every infected computer to stop the worm's activity. The containment mishap did not deter Shoch and Hupp from experimenting with worms. By 1981, they had tested five other worms that were designed to perform various useful functions such as running diagnostics on the network and delivering time-based alarms. They even designed a complex worm that would automatically create animated images, which were produced frame by frame by newly created worms.

The greatest application of worms was obvious to researchers and hobbyists right away. Writing a program to automatically exploit and copy itself to a seemingly endless number of new victims was all too practical. Even though these worms would show their effectiveness within a decade of their discovery, they would be used in later decades to build incredibly large networks of *bots*, or computers under the control of a single or small group of hackers. When used in conjunction with other methods in the 2000s and 2010s, worms turned into building blocks for much more destructive attacks.

Government in the 1970s

Private-sector research into computers and what could be done with them shed light on the types of threats that the U.S. government might have to deal with in the distant future. The fact that this research was still largely happening behind the closed doors of well-funded research labs in the United States, and shared across private linkages via ARPANET, insulated the immediate threat of malicious attacks involving worms and viruses. However, the possibilities of computer-based disruption were only becoming more and more obvious as computers grew in popularity.

Although the Cold War gave rise to the two world superpowers of the United States and Russia, the technological research being done by both nations wasn't always even. The United States and its satellite of ally nations had invested heavily in computer technology and maintained a significant lead in computerization throughout the Cold War. This technological lead in computing was maintained, in small part, through an active effort on the part of U.S. intelligence to deny the Soviet Bloc access to both computer hardware and software.

Of course, this lag in consumer electronics didn't mean that the Soviet Union was entirely bereft of computing technology until that time; it only means that the metaphorical walled gardens of computerized research were happening in elite academic institutions for much longer there than it was in the United States.

In the same way research into computer technologies that could be used offensively like worms and viruses happened inside of research laboratories, so too did research into how to defend against them. One of the biggest practical problems facing the most secretive computers in the nation involved the shared use of computing resources.

In the 1970s, many computers used for national defense still operated based on shared processing time. In other words, a computer used to process one type of information in the morning could be used later in the afternoon by another user to process information for an entirely different program. This operation method had important implications for computers that might be used to process classified information. By the late 1970s, the Defense Advanced Research Projects Agency (DARPA), which at this time had been shortened to ARPA, began a highly technical program to investigate this problem called the Protection Analysis Project. This project was designed to answer the questions of processing sensitive information on mixed-use processing machines and develop a model for determining whether processing could be done securely.

Using dedicated engineers whose job was to test these machines for operational security, DARPA employed some of the first professional computer *penetration testers* (who they called *penetrators*) to investigate these problems. What the Protection Analysis Project found was that many vendors providing the United States with computing technology said that they mitigated easily exploited problems in the operation of their computers but in practice offered little to no protection for problems above and beyond patching problems DARPA had found for them.[4]

The Protection Analysis Program was short-lived. The program's perceived technical challenges were overwhelming and were ultimately too expensive to sustain over time. ARPA published a report of its findings on the program in 1978, cutting the funding for the program soon after. However, the Protection Analysis Program was representative of a growing effort across the U.S. Department of Defense (DoD) into penetration testing and computer security.

Law Enforcement

The 1970s didn't bring substantial change in the way that crime involving computers was thought of or investigated within the

---

[4] Bisbey, R., Hollingsworth, D. Protection Analysis Final Report (May, 1978) Information Sciences Institute. https://csrc.nist.gov/csrc/media/publications/conference-paper/1998/10/08/proceedings-of-the-21st-nissc-1998/documents/early-cs-papers/bisb78.pdf

government. Among the crimes involving computers that were recognized in the 1960s and early 1970s, physical destruction of computer systems and embezzlement were among the most cited. What we might think of now as "classic cybercrime" was thought of more in terms of fraud than crimes of traditional material theft.

Such fraud cases often involved perpetrators with an ideological angle. In a legal report in the April 1975 *American Bar Association Journal* titled "Computer Abuses Raise New Legal Problems,"[5] Susan Hubbell Nycum referred to these criminals as having *Robin Hood Syndrome*. In other words, the attackers were driven by animus toward rich corporations and believed that stealing from these groups was morally righteous. Computerized heists were gaining popularity as the 1970s went on, with millions of dollars in stolen funds taken through the abuse of computer systems.

Within government, a completely different view of computerized crime was being observed. A Government Accountability Office (GAO) report published in April 1976 refers to 69 instances of computer-related crime with associated losses of $2 million in government programs alone. So-called computer-related crimes were seen as incidental crimes committed by actors with low technical skill. In response, the GAO's recommendation was to increase staff auditing to ensure that those who were given access to computers weren't abusing their privileges. From the government's perspective, the threat wasn't from outside actors but instead came from those who had been given legitimate access to government computer systems, the aptly named *insider threat*.

The FBI, slow as it was to catch up with modern technology, arrested Stanley Mark Rifkin in 1978 on fraud charges. Rifkin's indictment accused him of stealing more than $10 million USD

---

[5] Nycum, S. H. (1975). Computer Abuses Raise New Legal Problems. American Bar Association Journal, 61(4), 444–448. http://www.jstor.org/stable/25727139

from his employer, the Security Pacific National Bank. Rifkin's scam involved socially engineering the Irving Trust Company in New York to act as the intermediary in an international bank transfer using knowledge he gained as a contract employee for the Security Pacific National Bank. In his position with the bank, Rifkin knew the language used by agents of the bank for transferring money and had access to sensitive areas where bank transfer codes were written down and left in plain view of others. Rifkin memorized a four-digit code he had seen written down that was used for high-value daily wire transfers and used it himself to redirect millions of dollars to a Swiss bank account that he controlled later the same day.

After he had secured the money, Rifkin arranged for the purchase of $8 million in diamonds from a Soviet-based diamond distributor in Geneva, Switzerland. Rifkin packed his newly acquired 43,000 carats in diamonds into his carry-on luggage and smuggled them back into the United States. If the story wasn't already odd enough, Rifkin then attempted to extort his employer using the diamonds he bought to secure a contract to teach the bank how to prevent computer fraud.

Rifkin's hairbrained scheme caused him to be arrested, and while on bail for his Security Pacific National Bank heist, he began plotting a $50 million plan to rob another bank. It's at this point that Rifkin's story takes an even stranger turn involving multiple three-letter agencies. Rifkin's second, $50 million heist was the result of an attempted entrapment scheme involving the Drug Enforcement Agency (DEA). The DEA was in contact with a cooperating prison inmate who they were hoping to develop into an informant against organized crime. When the DEA agreed to secure the unnamed, prospective informant's release from prison, pressure mounted against their target informant. This led the DEA to cooperate with their informant to entrap Rifkin in a new scheme to rob a second bank to prove the trustworthiness in the eyes of the court for their would-be informant.

The entrapment scheme fell apart when FBI intervened in the second case against Rifkin, knocking down the pending charges for Rifkin's second planned robbery. Rifkin's defense chose not to pursue a case of illegal entrapment in the second case, and Rifkin ended up facing prison time only for the Security Pacific National Bank heist. Despite their late involvement, FBI did not seem to take away any lessons learned from Rifkin's robbery. For all intents and purposes, Rifkin's fraud case wasn't much different than any other fraud case that the FBI had dealt with before Rifkin's crime.

Rifkin's case added significant momentum to the technical and cultural inertia of the hacking community. In later years, famous hacker Kevin Mitnick, who would himself become the target of multiple FBI investigations, referenced Rifkin's story in his book *The Art of Deception: Controlling the Human Element of Security*.

The understanding of computer-borne threats was broadening within the safety of the Petri dish of academia. At the same time, this knowledge was beginning to find its way into the public sphere where it was expanded even further. As this discovery continued among hobbyist and criminally inclined hackers, the first legal and ethical questions began to appear.

When it came to computer security threats, the U.S. intelligence community had the most skin in the game. Advanced research into computer threats started as early as the mid-1960s within the intelligence community and picked up where research on older technologies left off decades before.

It had been known since WWII that the natural emanations of electronic encryption and teletype machines could be used as an illicit intelligence collection source. These so-called TEM-PEST findings applied to computers as well and led to increased security mitigations that included metal shielding. In 1968, the DoD began investigating its own program to identify electronic threats and mitigations, which included applying TEMPEST shielding.[6]

Research into TEMPEST signaled that the U.S. government recognized advanced issues related to the use of computers and made early efforts to mitigate the threats they found. However, early research and the development of computer security initiatives were only the beginning of the work that would need to be done to sufficiently protect American government computer assets from attack. This work managed to put the government ahead of the curve, but there were still internal blind spots that would need to be addressed, some of which would soon become known.

The ARPANET Spam Incident

Despite being a self-contained network, ARPANET had a culture of its own. By the late 1970s, ARPANET had amassed a collection of new network connections and hosts to its national footprint. Companies such as IBM, Digital Equipment Corporation (DEC), Hewlett-Packard, and VAX were busy providing high-ticket computing solutions to U.S. government entities in the intelligence community and throughout the military. Computer sales were booming, and there were plenty of salespeople on ARPANET looking to cash in.

First introduced in 1971, email had been put into use on ARPANET and had quickly become the primary mode of communication for most ARPANET users. Rules and regulations

[6] U.S. Department of the Army. (16 July, 1968). Memorandum for: Chairman, Computer Security Working Group, USIB Security Committee. Subject: Enumeration of Individual Agency Computer Security Problem Areas. (CIA-RDP89B01354R000100120008-0).

dictating appropriate conduct on official government systems weren't always well documented or understood, leading to complaints about user conduct. On May 1, 1978, a sales representative for the Digital Equipment Corporation (DEC) named Gary Thuerk, who had access to email on ARPANET, decided to test the limit of this unwritten code of conduct.

Gary's email, sent to 393 recipients on ARPANET, began like this:

DIGITAL WILL BE GIVING A PRODUCT PRESENTATION OF THE NEWEST MEMBERS OF THE DECSYSTEM-20 FAMILY; THE DECSYSTEM-2020, 2020T, 2060, AND 2060T.

Thuerk's marketing instinct overrode his sense of courtesy, knowingly blasting official government emails with a first-of-its-kind "spam" marketing email from within the gates of this privileged system. ARPANET users were furious. Complaints about Thurek's abuse of a government system for personal gain poured in from users who had received one of his unwanted emails. It was unclear exactly what should be done about this breach of unwritten etiquette. Thuerk had certainly caused a stir, but was it enough to sanction him?

As considerations were being made about how to respond to Thuerk's provocation, his gambit ultimately paid off for him. While the complaints about his actions spiked, so did the new orders for the DEC systems Thuerk had advertised in his email. Thuerk's daft act of corporate insurrection resulted in the codification of a code of acceptable behavior on government systems. Venders selling products to the U.S. government with access to official email would likely lose their valuable access to official communications for pulling the same stunt as Thuerk did in 1978.

5

Hacker Rehabilitation

It was a hot summer day in 1983, and a 17-year-old named Kevin Poulsen furiously typed commands into his computer terminal. He had just managed to get a shell on his latest victim network: a University of California Berkeley (UCB) system. This system was unlike any other he had breached before; it was connected to a growing U.S. military research network that spanned the entire continental United States called the Advanced Research Projects Agency Network (ARPANET). Poulsen knew he shouldn't have been there, but he wasn't there to make money stealing information to sell to another country. He was there chasing a thrill.

Since its establishment in the 1960s, ARPANET had grown from its initial four hosts to well over 200 by 1983. Poulsen had graduated from phone phreaking to computer hacking but was still an active participant in both activities. With his hack of ARPANET, Poulsen was taking a dramatic step toward his status as a legendary hacker.

America in the 1970s was a crucible of increasingly reactionary cultures and subcultures. The Vietnam War had exacerbated the growing political divide in America's post-war civil society. The cultural reach of the political polarization spurred on by a growing number of casualties in Vietnam, Laos, and Cambodia was reflected in the activities of the Youth International Party (YIP). Despite their best efforts, YIP's influence on the general public in the 1970s was limited, but it wouldn't be long before hackers would begin leaving a much larger cultural footprint.

Dark Dante and the ARPANET Breach

At that time, computers were treated in much the same way as telephones were at that time. These systems could be connected to telephone systems, and then accessed remotely by directly calling a telephone number corresponding to a computer system.

Amassing their collective knowledge on BBS across the country, phone phreakers had learned a strategy called *war dialing*, which gave them a way to learn about what systems could be connected to, by calling each one and recording information about the type of system that responded. This information was then read and shared by the various Bulletin Board System (BBS) members.

In 1983, 17-year-old Kevin Poulsen was sitting at his computer, trying a phone number for an ARPANET-connected computer that he received online from a friend. Like so many other hackers in the early 1980s, Poulsen got his start in phone phreaking and made his way into hacking computers from there. Benefiting from the BBS development in the late 1970s, Poulsen (under the handle "Dark Dante") was able to locate all sorts of information, freely flowing through the interconnected space of the BBS.

So-called *phreaker forums* became bastions of information sharing among the members of the phreaking community. In prior decades, phreakers relied on the mail system to expand and distribute relevant information. After the advent of BBS, phreakers had a natural pathway to widening the community far beyond the confines and limitations of the mail system. Phreaker forums quickly became the primary method for sharing phreaking knowledge like dial-up gateways connecting a computer to a government agency.

Poulsen found the dial-up number to a computer connected to ARPANET at the University of California, Berkeley. After successfully obtaining a password prompt from the ARPANET computer, Poulsen was able to guess the password and obtain remote access. He had opened a door to one of the most sensitive computer networks in the world simply by guessing his way in. Working with a friend by the name of Ron Austin, Poulsen and Austin spent weeks exploring complex interconnections within ARPANET. It wasn't long before their presence on the network was noticed by a UCB member who reported their findings to the Federal Bureau of Investigation (FBI). It wasn't too long after that the Feds came knocking on Poulsen's door.

At age 17, Poulsen was legally considered a minor and wasn't charged in connection with the breach of ARPANET. Ron Austin, however, wasn't so lucky. He was charged and served time in jail. The fact that Poulsen was a minor benefited him years afterward, when he began working the Stanford Research Institute International (SRI), which had become a defense contractor in the 1970s. At the time, SRI was providing services to the U.S. Navy and was searching for technical experts to join their ranks. Recognizing Poulsen's talents, an SRI employee recognized Poulsen's talent and took him under his wing.

Geoffrey Goodfellow knew he was taking a risk on Poulsen, but Goodfellow was determined to get Poulsen on the right technical path. The prospect of working for SRI was of mutual interest to Poulsen who was excited by the opportunity to get his very own ARPANET account. When Poulsen agreed to take the job offer from SRI, Goodfellow's plan to rehabilitate Poulsen's image began.

In the 1970s, Goodfellow's plan was considered a somewhat risky gambit. Entrusting known hackers with legitimate accounts on one of the most secretive military networks in the world seemed like tempting fate. Was it really possible for Goodfellow to pull off such an audacious move? Nobody really knew. The idea of *hacker rehabilitation* wasn't a well-settled trope in the same way that it is now. Some Navy staffers considered Poulsen's involvement in the legitimate business of the U.S. Navy a significant risk especially in light of his history of breaching the very same network Goodfellow was now lobbying to give Poulsen access to. Goodfellow's plan was, at best, counterintuitive if not ridiculous outright. Ultimately, Goodfellow's effort to give Poulsen a second chance succeeded, and Poulsen was awarded both a job, and his coveted account on ARPANET. But Goodfellow had spent all of his political capital on Poulsen's second chance. Poulsen's compatriot in the original ARPANET breach, Ron Austin, wasn't so lucky.

Citing the charges for breaching ARPANET against Austin, the Navy denied SRI's request to give him his own ARPANET account. Poulsen had narrowly avoided charges of his own due to the fact that he was a minor at the time of the ARPANET breach. Austin was charged as a legal adult, effectively disqualifying him from catching the same break Poulsen had. Nevertheless, Goodfellow considered his efforts successful. He may not have been able to save both young men, but even one was enough to prove his theory that young hackers could be saved from a life of crime as long as they were given a second chance and the right opportunity.

The Los Alamos National Labs Breach

The 1970s had witnessed an explosion of computer technology usage throughout Western governments, with ARPANET acting as the backbone of a rapidly growing national security bureaucracy. Powered by network-attached computers, ARPANET was the indispensable conduit of U.S. military research and development. In the closing years of the 1970s, ARPANET's foundational concept as a method for sharing information had been proven, and networked computing technologies were entering into even the most entrenched government agencies in the country. This trend even made its way into one of the most sensitive military research laboratories in the world, the Los Alamos National Labs (LANL).

It was just after working hours on May 9th, 1983, when an LANL researcher logged into his computer terminal and noticed something odd. He received an internal system message from an account that had been programmed into the system by default. The default system account on the Digital Equipment Corporation Virtual Address eXtension/Virtual Memory System (DEC VAX/VMS) used by LANL was called "DEMO".

The DEMO account was rarely, if ever used. This fact alone was enough to raise concern, but when the user behind the DEMO account began asking where to find computer games on the network, it was clear that something unusual was happening. Confused, the researcher began a conversation using the internal messaging system with the user logged into the DEMO account (figure 5.1). The confused, and slightly alarmed LANL researcher was beginning to suspect that the DEMO account was *not* under the control of a legitimate Los Alamos employee. The researcher made note of the strange conversation and reported it to lab security.

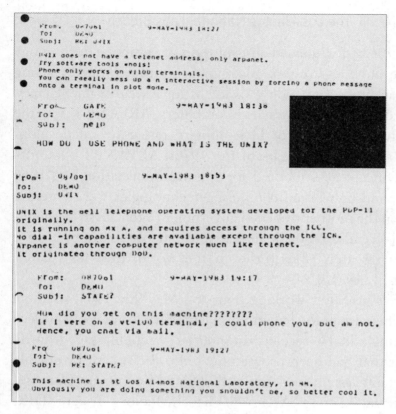

FIGURE 5.1 An LANL system operator talks to a 414 hacker on their compromised system

After a second breach of the LANL network in June an internal investigation was launched, which found that multiple default accounts had been accessed during both breaches. At the time, VAX/VMS came preloaded with a few different default accounts that could be used for various reasons. For example, accounts like "NETWORK" could aptly be used to configure networking while the "TEST" account could be used to test the functionality of the system prior to creating other user accounts. These default accounts were paired with common default passwords, which could be found in system manuals and were easily guessed.

For example, the password for the "NETWORK" account was simply NETWORK. As the internal investigation into the breach continued, they would discover that the compromise had not been the work of just one hacker.

The 414s

The investigation of the LANL breach turned up evidence that responsibility for the breach belonged to a group of teenage hackers in Wisconsin. The teenage members of the *414s*, as they called themselves, originally met in an IBM-sponsored tech mentorship program called the *Explorer Scout* program. The program provided resources to participants and opportunities to hone their technical skills. As was common for BBS operators in the 1980s, the group adopted their name from the Milwaukee area code they lived in. By all appearances, their intent had not been to cause any harm, but instead they took an opportunity to get into a sensitive military research network and digitally loiter. They seemed more interested in games hosted on the network than stealing sensitive information.

Ranging in age from 17 to 22, the core members of the 414s were Neal Patrick, Tim Winslow, and Gerald Wondra. As law enforcement began to focus on these three young men, it became clear that the breach of the LANL network wasn't the first time they had done something like this. Attacks on other organizations by the 414s included the Sloan-Kettering Cancer Center in New York and the Security Pacific National Bank, both breaches were under FBI investigation. The most pressing question resulting from the investigations was exactly how a ragtag collection of teens managed to gain access to a network used by one of the foremost nuclear research labs in the country. How were they even able to find the right number belonging to the LANL network among the 87 million American telephone numbers in use in 1983?

The 414s, cooperating with law enforcement, were happy to answer this question. The teens stumbled across a list of remote-access telephone numbers, which had been shared with them by other hackers. The hackers who shared the information had compiled the list using *war dialing* techniques. One of the numbers on this list was the telephone number to the LANL network. When the 414s connected dialed the number and connected their computers to the network, they were able to use the easily-guessed default accounts to get their access. The sheer simplicity of their breach was enough to rattle investigators.

Although they didn't cause any damage to the LANL network or its operations beyond a minor disruption, the cultural impact was tremendous. When the story of the LANL breach broke to the public in August 1983, Patrick became the face and de facto spokesman for the 414s. At age 17, he became an overnight celebrity and took advantage of his newly minted notoriety to speak directly to the press. Part of his media tour even included an appearance on Phil Donahue's popular daytime talk show. For many Americans, this was their first exposure to the concept of computer hacking, let alone the image of a hacker in the flesh. The fact that their notoriety came from allegations of hacking the government only fueled public intrigue. Patrick and the 414s' timing could not have been better.

WarGames, a popular movie starring Matthew Broderick as a teenage hacker named David Lightman who gains access to an American nuclear launch system, had been released only one month before the story about the 414s broke in mainstream news sources. The movie left such a deep impression on the American public that it even inspired President Ronald Reagan to begin taking the threat of amateur hackers more seriously.

Shaping the Hacker Image

Before the LANL breach, few major news stories involving computer-related fraud and hacking had made it onto the front pages of mainstream news. Suddenly, the public saw Patrick's teenage face on the cover of *Newsweek,* alongside a headline reading "Computer Capers." *WarGames* and Patrick's public appearances did more to define the image of the young white male hacker to the public at a crucial time in history. Speaking to the *Detroit Free Press* in August 1989, a security consultant named Donn Parker remarked that the 414s "fit the classic profile of computer bandits" as "young, male, intelligent, highly motivated, and energetic,"[1] which further cemented the stereotype to the public.

Many who saw Neal Patrick and the story of his cohort of young hackers began to ask serious questions about the security of American government computers for the first time. These questions were at least in part driven by Cold War anxieties. After all, if these fresh-faced, teenage hackers could run amok in a nuclear research network, imagine what the Russians could do. The American public demanded answers, and Congress was obligated to answer.

Congressional Testimony

The real-world consequences of the LANL breach culminated in a Congressional hearing on the issue of the U.S. government's computer security policies. Testimony was scheduled to be heard before the House Subcommittee on Transportation, Aviation, and Materials in the later months of 1983. Among those testifying was the Deputy Assistant Director Floyd Clarke of the FBI's

---

[1] https://www.newspapers.com/article/detroit-free-press-high-techhijinkswar/21801610

Criminal Investigative Division. In his remarks, Clarke high-lighted cases involving computer-based fraud and underscored the trope of the teenage hacker, citing a 1980 similar case out of the FBI's New York field office.[2] In this case, a group of middle schoolers accessed 20 computers at their school without permission.

Another piece of supporting testimony to the same House subcommittee came from none other than Geoffrey Goodfellow. At the time of his congressional testimony, Goodfellow was hard at work rehabilitating his co-worker at SRI, Kevin Poulsen. Standing before the House of Representatives, Goodfellow gave remarks about the nature of hackers in defense of the 414s. In his testimony, Goodfellow gave personal details on his own back-ground as a hacker, describing that he'd discovered computers at a young age and followed a similar path that the 414s had.

Goodfellow had been a high-school dropout before coming onboard with SRI. In his decade long career since, he had been promoted to the position of principal investigator at SRI, and he had done it all without any formal education. Goodfellow pro-fessed that he had been self-educated, and attributed his profes-sional success to the fact that he had not been caught for any of the supposed crimes he committed. Goodfellow saw himself in the story of troubled young hackers like Poulsen and the mem-bers of the 414s.

What Goodfellow failed to accomplish at the time, how-ever, was a more robust understanding of the nature of the hacking community. He trivially sorted hackers into two camps: the *good guys* and the *bad guys*. Influenced heavily by *Star Wars*, Goodfellow spoke of hackers in the binary terms of the movie's lore—aligned either with "the light side" or the dark side."

---

[2] https://www.muckrock.com/foi/united-states-of-america-10/414-hack-of-los-alamos-72665/#file-861321

But in his testimony, he did little to define what actions materially separated the two groups. As far as Goodfellow was concerned, his project to rehabilitate Poulsen had been a success in September of 1983. Goodfellow saw that the skills of wayward hackers could be put to good use within government, and with his young apprentice, Poulsen, as his token success, he was prepared to sell the concept of hacker rehabilitation to anyone who would listen.

Goodfellow's argument for leniency for the 414s was that they were merely curious kids who didn't see their activities as legal or illegal. He painted them as innocently curious, and this fact exempted them from the legal implications of their actions. Furthermore, he blamed the victims of hackers, suggesting that the responsibility for the LANL hack was with the system administrators of the LANL network for not protecting their computers well enough. Although federal law would eventually prove that Goodfellow's legal analysis was incorrect, his testimony helped set a standard, even for a short time, for the way hackers would be treated by federal law enforcement. What some like Goodfellow recognized is that the technical skills possessed by inquisitive young hackers were not easy to come by at the time, and adopting a rehabilitative approach to criminal justice in these cases had its benefits.

The Morris Worm

On December 6, 1988, the Department of Defense (DoD) Office of Public Affairs team issued an urgent press release. The headline on the press release stated, "DARPA Establishes Computer Emergency Response Team" and announced, "The CERT is intended to respond to computer security threats such as the recent self-replicating computer program ('computer virus') that invaded many defense and research computers."

In the previous month, the entire DoD had been in chaos, as a first-of-its-kind computer virus tore through ARPANET. The Morris worm began its spread on the evening of November 2, 1988, on the Massachusetts Institute of Technology (MIT) campus. Its first detection was recorded at 5 p.m. at Cornell University.[3] Before midnight, the overpowering worm had made its way into military networks. Within 24 hours, the Morris worm had infected 10% of all computers connected to the Internet.

Investigating the release of a computer virus is similar to how an epidemiologist might investigate the beginning of a new disease. Determining who and where "patient zero" is at the time of infection is a painstaking task that requires both the collection and analysis of huge volumes of information. In some cases, a human virus might spread far beyond the original host before it's even recognized. This wasn't the case for the Morris worm.

The worm was written by a graduate student named Robert Tappan Morris. To his credit, Morris had quickly taken responsibility for writing the worm when he realized that it had managed to spread out of his control. On November 5, 1988, the *New York Times* broke the story of the rampaging computer worm, identifying Morris by name. To some in government circles, Robert Tappan Morris was a familiar name. Morris' father (also named Robert Morris) was a career cryptographic mathematician working at the National Security Agency (NSA) at Ft. Meade, Maryland.

Two days after the story broke, FBI investigators met with Robert Tappan Morris' father, at his workplace. The NSA was already aware of the worm before the FBI had even met with Morris' father, who had shared a copy of the code with the NSA

---

[3] https://nsarchive.gwu.edu/sites/default/files/documents/6168246/National-Security-Archive-Office-of-the-Under.pdf

on November 3 and work was well underway to dissect and analyze the worm's code. The National Computer Security Center (NCSC), a group of NSA employees focused on computer defense, determined that despite its presence on ARPANET, the Morris worm had not made its way onto any computers containing classified information. It was another close call for the government and was instructive for future digital outbreaks.

At the time, computer researchers in the U.S. government didn't have the benefit of an experienced and dedicated organization capable of tracking and responding to the active spread of computer viruses. Like the 414 breach, the Morris worm was yet another wake-up call for leaders in the American government, and highlighted the critical lack of widely available high-tech skill within their ranks.

In post-mortem reports of the incident, the National Aeronautics and Space Administration (NASA) noted that, on the same day the worm had been released, it had already made its way onto ARPANET. Once the worm made it this far, it put all of the research organizations attached to the network at risk turning ARPANET into a conduit to spread the worm into NASA's dedicated research network. Once compromised, a computer infected with the Morris worm spawned multiple "shells" or terminal programs that would deplete the resources of the victim computer. In effect, this was the dreaded denial-of-service attack that had been imagined by Xerox researchers in the 1970s.

In a February 1989 paper titled "The Internet Worm," author Peter J. Denning wrote:

> *Attempts to kill these programs were ineffective: new copies would appear from Internet connections as fast as old copies were deleted. Many systems had to be shut down and the security loopholes closed before they could be restarted on the network without reinfestation.*

In an incredible stroke of luck, a pre-scheduled annual meeting of Unix experts was happening in Berkeley, California the day after the worm was released. Working with captured copies of the Morris worm's software, the Unix researchers were able to issue a patch later that evening, which helped stop the rapidly spreading infection. While the damage of the Morris worm seemed severe at the time, and a significant number of Internet-connected computers were impacted by it, the length of time the worm was allowed to spread without any mitigations to slow it down was isolated to less than a week. By November 12, 1988, the last of the backlogged emails were clearing, but the story of the Morris worm was only just beginning.

After turning himself in, Morris fully cooperated with the investigation, giving responders information about how the worm was written and how it had spread so quickly. Despite his help, Morris was the first person ever charged and convicted under the newly passed Computer Fraud and Abuse Act (CFAA) and sentenced to three years of probation. During his trial, he revealed that he had suffered from his own success, stating that his motive was "to demonstrate the inadequacies of current security measures on computer networks by exploiting the security defects" that he managed to find.

Morris's motivations were a common theme for many hackers and security researchers. Complex motivations are involved in finding computer security vulnerabilities. In many cases, these vulnerabilities are shared with the vendors responsible for fixing their products. But in the 1980s, it was just as common for vendors to ignore hackers sharing information with them as it was for vendors to accept security researchers' findings and fix the bugs. In a desperate effort to see their vulnerabilities fixed, hackers would sometimes release the vulnerabilities to the public, allowing anyone to actively exploit them. This, in turn, places pressure on the vendors to fix the vulnerabilities.

In the weeks after the release of the Morris worm, senior officials representing three-letter agencies met to discuss their recommendations and findings on November 14, 1988. One of the main prescriptions was that a government authority should be established to track and respond to computer-based threats. To meet this need, the Defense Advanced Research Projects Agency (DARPA) was tasked with creating that central coordination center. This new organization was called the Computer Emergency Response Team (CERT) and announced the following month.

Before the Morris worm, viruses had only been considered a major problem for personal computers. Any threat they may have posed to large, complex computer networks was nominal. When the dust settled from the Morris worm's spree of infections on ARPANET, the NSA's executive team was forced to consider the threat of domestically sourced viruses as a serious threat to national security.

Legal Implications of Hacking

A sharp increase in the availability and use of technology in the mid-late 1980s came with an increase in computer-aided fraud that was becoming an increasing problem for American law enforcement. Police at the local and federal level were working with outdated tools, often charging suspects with offenses that were only vaguely applicable to the crimes they had been accused of committing.

Relief first came with the passage of the Comprehensive Crime Control Act (CCCA) of 1984. This act included the first federal computer crime statute in American law and was a step toward a more suitable legal framework for cybercrime legislation. The CCCA was also a recognition that computer crimes could be an issue for federal law enforcement as much as local police, who had been responsible for enforcing rules against telephone fraud at the peak of the popularity of phone phreaking. Two years later in 1986, Congress passed the CFAA, which fundamentally changed the way that computer crime laws would be prosecuted and had impacts on the hackers this act meant to bind.

WANK and OILZ

As the 1980s ended, the changing state of computer security wasn't kind to America's premier space agency. In addition to suffering from the release of the Morris worm, NASA's Space Physics Analysis Network (SPAN) had also been infected by the Father Christmas worm in 1988. Both infections had been incidental. In other words, they weren't targeting NASA specifically but managed to infect agency assets regardless. While both the Morris and Father Christmas worms would leave their mark on NASA's computer security strategy, one infection in the 1980s, above all, would change the face of computer security forever.

On October 16th, 1989, NASA employees logged into their computers and found a crude text-banner filling their screens. Like the Morris worm, an infection appeared to be taking place on the SPAN, but it appeared to have a somewhat different purpose. The message displayed in the banner hinted at an opposition to the launch of the nuclear-powered Galileo spacecraft, which, at the time of the infection, was preparing for launch at Cape Canaveral, Florida.

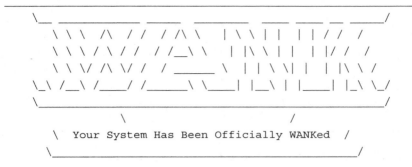

```
W O R M S   A G A I N S T   N U C L E A R   K I L L E R S
```

You talk of times of peace for all, and then prepare for war.

By the end of the first day of the infection, the code for the WANK worm had already been collected, analyzed, and response actions were underway. The following day, CERT issued an advisory on the worm, showing that the prescriptions made after the Morris worm were already being applied to new incidents. Within three days of the infection, a government-wide response had produced multiple scripts to combat the WANK worm's spread. It seemed that rapid mitigations, thanks to the lessons learned from past incidents, had worked as expected and ended the infection. However, any celebrations of the demise of WANK were premature.

On October 30, signs of a new infection once again began to emerge from NASA's networks. In networks that were believed to be free of WANK worm infections, a second, upgraded variant of the original WANK worm appeared. Named OILZ, the second variant fixed a problem in WANK, which had self-limited the spread of the initial infection. Improvements in OILZ allowed the new worm to spread much further, both gaining access to new accounts and changing their passwords. Fresh off of the investigation of the WANK infection, responders found that OILZ was forwarding information about infected machines to a server located in France. It was this persistent network connection that led investigators to believe that the source of both infections could be traced to French hackers (figure 5.2).[4]

Although OILZ isn't as well-known in historic context as the WANK worm despite being part of the same attack, the capability added to OILZ shows a level of maturity and automation that hadn't been seen before in attacks against the government. Course correcting mid-breach, the features present in OILZ were determined to have been authored by multiple participants, as had the original WANK worm. But not all of the conclusions made by investigators proved to hold up under scrutiny (see Figure 5.2).

OFFICE OF MANAGEMENT

INFORMATION RESOURCES MANAGEMENT

SPACE PHYSICS ANALYSIS NETWORK (SPAN) WORM INCIDENT

DESCRIPTION OF ATTACK

- ORIGIN TRACED TO FRANCE

- WORM CODE:
    - EXPLOITS POOR PASSWORD MANAGEMENT PRACTICES
        - NASA VICTIMS FAILED TO FOLLOW PUBLISHED AGENCY POLICIES AND PROCEDURES
    - CAUSES
        - DISRUPTION AND DENIAL OF SERVICE
        - EXPENDITURE OF RESOURCES TO TECHNICALLY DIAGNOSE AND DISINFECT AFFECTED SYSTEMS
        - DISPLAY OF BANNER ON USER SCREENS

- TWO PHASED ATTACK
    - OCT 16 ATTACK AFFECTED APPROXIMATELY 90 NODES
    - OCT 29 ATTACK AFFECTED OVER 500 NODES
        - USED IMPROVED VERSION TO EXPLOIT ADDITIONAL PASSWORDS

- SPECIFIC IDENTIFICATION OF PENETRATED NODES UNDERWAY
    - ONLY 3 IDENTIFIED AT NASA TO DATE

- ATTACK IS STILL ACTIVE

FIGURE 5.2 NASA's investigative record incorrectly attributed the origin of the WANK worm to France.

---

[4] Longstaff, T.A., & E.E. Schultz. (1993). Beyond preliminary analysis of the WANK and OILZ worms: A case study of malicious code. *Computers & Security*.

On its own, the message was rude, but it was the connotation of the abbreviation of WANK spelled out above the word that gave a major context clue to its origin. "Worms Against Nuclear Killers" hinted at a political motivation for the attack. Targeting NASA just days ahead of the launch of the Galileo space probe, which itself was carrying nuclear material, WANK was assumed to be part of a growing anti-nuclear technology movement, which believed that sending nuclear material to space was not in the best interests of humanity.

The worm's code gave additional context clues as to the nature of the worm's authorship. It appeared to use native English in its messaging, and its code was filled with more sophomoric humor (e.g., some variables were named "PHALIC" or "PHRACKED"), leading researchers to believe that the authors must have been young men.

In addition to DECNET at NASA, the WANK worm also infected another major government network at the Department of Energy. Remarkably, WANK seemed to be selective about which networks it spread to. This suggested some discretion on the part of the authors about which networks they wanted to use to send their message.

Investigation

Although the original WANK infection was traced to France during the breach's initial investigation, the true origin of the infection was Australia. One of the messages included in the original WANK code read, "*You talk of times of peace for all, and then prepare for war,*" which came from a popular 1980s song named "Power and Passion" by Australian band Midnight Oil. It's also likely that "OILZ" was named as a reference to the band.

Subsequent investigations into the attack's history would result in criminal charges for a small, but dedicated group of hackers living in Melbourne, Australia. Rumors of involvement in the

WANK/OILZ breach were also leveled against an individual who would become a household name some 30 years later: Julian Assange. Assange himself, however, has been coy about his knowledge of who was responsible for writing the WANK worm despite his involvement in the Melbourne hacking scene of the 1980s.

Hacktivism

Ultimately, the legacy of WANK and OILZ was to set the tone for future acts of what would come to be called *"hacktivism"* in the future. They were also among the first attacks against a world government with an apparent grassroots political motivation. Discussion of the efficacy of using nuclear power had become a hot topic of conversation in the late 1980s. The public's concern about nuclear energy was prompted by two major events that happened in 1986: the nuclear meltdown at Chernobyl and the midair explosion of the Challenger spacecraft that scattered nuclear material across Floridian civilian-inhabited areas.

As a case in isolation, WANK didn't have the intended effect on NASA's long-term operations. NASA continued with its plans and launched the nuclear-powered Galileo spacecraft on schedule, however, WANK did leave an enduring mark on the technology landscape of the early 1990s and proved that hacktivism could be a powerful tool of public influence.

Another important legacy of WANK/OILZ was the demonstration of the development and deployment of multiple generations of malware. Although WANK wasn't the first worm to infect a sensitive government network, it was one of the first to see a second version emerge during the cleanup of the original infection. WANK and OILZ had set a standard for politically motivated hacking that wouldn't be matched for many years, but future hacktivists had the Melbourne hackers to thank for proving the theory was possible.

CHAPTER

6

On the Other Side
of The Wall

Cliff Stoll was about as far from the archetype of a digital investigator as a person could be. He was a jack-of-all-trades who was as interested in electronic music as much as math, science, and astronomy, but against all odds, he would find himself in the middle of a tale of international intrigue. In 1986, Stoll was working as a system administrator at Lawrence Berkeley National Laboratories and had been tasked with reviewing a time-accounting ledger for the Unix system he administrated. As he read the monthly telephone billing invoice for his division, he noticed that the amount of time the university was billed for did not match the amount of time his users had logged when connecting into the computer systems he managed.

The difference on the bill amounted to a grand total of 75 cents, an amount that would have gone completely unnoticed to most other system administrators, but not Stoll. To him, a large inconsistency would have been less interesting, it was the fact that the difference in billing was so small that drew his attention. The unaccounted 75 cents would cause Stoll to launch his own investigation into the cost discrepancy and would eventually be documented in his popular book, *The Cuckoo's Egg: Tracking a Spy Through the Maze of Computer Espionage*, published in 1989. As Stoll pulled the thread on the mystery, he uncovered a breach of his university's network that would lead back to something much bigger than he ever could have imagined. He found that two hackers associated with a hacker collective in West Germany called the Chaos Computer Club (CCC) had been responsible for a breach into the Lawrence Berkeley lab network.

The two hackers were Markus Hess (aka Urmel) and Karl Koch (aka Hagbard).[1] Both Hess and Koch were West Germany residents and active in the Western German hacking community. Not only had they exploited their way into Lawrence Berkeley, but they had also breached U.S.-based military contractors, facilities, and universities, stealing information everywhere they went.

Although they had been involved in the hacking plot, Hess and Koch didn't set out to be spies. At the start, they were hobbyist hackers using the skills they had to gain unauthorized access to highly sensitive networks purely for their own amusement. They spent most of their time focusing on universities and telecommunications companies. But once they realized that some of the networks they breached contained information valuable to the Soviet government, they decided to go pro. Their decision to begin hacking for money was driven in part by financial problems brought on by the high telephone bills they accrued from their hacking activities. Not only would the money go to subsidizing their hacking, but it would also go to Koch, who was struggling with his addiction-related debts.

[1] https://www.guinnessworldrecords.com/world-records/612868-first-incident-of-cyber-espionage

To get the ball rolling, Hess and Koch contacted three of their acquaintances who they knew had contacts with the Soviet KGB. Those three men, Dirk-Otto Brezinsky (aka DOB), Hans Huebner (aka Pengo) and a local casino employee Peter Carl contacted the KGB through his affiliates and let them know about the pair's activities. Shortly after, the KGB arranged with Hess and Koch to purchase the stolen information. This type of agreement was common in the world of espionage, but it was new territory for hackers.

The story of the KGB hack stands as a historic first in hacking for geopolitical purposes. It's the first well-recorded case of hacking between world powers but as is sometimes the case in spy stories, it ends on a somber, mysterious note. After voluntarily coming forward to claim responsibility for the hacks, Markus Hess was arrested in 1987 and three years later, convicted on charges of espionage. His sentence was suspended, and Hess managed to avoid serving any time in jail. On the other hand, Koch's fate is unclear to this day.

On May 23rd, 1989, Koch appeared at his office of employment in Hannover, Germany. After leaving the office to deliver a package that afternoon, Koch disappeared. It was the last time he was seen alive. Koch was reported missing by his co-workers, and on a tip about an abandoned car in a forest area outside of Hannover, Koch's shoeless body was found burned in what appeared to be a controlled fire. Koch had left no suicide note, and strangely, he did not have any shoes on his feet when his body was found.

Immediately, questions were raised about Koch's death, and the German hacking community began to wonder if Koch's role in the KGB hack had played a part in his untimely death.[2]

---

[2] *Approaching Zero: The Extraordinary Underworld of Hackers, Phreakers, Virus Writers, and Keyboard Criminals*, by Paul Mungo & Bryan Glough, 1991.

Despite the suspicious circumstances that the state Koch's body was found in, local authorities ruled his death a suicide. With suggestions that the East German intelligence service, the Stasi, was involved in Koch's death, the evidence of murder remains circumstantial.

Had a vengeful intelligence service been responsible for Koch's death? Had local authorities acted complicitly in a case of international execution? Some historians point to Koch's history of mental illness and addiction to support the official case for suicide, but this fact does not answer all of the lingering questions about the case. If Koch's death had been a case of state-sponsored murder, it wasn't the only such case of extrajudicial killing in the history of Cold War espionage.

Many details of the KGB hack are now known, but one major question hasn't yet been answered. How did a world power without an obvious native hacking culture rivaling the West manage to pull off such a complex attack for its day?

Soviet Intelligence

Under Stalin, the USSR was a notoriously paranoid society. This environment of paranoia existed even before the Bolshevik communist movement seized power of Russia in 1922. The Soviet KGB, which operated in the post-war Soviet Union, can trace its origins back to the Tsarist secret police established in 1881. Named the *Okhrana*, it was the predecessor to the more recognized secret police organization run by the Soviet Union called the *Cheka*.

Unsurprisingly for a secret police organization, the Cheka had a reputation for brutality. Led by a man with a particularly cruel reputation, Felix Dzerzhinsky oversaw some of the Cheka's most barbaric operations, which included programs of widespread torture and execution of so-called "enemies of the people." This *"Chekist"* approach to dealing with the civilian population continued through the second world war and into the post-war period. Many of the same methods used by the Cheka would later be adopted by post-war Soviet intelligence after it reorganized into the KGB. Chekist brutality was one of the main enforcers of Soviet orthodoxy and contributed to the "closed society" for which the USSR came to be known.

It was this isolationist culture that led Winston Churchill to declare that "an iron curtain has descended" across the Asian continent. The closed Soviet society made communication beyond the borders of the Soviet Bloc nearly impossible for average citizens and suppressed information exchange even inside Soviet society. Even with all of these means of control in place, Soviet intelligence had difficulty keeping pace with the Western world in terms of computer technology development.

What Soviet intelligence lacked in technical skill, it made up for in human operations. Throughout the Cold War, Soviet intelligence was proficient in the recruitment of human spies, particularly against the United States and United Kingdom. Soviet intelligence had a talent for spotting potential recruits early and convincing them to work for the Soviet cause on the basis of ideology, as it had done in the case of the Cambridge Five spy ring, as well as spies in the Manhattan Project, Klaus Fuchs and David Greenglass. This was in contrast to Western intelligence agencies such as the National Security Agency (NSA), Central Intelligence Agency (CIA), Government Communications Headquarters (GCHQ), and MI6, which found more espionage success through the use of cutting-edge technologies like the U-2 spy plane and the Corona spy satellite program.

A "Closed Society"

Retrospectives on the U often draw contrast between the "open" society of Western nations during the Cold War and the "closed" society of the Soviet Bloc nations. Soviet protectionism did chill international trade and communication to the detriment of many different aspects of Soviet life, including the average Soviet citizen's relationship to technology. The closed, paranoid society fostered by Soviet state security is one major reason that a pervasive culture of hacking didn't develop on the world stage in the same way that it did in many others, but this isn't the full story. Technological development in the Soviet Union had different goals and values than Western nations, and as a result, some Western technologies didn't have exact Soviet equivalents.

This isn't to say that Western nations didn't have their own issues involving the suppression of social groups. The FBI's activity throughout the Cold War, suppressed civil rights organizations and even today, routinely puts its thumb on the scale against social change. Over the years, this activity, even in the context of the "open" Western society created an air of distrust and resentment among Western hackers and law enforcement. However, the comparative openness of Western nations did create a more relaxed approach to the development of subcultures and even countercultures like that of the American hacking community.

Glasnost and Perestroika

After decades of Soviet life defined by fear of repercussions by paranoid state-security, it was clear to Soviet leadership that something needed to change. In the 1980s under Premier Mikhail Gorbachev, the USSR undertook a sweeping social reform to relax state control and allow more outside influences into Soviet nations. The first of these reforms was known as *Glasnost* and preceded a further reform of the Soviet economy called *Perestroika*. Together, these policies somewhat improved the accessibility of commercial computing technology to Soviet citizens and allowed them to be exposed to aspects of Western culture.

Before Perestroika, computer access in the Soviet Union was limited. While Apple computers were becoming more widely available in the average American homes, home computers were far beyond the reach of the average Soviet citizen. The same walled-garden that existed in the United States in the 1950s not only existed in the USSR but persisted deep into the 1980s.

When Perestroika came to the Soviet Union in the late 1980s, it enabled private electronics enterprises aimed at importing and distributing computer technology to the Soviet public. Soviet computer cooperatives imported secondhand computer hardware and software from Western nations and sold both to a Soviet public hungry for more modern technologies.

Computers and Telecommunications

From the beginning, science and technology were major focus areas for Soviet domestic policy. In 1957, the USSR embarrassed the West on the world stage by launching the first satellite. Sputnik signaled to the world that the USSR was just as, if not more, adept at producing advanced technologies than the West. But what Western governments at the time didn't fully understand was that technological development in the Soviet Union was uneven and full of contradictions. For example, Soviet computing technology significantly lagged behind the West from the beginning of the post-war period. After the world's first digital computer Electronic Numerical Integrator and Computer (ENIAC) was revealed to the public in 1946, the Soviet Union saw the potential applications for advanced computing and tried to buy ENIAC designs so they could build their own version of the machine.

When that plan failed, the Soviet government then attempted to buy a fully assembled ENIAC.[3] However, by 1948, Western nations began economic sanctions against the Soviet Union, which constrained the export of computer equipment to the USSR. This forced Soviet leaders to find ways to develop their own hardware. The USSR had a telecommunications system, but it didn't always meet the needs of the public and suffered from inadequate automation.[4] While phreakers were fighting "Ma Bell" in the United States throughout the 1960s and 1970s, citizens of the Soviet Union were fighting a telephone system that hadn't even been digitized throughout the country.

As far as computers were concerned, what hardware the Soviet Union *did* have was often smuggled into the country along with the software needed to operate it. The USSR did have some of its own hardware designs, but by the late 1980s, Western-designed hardware and software were vastly preferred over domestically produced materials.

Soviet Phreaking

Despite the popularity of phone phreaking in the West, phreaking didn't develop in the same way in the Soviet Union. In the West, phone phreaking was advanced by amateur enthusiasts who were able to learn about the phone system through open communication with other phreakers and their own low-risk explorations.

---

[3] *Soviet Computing and Technology Transfer: An Overview* by Seymore E. Goodman, July 1979. https://doi.org/10.2307/2009909
[4] *The Soviet Telecommunications System*, by Robert W. Campbell, 1988.

In the Soviet Union, the telephone system was controlled by the state as opposed to being managed by a private company as they were in the United States. For Soviet citizens, theft of state property was punished much more harshly than similar crimes in the West. During the Stalinist era, theft of state property could earn a thief a trip into the dreaded Gulag carceral system, which was considered a stiff deterrent even for simple crimes. Even with this hefty punishment, theft of state property accounted for half of the inmates of the Gulags.[5] Breaking and entering and theft of computer manuals in the West were also considered serious crimes, but punishments in the American legal system for these types of crimes didn't typically come with such strict punishments, not to mention that Gulags were known for their cruel and unusual punishments.

Even with harsh penalties, theft was still a common crime in the USSR. This suggests that the fear of a sentence to the Gulag couldn't have been the only reason phreaking didn't develop in the same timeframe. A more likely explanation is that the Soviet telephone system was simply too old to hack. The phreaking community in the United States only grew in popularity thanks to the possibilities the digital telephone system offered. For example, blue boxes could work only because they could exploit the digital acoustic systems used by American telephone companies. This is how phreakers like Joybubbles were able to hack the American telephone system through whistling at different pitches.

A study conducted in 1970 concluded that the number of Soviet telephones connected to a manually switched system was around 14%.[6] The vast majority of the Soviet telephone system

---

[5] https://pure.manchester.ac.uk/ws/portalfiles/portal/84501912/EHR_Gorlizki_Theft_under_Stalin_AAM.pdf
[6] https://www.ucis.pitt.edu/nceeer/pre1998/1988-801-5-Campbell.pdf

was connected by analog switching systems, unlike the Western telephone network, which was in the process of going digital in the 1970s. These analog systems were electromagnetically actuated, requiring the electronic connections that connected one telephone to another to be physically switched. This meant that the analog system used by the Soviets was on the one hand, less efficient but also wasn't prone to the same sorts of exploits phreakers in the West had developed in the same decade. Electromagnetic switching continued to be the main form of telephone-switching technology in use in the Soviet Union into the mid-1980s, roughly a decade before mobile phones would hit Soviet markets for the first time.

Building a Soviet Internet

Western retrospectives on Internet history portray the idea that a large-scale project like the Advanced Research Projects Agency Network (ARPANET) were unique to the United States. However, the United States wasn't unique among nations in both imagining and demonstrating the proof of concept for networked computers. The Soviet Union was just as much a competitor in the development of cyberspace as the Western world. In the USSR, the first attempt to build a Soviet counterpart to ARPANET was called the National Automated System for Computation (OGAS). OGAS was ahead of its time. In fact, as was the case with Sputnik, Soviet science was further along in the creation of computer networking than the West.

Initial research into OGAS began in 1962, and was led by the Soviet mathematician and information technology pioneer Viktor Glushkov. The founding idea of Glushkov's OGAS was prophetic; he imagined that with the right funding OGAS wouldn't only change the way that Soviet citizens would communicate, it would also fundamentally change the economy. Glushkov predicted that OGAS-connected computers would bring about a cashless society, envisioning a complete move to electronic payments within 20 years.

In 1970, Glushkov requested a 100-billion ruble investment from the Soviet government to expand OGAS. This expansion would've made Internet technology rapidly available to the Soviet public. The sum Glushkov asked for was tremendous, totaling roughly $850 billion today, but his request was denied. This left Glushkov to pursue a much more modest maintenance project for existing OGAS networks, rather than expanding toward the full realization of his goals for OGAS.[7] OGAS ultimately failed to secure funding because of political conflicts within the Soviet government. But this wasn't the story's end of how the Soviet Internet came into being.

After the collapse of funding for the OGAS expansion, the Soviet government began to look at building a computing network for the purpose of research in 1978. The development of Akademset was driven by the Institute of Electronic Computing Technology (IEVT). Akademset's main goal was to enrich the scientific community across the Soviet Bloc, rather than the dual purpose of also enriching the military apparatus as ARPANET did.

Akademset's presence in the Soviet Union (see Figure 6.1) represented a new possibility for an opening of communications into the heavily isolated Soviet Union. When computers were available, they were most likely to be found within education and academics.

---

[7] Peters, Benjamin, *How Not to Network a Nation: The Uneasy History of the Soviet Internet* (Cambridge, MA, 2016; online edn, MIT Press Scholarship Online, 19 Jan. 2017)

FIGURE 6.1 A map of Akademset nodes throughout the Soviet region

These computing resources were typically reserved for use in economic enterprises before they were made available as educational tools. Software development was a particular weak point for Soviet nations. In addition to relying on Western hardware, the USSR depended on Western software to run their computers.

Soviet Programming

A 1989 publication from the Hudson Institute titled "Soviet Computer Software and Applications in the 1980s" asks, "Can Ivan compute?" Citing examples such as the success of the automated Soviet space shuttle Buran, the authors conclude that "Ivan can compute, but the fact is that he does less of it than Johnny. . .or Pierre or Fritz. Indeed, it seems that he does proportionately less of it than anybody in the developed world."

Despite being awkwardly phrased, it reflects the perception outside the Soviet Bloc that their computing and programming ability lagged significantly behind the rest of the developed world. However, this shouldn't diminish the value of early Soviet research into computer networking.

Soviet Understanding of Hacking

Pre-Perestroika, there doesn't appear to be a term in the Russian language for what we refer to as a hacker. Of course, there were people who worked with computers in a technical capacity. But it wasn't until MIT professor Joseph Weizenbaum's book, *Computer Power and Human Reason*, was translated into Cyrillic in the mid-1980s that the term *hacker* was introduced to the Soviet lexicon.

Once the term was introduced, it quickly became popular among technically inclined Soviet citizens. Despite having a term to describe what hacking was, the average Soviet citizen still didn't have access to computer technology immediately following Perestroika. It wouldn't be until the 1990s and the broadening of available technologies that more Russians would identify with this term.

Post-Soviet Russia

When the Soviet Union was officially dissolved in 1991, it set Russia and its former-Soviet satellite nations on a new trajectory. The end of the Soviet Union spelled doom for the production of domestically-produced hardware and software, but Soviet users of computer technology had already become quite accustomed to using Western products anyway.

As for the availability of technologies that had been considered ubiquitous by Western standards, ex-Soviet citizens would finally get a much-needed upgrade. Perestroika had made significant progress in opening Soviet society to the rest of the world, but it wasn't until after the fall of the Soviet Union that basic computer technology would become widely available to the Soviet public. By this time, the global hacking community had a full 20 years of development that rushed in to fill the void. Globally, the hacker culture of the 1990s reflected punk-rock roots. This alt-rock aesthetic was on full display on the covers of the earliest mainstream tech-focused publication, *Hacker* magazine.

A New Class of Criminal

The flood of new technology available to the post-Soviet Russia, and a newly marketized economy helped fill the apparent vacuum of hackers in Russia. Not long after the fall of the Soviet Union, Russian black hats quickly made their mark on financial global financial services. One such crime rumored to have started in Russia in the early 1990s was a form of private information theft referred to as "carding." As the name implies, carding involves the theft of credit card information, which became an increasingly severe problem in the early 2000s. The crime of carding grew out of the community of cybercriminals in the early 1990s, who were actively finding new ways of stealing and exploiting prepaid phone cards. These forms of theft were fairly easy for hackers to get away with and naturally evolved over time as electronic payment systems, and the ubiquity of customer databases grew in the early 2000s.

But organized Russian cybercriminals weren't only cutting their teeth on petty electronic theft in the early 1990s, they were also targeting bigger fish. It was Russian hackers who were responsible for the high-profile hack of Citibank in 1994, in which the Russian hacker Vladimir Levin made off with $10 million. Levin and his associates stole the money by transferring the funds to accounts that they had access to, and the money was withdrawn from banks in Europe. For this crime, Levin and his accomplices were arrested, and Levin himself was extradited to the United States for trial after being arrested at Heathrow Airport in London.

The Western world has always taken a narrow, self-centered view in understanding how different nations developed their own native hacking cultures. There are still very few names of Soviet hackers that can be studied in Cold War documentation, but the threads of evidence for the presence of Soviet hacking expertise are a tantalizing hint that more is yet to be learned about how hackers exist behind the Iron Curtain.

7

Hackers of the World, Unite!

In February 1971, a man with a well-kept beard and mustache exited the international terminal at Comodoro Arturo Merino Benitez International Airport in Santiago, Chile. His name was Stafford Beer, and he was one of the foremost experts in a cutting-edge field of technological research called "cybernetics." For Beer, his time in Santiago was a major opportunity to demonstrate the future of cybernetics on the world stage.

Building a full-scale man/machine network at a time when the foundational technology of packet switching was still in its infancy in the United States was a major gamble on the part of the newly elected Allende government in Chile. If Beer's project was a success, it would have put Chile on a fast track to being a major world power in the Southern hemisphere. The stakes could not have been higher for the nation, and the technological possibilities were immeasurable. But when Beer stepped off his plane in 1971, he had no way of knowing that in a few short years, world events would doom not only his project, but the entire Allende government.

Project Cybersyn

As the 1960s drew to a close and the space race found its winner in the United States, a new arms race was heating up. The clash between capitalist and communist nations had gone global, resulting in 20 years of proxy wars throughout the world by the early 1970s. The great irony of the Soviet Union's National Automated System for Computation ("OGAS") failure was that management of the OGAS's development involved the type of return on investment (ROI) politics typically more emblematic of capitalist economies than the general welfare concepts championed by their own Soviet government.

Much of the way that Advanced Research Projects Agency Network (ARPANET) Director Dr. Licklider imagined interconnected computers as a beautiful utopian project depended on a socialized model of funding for its success. The reality of the success of the American Internet project is that its development was aligned with well-funded public military interests. As a result of its alignment with economic goals, the success of OGAS ultimately required it to be a profitable project.[1]

In November 1970, Chile elected President Salvador Allende on the promise of delivering socialism to the Chilean people by prioritizing teachers and nationalizing the mining industry, redistributing land, and expanding the rights and earnings of Chilean workers. When Allende took office, he inherited a government in turmoil. Facing an oppositional congress led by a

[1] *How Not to Network A Nation: The Uneasy History of the Soviet Internet*, Peters, Benjamin, 2016.

Nationalist party faction, strong headwinds challenged Allende's lofty plans; he needed all the help he could get to make good on the promises he made to voters to transform the economy.

Early on, Allende took interest in the science of *cybernetics*. Cybernetics seeks to study the combination of animals and machines, defining how social and biological systems communicate and interact. Allende believed that cybernetics and the unifying social visions of interconnected computers could be leveraged to provide untold benefits to Chile's economy and for the overall quality of Chilean life. In 1971, shortly after being elected, Allende launched Project Cybersyn to accomplish his agenda.

For most of the world, computer technology was still new and exciting. Even the concept art for Project Cybersyn's operations rooms reflected a science-fiction–esque optimism. Designed around the Gestalt principles of human perception, they looked as if they had been ripped straight from the set design of *Star Trek*. Despite the somewhat hokey veneer, the aims of Project Cybersyn were serious, and the theory behind its cybernetic roots was sound. If Chile managed to finish the ambitious project, it would have been a prototype for economic systems across the world.

Get Me Beer!

For Allende's plan to be successful, they would need a field expert. For this role, they eyed the British cybernetics researcher Stafford Beer. As Project Cybersyn's initial plan was coming together, Allende's finance minister, Fernando Flores, invited Beer to come work on-site in Chile to build the prototype cybernetic system that he hoped would supercharge Chile's economy. Flores' invitation couldn't have come at a better time for Beer who was unable to gain attention in Britain for his ideas about creating large socially integrated cybernetic systems. An adventure in Chile was exactly the sort of opportunity Beer had been waiting for.

As far as adventure was concerned, Beer had already been leading an exciting life when Flores reached out to him. Beer was born in London in 1926, the son of the chief statistician for Lloyd's Register of Shipping. He left college in 1944 to join the military and served in India as a company commander of the 9th Gurkha infantry regiment.

After the war, Beer took a job working for United Steel and began early operational research into cybernetics in 1956. This position brought him into contact with cutting-edge computing technology of the time that included the gargantuan Ferranti Pegasus computer system, the first computer system dedicated to cybernetic management. In 1961, Beer left United Steel and cofounded a cybernetics research consultancy called Science in General Management (SIGMA). He continued his work as an independent cybernetic consultant after a stint with one of his SIGMA clients, the International Publishing Corporation in 1970.

Beer had established himself as an eccentric with revolutionary socialist politics, which found good company among Allende's government. Sporting a long beard and known for teaching tantric yoga, Beer can be seen examining documents with a functional monocle in one photo taken in 1990. Stafford Beer's expertise with Project Cybersyn was a sign of how dedicated the Allende government was to making the project a reality. When Flores contacted Beer in 1970, his expertise as well as his politics preceded him.

Building the Network

One of the main features of Project Cybersyn was a system designed to support economic leadership on economic reforms. Cybersyn needed to be able to collect and interpret complex economic information in real time and produce on-demand reports for government leadership to help drive decision-making. To do this, the project was given 500 telex machines that were to be interconnected and installed throughout the Chilean supply chain. These telex machines could be used to collect up-to-date information on various aspects of production, including how many factory workers were available, how much energy a facility was using, and what its ultimate output was. This information could then be instantly shared with leaders in Santiago, who could quickly adjust and improve production efficiency.

Ultimately, the global political environment proved too unstable for the dream of a Chilean cybernetic economy. The success of Project Cybersyn depended on having the time it needed to mature, but tragically Project Cybersyn would never be completed. After only two years of development, the project was abandoned when a wave of ultranationalism swept over Chile, unseating Allende and his government.

Operation Condor

On September 11, 1973, the Chilean military led by the notoriously violent General Augusto Pinochet seized the capital city of Santiago. Two days later, Pinochet dissolved the Chilean congress and installed Pinochet as a junta dictator. In the ensuing months, the Chilean national sports stadium would be appropriated into a torture center, eventually detaining tens of thousands after a CIA-backed coup d'etat (named Operation CONDOR) unseated Allende's democratically elected government. In a cruel twist of fate, some of the same telex machines allocated to achieving the utopian goals of Project Cybersyn were likely used to coordinate Operation CONDOR's death stroke against the Allende government. In 1975, the illegitimate Pinochet government hosted the first meeting of "Southern Cone," which included other South American military dictatorships supported by the United States. At this meeting, Pinochet encouraged these nations to adopt cipher machines, which were used to coordinate targeted murders and a suppression of dissidents. After an initial batch of cryptographic machines was decided on by the Southern Cone nations, Brazil later provided a set of common-cryptography machines to each member nation.[2]

These cryptographic machines were made by Swiss cryptography company Crypto AG, which was reported in 2020 to have been widely compromised by American intelligence services. It would've allowed American intelligence to keep tabs on their subordinate regimes.

In her book *Cybernetic Revolutionaries: Technology and Politics in Allende's Chile*, Eden Medina notes that what drove Project Cybersyn was the unification of two utopian ideas: one political and one technological. These two ideas have been a driver of the broader global hacking community since the beginning and have been a challenge that Western governments have had to reckon with in their pursuit of technical talent. For Beer, Allende's Chile didn't force him to compromise his values for the job. In Project Cybersyn, Beer could indulge both his technical interests and socialist leanings. For later hackers in the United States, taking a government job wouldn't offer the same luxury.

Project Cybersyn's Epitaph

Beer himself was a true believer in the Marxist cause championed by Allende and his government. In a lecture given in February 1973, titled "Fanfare for Effective Freedom: Cybernetic Praxis

In Government," Beer mused in retrospect on his work with the Chilean government. In this speech, he discussed the idea that revolutionary technologists needed to lend their expertise to the global socialist movement to promote its success.

Chaos Computer Club

On September 1, 1981, a short note was published in the leftist German newspaper *Die Tageszeitung* (TAZ), under a bold heading reading "Aktionen." The note's authors expressed fears that computer technology was being abused by corporations and poised to begin replacing humans. The authors stated, "Today, everyone in power believes that internal security is only possible through the use of computers. The fact that computers don't go on strike is slowly gaining acceptance even among medium-sized companies . . . ." The authors also make an appeal against large, centralized organizations and urged the readers to "do something." The note was signed by "Tom Twiddlebit" and "Wau Wolf Unnamed."

Tom Twiddlebit and Wau Wolf encouraged readers to join them 11 days later in the main building of the TAZ newspaper to talk about international computer networks, law and data privacy, and all manner of other technical interest topics (see Figure 7.1). Many topics the two authors encouraged leftist readers to come out to discuss are still relevant today. The two authors were hackers themselves by the names of Klaus Schleisiek and "Wau" Holland, and the meeting they planned on September 12, 1981, would be the first meeting of the Chaos Computer Club (CCC).

Since the beginning, the CCC was Europe's largest public hacking club, spreading out to smaller local chapters throughout Germany and even reaching out to neighboring countries. Like

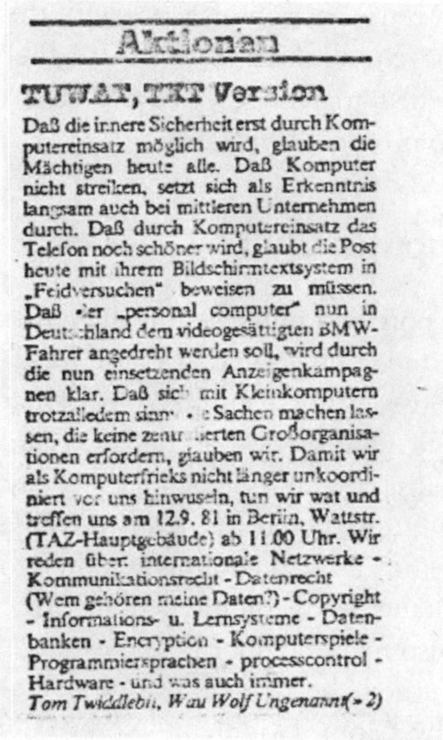

Aktionen

TUWAT, TXT Version

Daß die innere Sicherheit erst durch Komputereinsatz möglich wird, glauben die Mächtigen heute alle. Daß Komputer nicht streiken, setzt sich als Erkenntnis langsam auch bei mittleren Unternehmen durch. Daß durch Komputereinsatz das Telefon noch schöner wird, glaubt die Post heute mit ihrem Bildschirmtextsystem in „Feidversuchen" beweisen zu müssen. Daß der „personal computer" nun in Deutschland dem videogesättigten BMW-Fahrer angedreht werden soll, wird durch die nun einsetzenden Anzeigenkampagnen klar. Daß sich mit Kleinkomputern trotzalledem sinnvolle Sachen machen lassen, die keine zentralisierten Großorganisationen erfordern, glauben wir. Damit wir als Komputerfrieks nicht länger unkoordiniert vor uns hinwuseln, tun wir wat und treffen uns am 12.9. 81 in Berlin, Wattstr. (TAZ-Hauptgebäude) ab 11.00 Uhr. Wir reden über: internationale Netzwerke - Kommunikationsrecht - Datenrecht (Wem gehören meine Daten?) - Copyright - Informations- u. Lernsysteme - Datenbanken - Encryption - Komputerspiele - Programmiersprachen - processcontrol - Hardware - und was auch immer.
Tom Twiddlebit, Wau Wolf Ungenannt(= 2)

FIGURE 7.1 A copy of the original post made in TAZ by the founders of the CCC

many of its American counterparts, CCC grew out of a politically conscious and active group of high-tech geeks. Concerns over the use and abuse of modern technologies drove the CCC organization, especially in the early days. Over the next five years, the CCC would begin its own hacker publication and become known across Europe. It didn't take long for CCC to get the attention of international authorities.

On September 16, 1987, the *Boston Globe* published a story by Girard C. Steichen, titled "Hackers Penetrate NASA Data Network."[3] In it, Steichen explained that hackers located in

---

[3] https://archive.org/details/1601977-0-section-1

Frankfurt, Germany, managed to exploit their way into the computer network of the National Aeronautics and Space Administration (NASA). In the act, the hackers made off with sensitive information about NASA's future space projects and reports detailing notable launch failures. Steichen's story was short and to the point but excluded several important pieces of context about the attack.

According to FBI files obtained through the Freedom of Information Act (FOIA), the FBI was working with a cadre of other law enforcement organizations across Europe, including authorities from Germany, Switzerland, France, the United Kingdom, and even Interpol, which provided the FBI with the original tip-off on the breach of American concerns. What's particularly interesting about this case is that despite lacking important legal tools and the precedent to legally prosecute hackers domestically, the FBI was prepared to meet the challenge of coordinating international investigations with overseas partners. Not only were they capable of coordination, but were also capable of developing clandestine sources known as confidential informants (CIs) to act as counterintelligence assets against investigation targets.

One file included in the FBI's CCC investigation mentioned overt cooperation between CCC members and FBI agents and a willingness to collaborate with American authorities to close the vulnerability that the CCC used to gain access to NASA and other American targets. What those collaborating members might not have known at the time is that the FBI had already developed two informants with CCC knowledge who were providing the bureau with valuable information identifying potential suspects in the breach. This information was particularly valuable to FBI, as they pointed out in their internal reporting, because the terminal used in the attacks on American targets was located in a room maintained by CCC with open privileges for anyone in the group to use. In retrospect, it's likely that the CCC-affiliated hacker the FBI was looking for was in fact Karl Koch, the hacker responsible for the KGB hack.

Chaos Computer Club France

As new CCC offshoots were popping up throughout Europe, one localized organization was established in France in 1989. The Chaos Computer Club France (CCCF) was sold as a French national association of hackers to complement the central German association. Primarily organized by one man, Jean-Bernard Condat, the CCCF attracted membership primarily within the city of Lyon and gave French hackers a place to organize and coordinate with one another.

Condat made a name for himself, often appearing on television discussing hacks he had performed and privileged information he possessed. In one case, Condat was seen on a French news program reviewing a technical manual for weapons systems in Iraq, which he had ostensibly stolen from Saddam's military computer networks. Condat also published a regular newsletter titled *Chaos Digest* between January 4, 1993, and August 5, 1993. This digest was so widely sourced, that it could even be found on U.S. government lists around this time, documenting reliable sources of hacking-related information. CCCF seemed by all appearances to be a fairly standard European hacking organization for its time, but Condat wasn't the forthright hacker he'd made himself out to be on national news.

Condat and his entire CCCF group was a front organization for French domestic intelligence. At the same time that the French government was collaborating with U.S. authorities investigating leads that the source of the WANK worm was in France, French intelligence agency La Direction de la Surveillance du Territoire (DST) was in the early stages of building the

CCCF. French intelligence was desperate to find its footing in cybersecurity investigations, and the CCCF's goal was to produce intelligence material on hackers within France.

As the first internal intelligence service after World War II, DST's mission was to collect intelligence on security matters inside France. DST's predecessor organization prior to Nazi occupation, the Surveillance du Territoire (ST), was responsible for arresting German spies. At the outbreak of the war, many of the constituent members of the ST's staff went on to become maquis fighters for the French Resistance.

With a similar internal structure to other domestic intelligence agencies around the world such as MI5 and the FBI, DST's investigators had broad authority to conduct counterterrorist operations, collect intelligence through surveillance, and make suspect arrests. When computers became more commonly used in both French foreign and domestic crimes, DST found its focus shifting more toward investigations involving hackers. However, like many other governments at the time, France found itself in need of hackers yet didn't have a reliable source willing to work in government service.

Under the direction of Intelligence Officer Jean-Luc Delacour, the DST conducted surveillance on and arrested hackers who joined the CCCF. Some hackers who had joined the organization and were invited to private gatherings at Condat's Paris apartment were shown photographs of themselves inside that apartment, suggesting that DST had gone as far as to have cameras installed within.

Like many other hackers, Condat started hacking at a young age. While at university, he managed to gain access to unprotected U.S computers, which attracted the attention of American authorities. As Condat tells it, he was confronted by an FBI agent in his youth, who then passed Condat on to local DST authorities for handling. At the time, DST was struggling to find competent hackers to join its ranks. The apparent compromise of a hacker within France exposed an opportunity for French authorities. Condat was convinced to join DST and given the codename "Cucumber."

The targets of the CCCF organization were young hackers who could be coerced into working as informants. What French authorities didn't count on was just how skeptical hackers could be. Retrospectives on the CCCF have concluded that the program more or less failed in its goal to recruit prospective hackers. On the contrary, French hackers looking back on the CCCF operation believe that it fueled national distrust among native French hackers. If they were skeptical about working for the French government before the exposure of Condat as a DST informant, they were even less likely to cooperate afterward.

The DST operation was hastily put together with opposing goals that ultimately drove a deeper wedge between French hackers and their government. It wasn't a novel idea to attempt to recruit hackers by threatening legal action for known crimes, but the mistake French authorities made was in going after young hackers with incredibly minor charges.

The true goal of French intelligence was to turn "pirates" into "whales" by way of recruitment into government service. In CCCF's case, the modus operandi of the French government was to accomplish this through the process of coercion. The case of the CCCF is emblematic of the types of complex legal and operational trickery that advanced nations would resort to for the purpose of improving their access to those with the technical skills they needed to operate.

Building Teletext

Just prior to the advent of email, a noticeable gap existed in the market of consumer communication protocols for the coming-of-age Internet. In the 1980s, home computers were still fairly expensive for the average person. However, communications technologies using existing telephone lines were being eyed as a carrier to deliver important information. The market's niche for these services involved using television sets, to which, by the 1980s, most homes in Western nations had access. Any service that could make use of the fact that Americans wouldn't need to buy a fancy new computer (which most people didn't know what to do with in the first place) was well-positioned to be successful.

In these heady days of early Internet service, one of the contenders for next-generation communications technologies was called *teletext*. Teletext services were provided to home television sets via television signal and could deliver important information like train schedules, consumer reviews, and even movie times straight to a user's television. The blocky typeface of the teletext service was often presented with an eye-catching array of 16-bit colors and even had rudimentary animations that made users feel as if the future was finally right there in the center of their living room. One major limitation of teletext is that it was, in essence, a dumb terminal. Teletext was a one-way information transfer system on which information could be viewed but not interacted with in any meaningful way.

In this way, early adopters of teletext services didn't see its obvious benefits over more traditional means of information communication over telephones or even a daily newspaper. It's partly due to these reasons that we don't use teletext today.

The Prestel Hack

In the United Kingdom, one such teletext service was named Prestel. Prestel was invented by the British post office, which was responsible for maintaining the British telephone service in addition to running the mail. While teletext was available through providers like the BBC's Ceefax offering, researchers at the U.K.

Postal Service aimed to create a more interactive service using not only television signals like teletext but also telephone lines to provide a return flow of information that users could use to have a more interactive experience.

Sadly, similar to teletext, the Prestel service didn't quite catch on with the British public, attracting only 6,000 users by 1981. As the service limped along, it explored adding "mailbox" services and online banking in 1983. Prestel even attempted to provide an online grocery delivery service and "Beer at Home" service for beer delivery. Users could consult a printed directory, which was regularly mailed to them with services they could connect to, including a special numeric code that could be used to find the Prestel service. Even though Prestel wasn't particularly popular outside of business clients, there was at least one high-profile system user.

In 1985, journalists Steve Gold and Robert Schifreen stumbled across a highly privileged Prestel user account with the password 1234. In the course of exploring the Prestel Viewdata system, Schifreen had discovered a Prestel mailbox belonging to Prince Philip, the Duke of Edinburgh. Schifreen notified a Prestel affiliate, who called in the London Metropolitan Police, who arrested Schifreen not long after.

While American hackers were generally being charged with telecoms fraud, U.K. citizens Gold and Schifreen found themselves the first two defendants against the interesting charge of "deceiving a non-human entity" under a forgery statute written in 1981. Ultimately, the charges against the two men were dropped. Schifreen would go on to become the editor of .EXE Magazine, a publication dedicated to computer programming. He would also start a private computer security consulting service, following a long-term trend of hacker rehabilitation.

Overseas Cooperation

In the modern era, the United States and United Kingdom have been close allies. Their international relationship was tested and strengthened several times throughout WWII, including through the Lend Lease Act and the 1941 Atlantic Charter. In 1943, both nations drew up a treaty called the "BRUSA" Agreement, which established a basis for which war-related code and cipher intelligence could be shared. After WWII, the two nations deepened their commitments to intelligence sharing. The so-called "Five Eyes" intelligence pact was established that formalized intelligence partnerships between Western nations and widened the partnership to include other English-speaking nations including Canada, Australia, and New Zealand. As computers made the world a smaller place, leadership in Five Eyes nations sought out more cooperation areas.

One such area of cooperation was in the investigation and prosecution of a newly developing form of international crime: so-called cybercrime.

The Australian Scene

For Australian hackers of the late-1980s, Melbourne, Australia, was the place to be. Melbourne played host to several small hacking groups that had an outsized impact on the world stage. Australian hackers were considered among the best in the world, in part due to their participation and contribution to the larger global hacking community.

The hack that would put Australian hackers on the map was the 1989 Worms Against Nuclear Killers (WANK) NASA breach. Initially, when NASA investigated WANK, they concluded that the attack had originated from France. When

American authorities passed this information on to French law enforcement, the DST was already working on their effort to entrap French hackers through the CCCF. Although the WANK's source wouldn't be known for many years, it still put Australian hackers on the map.

AFP Tracking of Realm

Among the most prominent Australian hacking groups of the 1980s was The Realm. Even before WANK was making headlines, other Australian groups like The Realm were forging a reputation as some of the most skilled on the scene. The Realm was a tight-knit group of young hackers, each bringing their own skillsets to the table. The three core members of the group, Electron, Phoenix, and Nom, are featured prominently in Suelette Dreyfus's 1997 book, *Underground: Tales of Hacking, Madness and Obsession on the Electronic Frontier*. In her book, Dreyfus chronicles the exploits of this early group and details some of their interpersonal connections.

Notably, members of The Realm were active on a West German–hosted hacking forum named Altos. The Altos forum was shared between hackers all over the world, but it was there that they would meet Pengo of KGB hack fame. One advantage that Australian hackers had over their international peers was a keener sense of discretion. While hackers in other countries were being caught for their crimes due to sloppy decision-making, members of The Realm had a healthy paranoia that led them to make more careful decisions about how they approached their hacks.

They also didn't openly boast about their exploits in the same way as other hackers. Members of The Realm preferred sharing their best information only to other trusted group members.

For example, Phoenix maintained a program called DEFCON (not related to the Las Vegas hacker conference by the same name), which could be used to scan computers with attached modems.

One night while using DEFCON, Phoenix managed to find a trove of high-limit credit card numbers and accompanying transactional records. He shared this information with other members of The Realm, who realized that these credit card numbers originated from the U.S.-based Citibank corporation. For its part, Citibank had caught onto the breach and contacted the U.S. Secret Service. Members of The Realm were not only involved with hacks against Citibank, they also had targeted several American government networks, including American defense networks.

The Australian Federal Police (AFP), in cooperation with U.S. authorities, received a warrant to tap Phoenix's computer in the first remote computer monitoring operation in world history. The evidence produced by this tap justified a raid by AFP six weeks later in April 1990 against the three core members: Phoenix, Nom, and Electron. The trial against these three members took a similar path to other hacking cases around the same timeframe, amounting to a few months of jailtime deferred by bail and community service.

The legal heat against hackers was rising worldwide as governments began developing and using legal frameworks to understand and interpret cybercrimes. International cooperation on these issues was possible only after domestic policy was created, but once those laws were established, the floodgates for federal law enforcement were open wide.

CHAPTER

8

Electronic Delinquents

In 1982, regular viewers of the popular investigative news program *20/20* turned on their television sets and were greeted by the familiar face of Hugh Downs, the program's trusted cohost alongside Barbara Walters. In his trademark newsman voice, Downs read the segment's introduction accompanied by the image of a computer screen with the words "*Electronic Delinquents*" spelled out in green text. In his introduction, Downs described hacking as "*a growing and perplexing phenomenon of our time.*" This may have been the first time that many viewers of the program had ever heard the word "*hacking*" in the context of computers.

After his introduction, Downs passed the segment onto the infamously mustachioed visage of reporter, Geraldo Rivera. Long before he was known as a ringmaster for trash television, Rivera was a true journalist. His segment on electronic delinquents introduced the concept of youthful hacking to tens-of-millions of viewers. To Geraldo's viewers, hackers weren't just fodder for fictional TV and movies, they were now the topic of serious news programs.

Among the delinquents featured by Geraldo was a young hacker named Brian "System Cruncher" Catlin. By age 17, Catlin was a talented hacker who had already landed in court on charges of theft by using a computer belonging to his high school to access a payment system at DePaul University in Chicago. Catlin's hack caused the university's enrollment system to undergo maintenance during the week of student registration, causing a total of over $22,000 in damage.[1]

Rivera spoke to another phreaker using the name "Susy Thunder" demonstrated how to enumerate government computer systems to a perplexed-looking Geraldo. Susy Thunder was an accomplished hacker, and phreaker in her own right. Like her Roscoe Gang cohorts, Kevin Mitnick and Lewis DePayne, Susy was an outcast who found freedom in the never-ending telephone system.[2] Susy also described the harassment they would level against anyone who crossed them: *"We might disconnect his phone, cancel his insurance, repossess his car. Just little things, little harassment things."*

Behind the scenes, the exploits of Geraldo's electronic delinquents were not surprising to engineers working on building resilient computer networks for America's foremost intelligence agencies. To these engineers, teenage hackers were the least of their concerns.

Digital Spycraft

The arrival of digital communications technology offered both new threats and new opportunities to American intelligence services. These agencies, which had historically relied on a

---

[1] https://www.newspapers.com/newspage/302452696
[2] https://www.theverge.com/c/22889425/susy-thunder-headley-hackers-phone-phreakers-claire-evans

collection of intelligence collection methods, had a new domain to protect and exploit. To do this, they would need the technical expertise of the same types of hackers featured prominently on nightly news, but they didn't yet grasp how important these hackers would be in the coming decades.

Protecting America's Defense Networks

Even before the Advanced Research Projects Agency Network (ARPANET) was created in 1969, the U.S. Intelligence Community (USIC) was experimenting with computer networks of their own. On December 1, 1966, the USIC launched an ambitious project to create a computer network for sharing files between American intelligence agencies. The system, called the Community Online Intelligence System (COINS) experiment, was the first attempt at a multi-agency intelligence sharing network, which would bring the business of intelligence analysis into the modern age.

To build this network, COINS called for the deployment of computer terminals across intelligence agency offices. Once these terminals were installed, they would then be joined together in a unified network which allowed agencies to share information with each other. As packet-switching technology became more common in the early 1970s thanks to ARPANET, the COINS II project was launched in the mid-1970s.[3] COINS II brought much needed infrastructure improvements, and a more rigorous set of standards for the care and maintenance of intelligence community computer systems.

Given that COINS II was built to contain information at the highest classification, the computer network's security was paramount. A 14-page document titled *"Central Intelligence Agency*

---

[3] https://www.cia.gov/readingroom/docs/CIA-RDP89B01354R000400520001-0.pdf

Community On-Line Intelligence System (COINS) Security Procedures"
documented the forward-thinking policies that governed the
agency's approach to securing COINS terminals. These policies
were so thorough that they even included guidance on electronic
"TEMPEST" emanations and what to do in the event that information "spills" occur via one of these terminals.[4]

American Code Making

While most U.S. government agencies outside the intelligence
community were decades away from widely integrating computer technology into daily operations, the NSA was ahead of
the curve. The NSA's stewardship of American cryptographic
systems during and after WWII gave it a unique position to
influence encryption standards in the post-war decades. With
the growth of digital computer technology on the horizon, securing these devices through standardized encryption became a
major concern for the U.S. government in the 1970s.

One such standard was the Data Encryption Standard (DES),
an algorithm developed by IBM in the early 1970s. The DES was
poised to be accepted by the U.S. National Bureau of Standards
(NBS) for encrypting unclassified government communications,
the implications of which would be far-reaching. The NBS
selected a version of DES, which had been changed slightly by
the NSA after their consultation in 1976 on the algorithm that
raised concerns among privacy watchdogs. The NSA's involvement in the development of the DES led some researchers to
believe that the agency had selectively weakened aspects of the
standard for their own benefit, thereby compromising the overall security of the algorithm. Critics suggested that this represented a conflict of interest between the NSA's mandate to both

---

[4] https://www.cia.gov/readingroom/docs/CIA-RDP80B01139A000100100012-9.pdf

create encryption algorithms for the purpose of defending American government systems, and break the encryption used by global adversaries for the purpose of intelligence collection.

Suspicion of the DES led cryptography experts to warn against the implementation of the algorithm for decades despite a lack of strong evidence that the NSA had indeed tampered with it. According to *Wired Magazine*, since 2007, some researchers claim to have found evidence of the NSA's weakening of the DES algorithm[5], but NSA cryptographers maintain that the changes NSA proposed could not have contained a weakness that auditors would not have found themselves.[6] Regardless of whether or not the NSA indeed weakened the DES in the 1970s, suspicions of the NSA gained traction in the eyes of many in the public.

Church and Pike

Concerns about exactly how the NSA had contributed to the DES algorithm came at a turbulent time for American intelligence agencies that were being irritated by the fierce Cold War politics of the early-1970s. Driven in large part by frustrations over the war in Vietnam, a deep political rift divided the public on the legitimacy of American institutions. In the hacking community, the growing West Coast contingent of hackers empathetic to antiwar policies gave some hackers a political dimension to their work.

The first major scandal to bring attention to intelligence agency surveillance efforts came after the break-in at the Democratic National Committee headquarters inside the Watergate hotel in Washington, D.C. The 1972 investigation of the Watergate incident led to the arrest of five suspects working for a

---

[5] https://www.wired.com/2013/09/nsa-backdoor
[6] https://web.archive.org/web/20240123050249/http://www.ams.org/notices/201407/rnoti-p772.pdf

Nixon-affiliated organization named the Committee to Re-Elect the President (CREEP), one of which, Howard Hunt, was a former CIA officer. Another conspirator of the break-in with a wild backstory of his own, G. Gordon Liddy, had a history of working for the Federal Bureau of Investigation (FBI).

The involvement of Hunt and Liddy in the planning of the Watergate break-in raised questions about exactly how much influence America's intelligence agencies had over presidential elections. Congress had questions that needed to be answered about the nature of the intelligence community's surveillance against the American public, not the least of which was whether or not the FBI and CIA had any institutional responsibility in the wake of the Watergate break-in.

In 1975, two members of Congress formed a joint investigation known as the "Church and Pike" hearings. The hearings called for the testimony of USIC witnesses about exactly what happened behind the locked doors of their agencies. The Church and Pike hearings were an unprecedented investigation into the activities of America's most secretive and highly funded intelligence agencies, and what they found shocked both Congress and the American public.

Throughout the 1960s and 1970s, America's top-secret agencies were kept as far from the public eye as possible, conducting their operations beneath a veil of secrecy. The Church and Pike hearings put a bevy of top secret programs on full display to the American public, detailing operations aimed at curtailing opposition to both the war in Vietnam and criticisms of capitalism more broadly. These programs were a part of long-term Cold War strategy to limit the reach of socialist movements no matter where in the world they appeared, including within the United States itself.

Among the Church and Pike committee findings were documents and testimony proving that the NSA and CIA had illegally spied on private American citizens for their political views. Operations CHAOS, SHAMROCK, and MINARET, used intelligence assets to surveil American anti-war protesters. The revelations of the Church and Pike hearings put American defense institutions at odds with hackers, particularly those on the West Coast like Jude Milhon and her associates in the Community Memory project.

The Church and Pike committee hearings changed the way the USIC did business, and created layers of oversight promising to avoid future incidents of unfair targeting of U.S. citizens. Even with these sweeping changes in place, mistrust of intelligence agencies persisted, particularly within the hacking community.

The Rainbow Series

With the Church and Pike hearings behind them, the NSA refocused its effort on defending electronic communications. In 1978, the Department of Defense (DoD) Computer Security Initiative was introduced, aimed at improving the security of computers both inside and outside of government. The initiative itself was short lived, but it was a first step toward modernizing the NSA's relationship with new technologies. When the DoD Computer Security Initiative presented its results in 1981, DoD leadership created an organization with a mandate dedicated to computer security named the DoD Computer Security Evaluation Center (CSEC). Although there were some overlapping areas of interest, this organization would be completely independent of preexisting communications security (COMSEC) organizations within the NSA.

The DoD CSEC, which was renamed to the DoD Computer Security Center (CSC), published the first of a series of authoritative computer security books called *The Trusted Computer System Evaluation Criteria* in 1983. Named for the bright color of its binding, it was lovingly referred to by its readers as "The Orange Book." The CSC went on to publish several other authoritative texts covering the best cybersecurity practices for various digital applications, each with their own distinct color. This series of books came to be known as "the Rainbow Series" and earned a cultural following of its own.

The Rainbow Series was written to establish guidelines and standards for highly secure systems. It represented a major milestone in institutionalizing computer security as a discipline in government and showcased how seriously DoD was taking its own computer security. The influence of the Rainbow Series went far beyond the NSA's wall of secrecy and became iconic in their own way with hackers outside of government acting as indispensable references for building high-security computer systems.

The CSC published four entries in the Rainbow Series through June of 1985, and work on the series was taken over by its successor organization inside the NSA, the National Computer Security Center (NCSC). The Rainbow Series and the NCSC itself made inroads into a hacking community that had come to be skeptical of USIC since the Church and Pike years. The Rainbow Series showed that the NSA did, at least in part, have a genuine interest in sharing information with the public to improve computer security. It became a case-study for how sincere outreach to the hacking community could build important relationships and helped restore some of the trust that had been lost after the Vietnam era.

The Clipper Chip

Even after the NSA's 1970s dealings with the DES, lessons about how the public viewed their work had not been fully realized. In 1994, the NSA once again faced a public scandal claiming renewed efforts to spy on American citizens. This time, the target of their surveillance weren't anti-war hippies as it had been during project MINARET, but rather the American population writ large.

When the "Clipper Chip" was announced in 1993, it was billed by its U.S. government creators as the cutting edge in data encryption, and would be installed in all new telecommunications devices. The ostensible benefit of this change was better communications security for all American citizens and businesses, but behind the scenes the plan for the Clipper Chip wasn't as noble as its NSA developers claimed.

According to researchers, the aim of the Clipper Chip program was to create a widely adopted encryption system that would allow the NSA to listen into any call that used the chip at any time. This capability would have been enabled by a concept called *key escrow*, which meant that the NSA would hold a sort of master key to anything encrypted using the Clipper Chip. This placed the NSA in the privileged position of being able to decrypt any of these communications at will, effectively creating a panopticon effect with the NSA at the center of all encrypted communications.

When details about the design of the Clipper Chip program came to light, it became a national PR disaster for the Clinton administration, which scrambled to contain the blowback. Groups like the Electronic Frontier Foundation (EFF), which had only been established a few years before, and energized by recent cases like Operation Sundevil, took part in publicly criticizing the project. In particular, hackers in academia came out in strong opposition to the Clipper Chip, publishing their own white papers on the dangers of allowing Clipper Chip key escrow to continue.

One write-up, titled *"Protocol Failure in the Escrowed Encryption Standard"* published in 1994 by cryptography researcher Matt Blaze, pointed out a serious vulnerability in the implementation of the Clipper Chip's Skipjack encryption algorithm.[7] In his study, Blaze noted that the Clipper Chip transmitted enough information in an unencrypted header used by law enforcement to compromise its encryption key. This oversight nullified the reliability of even the marginal legitimate encryption the Clipper Chip offered, which underscored what made the idea behind the Clipper Chip so dangerous.

As Americans became more familiar with the technology in their daily lives, the efforts of the U.S. government to snoop on the communications of private citizens became more relevant to everyday Americans. The Clipper Chip scandal itself wasn't the first public controversy, and it wouldn't be the last for the NSA. In attempting to build a surveillance machine as far-reaching as the Clipper Chip would have been, the government underestimated the ability of hackers to communicate the nuances of new technologies to the public in a way that could be understood.

Prosecuting the 414s

While the technical grunts in the U.S. government worked to understand the new reality of needing to protect U.S. government systems from hackers, lawmakers were grappling with the changes that needed to be made to the legal system to accommodate them.

Until the mid-1980s, law enforcement had to resort to outdated legal definitions and ill-suited legislative tools to use against a steady rise in high-profile computer-aided fraud. After a string of high-profile computer network breaches and thefts via high-volume wire transfers, calls for lawmakers to act were getting louder. At the end of the 1970s, the government made its

[7] Protocol failure in the escrowed encryption standard | Proceedings of the 2nd ACM Conference on Computer and communications security

first attempt at curbing computer crime against the U.S. government and financial systems. Passed in 1978, the Federal Computer Systems Protection Act made it illegal for an individual to access a U.S. government computer or a computer belonging to a financial organization without authorization.[8]

Although the law was written in 1978, the law wasn't yet in force to be used against hackers like those of the 414 gang. Even if it had been in full effect, it may not have been possible to use it against the type of hacking that the 414s were guilty of, which was referred to as *joyriding*.[9] Joyriding was seen as less serious than an outright malicious, criminal attack. The purpose of Joyriding was confusing to lawmakers and police who had trouble understanding crimes with nontraditional motivations. In comparison, crimes like theft and sabotage were easy to understand, but hacking a system for fun didn't fit into a tidy legal framework, which made the task of figuring out how to handle gangs of teenage hackers like the 414s a difficult puzzle for lawmakers to solve.

Hackers on Trial

In the wake of the 414 computer break-in at Los Alamos National Labs (LANL), both Gerald Wondra and Timothy Winslow were charged with two counts of making abusive interstate phone calls. This oddly suited set of charges were brought against the teens for breaching computer networks belonging to the Sloan-Kettering Cancer Center and the Security Pacific National Bank in Los Angeles, and showed just how vexed the legal system was by their crimes. During the legal proceedings, Assistant U.S. Attorney Eric Klumb remarked that the crimes of the 414s were

---

[8] https://www.congress.gov/bill/95th-congress/senate-bill/1766?r=5&s=1
[9] https://www.computerworld.com/article/2523544/hackers-steal-legislators--attention.html

the first of their kind not done with a financial motive proving just how unprepared the American legal system was to deal with the onset of digital-age crimes.[10]

Even though the pair pled guilty to the charges against them and received probation as a result, Wondra and Winslow were excused in the court of public opinion. In fact, the charges of making harassing phone calls as a result of illegally accessing the computer systems of a national nuclear laboratory appeared to be rather amusing to the public. More than any other outcome, their trial became a promotional opportunity for the teen hackers.

Wondra and Winslow's shared lawyer, Paul Piaskowski, admitted that his approach to defending them was "*to portray the young men as computer hobbyists who were merely doing intellectual gymnastics*" and stated that, "*they had not meant to do any harm and certainly they were not criminals.*"[11] In a way, the teenage hackers of the 414s were not the only ones on trial. Their story represented an entire generation of young hackers and their motivations to the public. One member of the 414s, Neal Patrick, helped win their public relations battle by going on a media campaign to define their actions, providing interviews to media outlets like *The Phil Donahue Show* and even landing on the cover of *Newsweek*.

The 414s managed to successfully avoid severe consequences for their actions, and at least for a short time, managed to maintain the image of their own innocence. However, three years later, another teenage hacker would test how resilient the innocent image of the teenage hacker was in the eyes of the legal system.

In 1986, 18 year old Michael P. Wilkerson (going by the alias "The Sprinter") was charged with four counts of illegal computer trespass against major American companies such as Microsoft

---

[10] https://www.nytimes.com/1984/03/17/us/two-who-raided-computers-pleading-guilty.html
[11] http://timeline.textfiles.com/1983

and the trucking manufacturer, Kenworth. Ultimately, Wilkerson received more severe treatment by the legal system during his trial than the 414s had, due in part to the development of new laws passed after the case of the 414s.

Wilkerson's sentence was still relatively light, receiving a two-week jail sentence, a $2,000 fine, 200 hours of community service, and two years of probation. Wilkerson's sentencing set a new trend of treating hackers more like criminals than innocent children. Hackers who would come later could only dream of receiving the same gentle treatment that the 414s had.

Operation Sundevil

Following the new trend set by The Sprinter's trial, the federal government opted for a more aggressive path to investigating and prosecuting hackers. Under their mandate to investigate financial fraud, the U.S. Secret Service (USSS) began investigating online financial crimes. Under the dual mandate to both protect the president *and* investigate federal financial fraud, the USSS began planning a sting to takedown electronic fraud, which they felt hackers had been facilitating.

Named after Arizona State University's mascot (Sparky the Sun Devil), Operation Sundevil was coordinated between several local law enforcement jurisdictions and federal investigators at the FBI. The aim of the operation was to investigate and disrupt online credit card fraud by targeting the servers where the USSS believed this information was being actively traded.

A year after the investigation started, federal agents launched raids in 15 major cities across the United States in cooperation with local law enforcement. In total, 25 Bulletin Board System (BBS) were seized, and three hackers were arrested: Tony the Trashman, Electra, and Bruce Esquibel, aka Dr. Ripco. During the raids, investigators impounded thousands of dollars in computer equipment belonging to accused hackers, taking them in as evidence for further investigation. The raids sparked immediate concern from hackers, who rallied around Esquibel in particular, arguing that he was not guilty of the charges being brought against him.

Sundevil Blowback.   The case against Esquibel hinged on his position as the owner and operator of a forum called "Ripco BBS." At the time, Ripco BBS was one of the most popular online places for hackers to learn technical basics and meet other hackers they could collaborate with. Much of the information shared on Ripco BBS wasn't illegal in and of itself and, therefore, didn't constitute a crime that would warrant a full-blown raid by the USSS.

Interestingly, the case against RIPCO BBS was based, at least in part, on information provided by an informant known as "Dictator." Dictator had acted as a foot-in-the-door for USSS agents, accompanying them to the hacker conference Summercon where agents used Dictator's hotel suite to conduct surveillance of Operation Sundevil targets. These targets were lured into the room and observed interacting with Dictator in hopes that they would disclose admissions of digital crimes. Despite having an informant with supposed connections in the hacking community, the USSS apparently found no evidence of crimes occurring between Dictator and anyone he spoke with over the 15-hour stake out.

This was the first time the government had used an informant to establish evidence in a cybercrime case, but the gambit had not paid off. Despite the government's heraldry of Operation Sundevil as a landmark raid on cyber-fraud, the mass raids didn't result in a significant number of criminal charges or convictions. In fact, the raids called several of the methods the USSS used during the raids into question. Esquibel wasn't charged and eventually did get his impounded computers back, albeit wiped of all information, which only added insult to injury.

Operation Sundevil's long-term legacy was the secondary effect of creating an advocacy organization dedicated to improving technology and privacy related laws. The Electronic Frontier Foundation (EFF), founded to protect online civil liberties during the emergence of digital spaces, was a direct result of the shortcomings of Operation Sundevil. It was clear to EFF's founders, some of whom had been directly involved with Esquibel's case, that the government fundamentally didn't understand digital technology well enough to be able to competently investigate or prosecute it.

Within a few years of the raids, the EFF had made a name for itself with its advocacy. Foundational funding for the EFF's activities came from tech luminaries like Mitch Kapor, who had marketed a successful spreadsheet application called Lotus. A promise to match Kapor's donation came from none other than Steve Wozniak, the technical mind behind Apple Computers. In the years following Operation Sundevil, the EFF opened litigation against the U.S. government several times, litigating for issues related to personal privacy and online liberty.

After Operation Sundevil, trust between hackers and law enforcement was at an all-time low. Even as elements of the U.S. government realized their need for skilled technical experts, they couldn't seem to stop alienating the hackers by needlessly applying aggressive investigative methods against hackers. This was at least in part thanks to a fundamental misunderstanding by many in law enforcement about exactly who hackers were, and what motivated them.

Even as the process of hacker rehabilitation was being explored in the late-1980s, government officials had never truly digested the concept of accepting hackers into their ranks. In the minds of many in federal law enforcement, all hackers were simply criminals who would eventually be arrested for one crime or another. The actions of law enforcement in the early-1990s chilled the potential for better cooperation between hackers and law enforcement at a time when it was desperately needed. With a difficult domestic situation developing for hackers inside the U.S., misunderstandings between lawmakers and the technology they were responsible for regulating was poised to become even more complicated as questions of international policies came into play.

The Crypto Wars

As world powers rebuilt war-torn Europe in the post-war era, a host of new bureaucracies arose to control the flow of weapons and ammunition. The United States established the Coordinating Committee for Multilateral Export Controls (COCOM). The mission of COCOM was to establish a list of goods, which the U.S. considered to be dangerous to government interests. These goods could be placed under embargo, which government leaders felt would protect the interests of national security. This regulatory approach created a new body of rules, which came to be called International Traffic in Arms Regulations (ITAR) and required that these protected materials could not be exported without a proper license.

Under this legal premise, cryptographic materials came to be considered ITAR protected materials, which included algorithmic information for protecting digital communications. As digital exchanges of information became more ubiquitous in the 1970s and 1980s, concerns about how ITAR applied to information exchanges came to the forefront of digital politics. Once again, hackers had been left out of the conversation, and the consequences of this had international implications.

Digital Bullets

In June 1991, a new cryptographic algorithm called Pretty Good Privacy (PGP) was published to the internet by a private American citizen named Philip Zimmermann. Zimmermann's PGP promised to deliver free, high-quality encryption for email users. Quickly after its publication, PGP became the most commonly used form of email encryption in the world, effortlessly crossing international borders with the help of the internet. The availability of PGP's code to international users put a target on Zimmermann's back.

In 1993, the U.S. officially launched an investigation into Zimmerman and PGP for ITAR violations, once again, drawing the ire of hackers who had unwittingly became targets of the government's outdated regulations. COCOM's position that information could be classified as "munitions" in the same way as traditional weapons material like bullets and bombs was a tricky sell.

As they always did, hackers trolled the government, taunting regulators by printing the code for the Rivest, Shamir, and Adleman (RSA) algorithm on T-shirts, which they would wear on international flights. Under the governments reasoning, wearing these shirts without a proper license constituted an ITAR violation, which could incur legal action against the wearer. With this demonstration, hackers aimed to underscore the absurdity of prosecuting hackers with ITAR laws in the same way they had against Zimmermann.

The subtext of the case against Zimmermann was that hackers held considerably more power in the eyes of the government than they realized.

After a lengthy legal battle, the U.S. government dropped its case against Zimmermann and PGP in 1996. It was a major victory for hackers and overturned COCOM's broad export restriction on encryption. On the 30th anniversary of the release of PGP, Zimmermann published a blogpost admitting that his goals for PGP from the beginning had been true to the hacktivist spirit.

> I wanted PGP to be used for human rights applications. I wanted it to spread all over the world, especially to places where people needed protection from their own governments. But I couldn't say that out loud during the criminal investigation because it would help the prosecutor prove intent.

Ultimately, Zimmermann's goals for PGP were realized. PGP has been a powerful tool for humanitarian missions for decades, enabling aid workers to communicate with victims of violent conflicts where anti-surveillance technologies could mean the difference between life and death. According to Dr. Patrick Ball of the Human Rights Data Analysis Group, PGP has saved countless lives across the world from Guatemala to Kosovo.

9

Hackers Go Mainstream

An FBI officer wearing the Bureau's trademark navy blue windbreaker with "FBI" printed on the back in large, yellow block-print letters explored the kitchen of their most recent apartment raid. He stopped at the refrigerator, opened the door, and swore loud enough for their suspect to hear, who laughed to himself from an adjacent room. Inside the refrigerator was box of donuts from Winchell's Donut House with a message reading, "*FBI Donuts*" written on top in black marker. The suspect they had in custody knew the agents were coming and had used his last moments of freedom to pull one last prank on them.

Kevin Mitnick was finally in the hands of FBI agents after a two-and-a-half-year run from the law that made him a legend inside the hacking community. Mitnick fought the law, and the law finally won, but their win came with a cost. The FBI's inability to capture Mitnick drew attention to the fact that Mitnick, a jovial hacker with a penchant for harassing and pranking his enemies, managed to elude the preeminent federal law enforcement agency in the country.

In the same way that law enforcement brought the Old West era to an end, so, too, did the long arm of the law end the untamed digital frontier. As the freewheeling age of boundless possibilities came to an end, a cultural showdown was bound to happen. That showdown came thanks to two men named Kevin.

Computer Fraud and Abuse

The cases of the 414s and The Sprinter in the 1980s, proved that existing laws meant to regulate the use of modern computer technology were a work in progress. Hackers were being arrested and prosecuted, but the laws they were being charged with were often awkwardly applied to crimes that seemed at times to be completely unrelated.

To address the shortcomings of existing laws, Congress passed the Comprehensive Crime Control Act (CCCA) of 1984. The CCCA was a set of sweeping criminal justice reforms, which addressed several areas of the criminal code that hadn't been revised in nearly 80 years. In its reforms, Congress included new federal powers to prosecute computer-involved crimes along with other changes, including new livestock protection statutes and changes to how the government handled the insanity defense. The CCCA wasn't a dedicated piece of legislation aimed at hackers, but it was a step in the right direction.

The CCCA attempted to define computer crimes as a broader criminal offense, rather than one that was applicable only to government and financial interests. As a steppingstone, the CCCA was a crude attempt at defining computer crime, but if nothing else, it was better than allowing these crimes to continue to be defined by inapplicable postal and telephone laws.

In 1986, two years after the CCCA was passed, it was proceeded by a much more focused piece of legislation called the Computer Fraud and Abuse Act (CFAA). The CFAA was a much more comprehensive approach to addressing computer-related crimes, and became the modern legal standard for how hacking-related crimes would be prosecuted for several decades after.

Rather than treating these crimes as an esoteric misuse of the telephone system as the 414s had been charged with, the CFAA recognized computer crimes as worthy of their own legal category in criminal law. All in all, the CFAA was a competent legislative effort that transformed the way hackers would be treated by the legal system and set the boundaries for both where hackers could go, and how they could get there.

Kevin "Dark Dante" Poulsen

Despite taking a job as a military contractor and receiving the largess of his benefactor, Geoffrey Goodfellow, Poulsen couldn't give up the excitement of the life of a black hat hacker. He was simply having too much fun to quit and settle into the comparatively less exciting life that had been offered by the Stanford Research Institute (SRI). In 1988, Poulsen lapsed on his payments for a storage locker that he maintained under an alias, which caused the owner of the rental space to evict him. When the locker was opened by the owner, the contents belonging to their mysterious tenant prompted them to contact law enforcement.

When the FBI inspected the locker, they found a treasure trove of evidence of Poulsen's ongoing life of digital crime. In addition to false identity documents, Poulsen also retained telephone numbers for high-profile organizations, including the Soviet Embassy, which caused investigators to fear that he might have been acting as a Soviet spy.

The following year, Poulsen was indicted for breaching U.S. military computer networks and repeated attacks on the Pacific Bell company. It seemed that Poulsen had picked up right where he left off shortly after going straight with SRI. Rather than face his federal charges, which wasn't much fun, he opted to go underground. Poulsen went on the run from the FBI evading agents for 17 months. While on the run from the FBI, Poulsen performed his most legendary feat of phreaker expertise. Working with his old partner-in-crime, Ron Austin, who had been jilted in his quest for a military clearance in years past, the two hackers planned to rig a recurring radio call-in contest hosted by the famous Los Angeles rock and roll station KIIS-FM.

The grand prize offered by the radio station in their contest was a Porsche 944 worth $50,000, too tempting for the two young phreakers to pass up on. The contest prompted thousands of calls from listeners across the state who were all eager for a chance to win the impressive prize, but none of them stood a chance at winning when Poulsen and Austin decided to enter the contest.

When the moment came, the radio station announced that the call-in lines were open and that the 102nd caller would be the winner of the contest that day. Poulsen and Austin managed to maintain control of all of the radio station's phone lines for the contest, keeping them all closed except for the 102nd call-in line, which the pair reserved for themselves. The two hackers stopped all other callers from being able to get through the phone lines, locking out any legitimate callers and winning the grand prize for themselves.

Poulsen's time as a fugitive finally came to an end in April 1991, thanks in part to a segment, which featured Poulsen's story on the call-in television program *Unsolved Mysteries*. In his mugshot, a young Poulsen with bleach blonde hair smiled wide for the camera, looking more like he had been arrested for a party foul than federal fraud and wiretapping. Included in the charges brought against him were accusations that he had stolen secret classified flight orders related to a military exercise at Fort Bragg, North Carolina, in 1986, which resulted in the first federal espionage charges ever brought against a hacker in the United States. The espionage charges briefly raised the stakes for Poulsen, but these charges against him were ultimately dropped.[1]

Kevin "Condor" Mitnick

Mitnick, aka "Condor," developed a long career of digital crimes throughout the 1980s and early-1990s. First making his mark on phreaker forums, Mitnick was one of the hacking scene's first "rockstars" who even gained notoriety with the mainstream public. It seemed as though hackers like Mitnick and Poulsen were unstoppable, but after the passage of the CFAA, the tables had turned on hackers.

Fugitive Mitnick.   Mitnick first landed himself in legal trouble in 1979, when he breached a high-performance computer system called "The Ark" belonging to government computing vendor Digital Equipment Corporation (DEC). DEC's U.S. government contracts made the corporation and its products an attractive target of hackers since the late-1970s.

At 16 years old, Mitnick managed to socially engineer his way into DEC on a dare from his phreaker colleagues, who couldn't believe that he managed to get access to the company network. In the breach, Mitnick stole code and manuals for DEC's proprietary Resource Sharing Time Sharing Extended (RSTS/E) operating system. After Mitnick gave access to his

---

[1] https://web.archive.org/web/20130131131901/https://www.nytimes.com/1992/12/08/us/hacker-indicted-on-spy-charges.html

friends for them to use, one of them contacted DEC's corporate security, notifying them of the details of Mitnick's breach.

While investigators followed this lead, Mitnick kept up his antics. In 1981, Mitnick was caught inside a Pacific Bell switching office attempting to steal company manuals for the Pac Bell telephone system. The investigators of Mitnick's Pacific Bell trespassing were unwitting of Mitnick's activities within DEC in 1979, and he was not charged for the DEC breach until several years later.

Since Mitnick was 17 years old at the time of his trespassing into Pacific Bell, he was charged as a minor and only sentenced to probation. A year later, he was right back to his old tricks, this time he was arrested for breaking into computer systems belonging to the University of Southern California (USC). But this time he didn't get off as easily as he had before. For his USC break-in, Mitnick was given a 6-month jail sentence.[2]

Mitnick continued committing similar crimes throughout the 1980s, managing to avoid significant jail sentences each time, but his luck ran out in 1988, when the accusations against him for his 1979 breach of DEC's ARK finally caught up with him. At his trial, Mitnick was sentenced to a year in prison. Mitnick was not out of prison for long after his release from his 1988 prison sentence when he was caught, yet again, for attacking Pacific Bell while he was on probation for his last prison term in 1992.

This time, Mitnick decided to become a fugitive. Mitnick's run from the law became as iconic to his fellow hackers as the exploits that earned him the FBI's attention in the first place. As Mitnick ran from the FBI, he added insult to injury by taunting the FBI agents who were actively hunting for him. By his own account, Mitnick adopted several techniques to hide his tracks including changing his appearance, creating new identities for

---

[2] https://archive.nytimes.com/www.nytimes.com/library/cyber/hackstock/94074s-most-wanted.html

himself, and even changing the appearance of his walking posture by putting a pebble in his shoe.

While on the run, Mitnick even went on the offensive against his FBI pursuers, using techniques he learned as a phreaker to spy on telephones his investigators used, which helped him evade capture during his time running from them. Finally in 1995, FBI agents with the help of security consultant, Tsutomo Shimomura, (who was also subjected to merciless harassment from Mitnick while he was on the run) finally cornered him in his apartment in Raleigh, North Carolina.

Free Kevin.   After his arrest, a movement within the hacking community to free Mitnick began, encompassing many of the grievances raised by hackers after previous law enforcement actions like Operation Sundevil. In the eyes of many hackers, Mitnick's case was Dr. Ripco all over again, despite the fact that the crimes Mitnick was repeatedly charged with were significantly different from the charges, which were ultimately dropped against Dr. Ripco. Defenders of Mitnick felt that the law was once again being abused to lock up innocent hackers whose only crime was curiosity, but this defense was strained by the multiple clear legal violations committed by Mitnick. This perception led a contingent of hackers to start the "Free Kevin" movement, which aimed to have Mitnick released from jail.

Regardless of how badly hackers wanted to see Mitnick exonerated, he served five years in prison, eight months of which he controversially spent in solitary confinement.

Fallout from the Arrests

The arrests of Poulsen and Mitnick marked the end of an era for prominent cyber criminals who began their careers as phreakers and followed their technical interests into the new age of computer hacking.

After being released from custody, Poulsen was barred by courts against the use computers of any kind for many years. This punishment was shared by Mitnick as well in the years after his arrest and prosecution by the FBI. The court order was so serious that Poulsen had to get permission to drive a car due to the fact that it contained simple computer technology.[3]

Hackers who would come after the two Kevins would exist in a world where the weight of the American justice system could come down on anyone for activities that hadn't been seen as risky in years past. The FBI proved that, even in the digital age, criminals could run from them, but they couldn't hide. Even so, both Poulsen and Mitnick had embarrassed law enforcement at every level, forcing them to reflect on institutional changes that needed to be made to avoid embarrassment by hackers in the future.

However, this wasn't the end of their story. Both Kevins would serve time in prison, and both would take very different paths later in life. Yet, they also both got a new lease on life after their time in jail thanks in part to the concept of hacker rehabilitation, which Poulsen was already a beneficiary of. Their time running from law enforcement had inspired a whole new generation of hackers at a time when the government was making the prospect of becoming a young hacker a much riskier proposition. The types of hackers that the Kevins would inspire were a generation of smarter risk-takers.

After his time in prison, Poulsen retired from black hat hacking and became a renowned tech journalist breaking some of the most important stories in tech of the new millennium. Mitnick took a path familiar to other hackers before him, starting his own

[3] Computer hacker has to quit cold turkey; After prison term, he seeks relief from order barring proximity, *The Sun*, August 19,1996.

computer security consultancy using the hacker image he cultivated to promote his services.

In his final years, Mitnick became a mainstay of hacking conferences, handing out his business cards that doubled as a functional lockpick set. In July 2023, Mitnick passed away after a two-year struggle with pancreatic cancer leaving behind the legacy of a bygone era of hacking.

Forging the Hacker Image

The impact of popular media on the public's understanding of hackers can't be understated, particularly through the media-conscious lens of the Reagan administration. At different times, the media has carried messages of hackers as sympathetic and awkward young men who perhaps spend too much time on computers and at other times, shown hackers as reckless and even dangerous agents of chaos.

Scholars often ask a philosophical question, does art imitate life, or does life imitate art? Through the decades, the artistic balance of the media's portrayal of hackers has shifted several times. Each time it shifted, the depictions of hackers in the media mirrored the way that hackers were understood by the public and treated by law enforcement.

1960's Movie Hackers

Representations of hacking as we know it have been present in popular media since the 1960s, and have influenced popular perception of what a hacker is. One of the earliest film portrayals of hacking came in the 1969 movie *The Italian Job*, starring Michael Caine. In it, Caine masterminds a gold heist from a convoy in Italy, but to successfully pull of the scheme he needs to create a traffic jam. One of Caine's associates, a hacker, reprograms traffic signals on an important escape route to malfunction, causing traffic to stop. Thanks to the work of their trusted hacker, the protagonists escape.

The Italian Job portrays hacking as a means to an end. There's no positive or negative commentary about hacking as an activity, but rather as a means to an end. *The Italian Job* isn't the first hacking movie that springs to mind for most people, but it does highlight an old anxiety that persists even today in the minds of average Americans. Could a hacker really cause a critical service malfunction or outage? Making traffic signals go haywire through hacking would have been unlikely in 1969, and isn't much more likely to happen today.

1980's Movie Hackers

A major change that characterized hacker movies in the 1980s was the introduction of narratives focused on hackers themselves. In previous decades, if hacking was present in a movie's plot, it was merely a device used to progress the plot. The 1982 film *Tron* was the first feature-length film to showcase a main character, Kevin Flynn, who was employed as a software engineer, and his background as a hacker was central to the movie's plot.

Early in the film, Flynn hacks into his former company's mainframe to prove the company stole his ideas. Flynn's character adopted aspects of the hacker ethos that were seen as typical for hackers at the time. For one, Flynn's heroic struggle against a large evil corporation was reflective of the anti-establishment sentiment many hackers had in the 1980s and that many still have today. When Flynn is accidentally transported into the computerized world of *Tron*, he becomes a stranger in a strange land. Flynn is a curious outsider exploring an unfamiliar place, driven by curiosity.

Falken's Maze.   The clear standout in the 1980s portrayal of hackers was 1983's *WarGames*. In *WarGames*, young hacker David Lightman takes an interest in a computer he believes is hiding something important and attempts to gain access to it. Not only did *WarGames* play a role in promoting the young male archetype of hackers, but it also showed techniques hackers may have used at the time in a way that was at least based on reality.

Having tried to hack his way deeper into the mysterious computer Lightman connects with, he is unable to proceed when his attempts at playing through a list of games on the computer fail to show the computer's secrets. In desperation, he meets with a friend at a local computer lab who has some knowledge of how the system might work. Lightman's conversation is disrupted by the screeching voice of "Melvin," who pipes in with his own theory.

"Oh yeah, Melvin? How would you do it?" Lightman asks.

"The first game on the list!" Melvin replies confidently, *"Go right through Falken's Maze!"*

In the movie, Falken's Maze turns out to be a *backdoor*, allowing users with knowledge of its existence an easy way into the system. The use of a backdoor is a common trope in hacker fiction and in many ways, sounds as if it should be too simple to be true. In reality, backdoors exist in many forms and are often used by hackers themselves to establish access to a previously compromised system. The concept of Falken's Maze lives on as a throwback to an older era of hacking that is still a fun cultural touchstone for hackers today.

Matthew Broderick.   No analysis of hacker culture in entertainment would be complete without a nod to Matthew Broderick's work in the 1980s. He played David Lightman in *WarGames*, which as mentioned was perhaps the most influential hacking movie of the decade. Its impact was so profound that it didn't only change the perception of hackers, it also changed government policies.

Despite having been released the year before, *Tron* didn't affect the mainstream perception of hackers in the same *WarGames* had. Part of the reason for this was likely because of how closely *WarGames* mirrored the reality of the time. In *WarGames*, Broderick's character unwittingly finds an internet-connected computer responsible for nuclear command and control. The computer is disguised as a computer offering games to users who connect and includes games like chess, checkers, tic-tac-toe, and one called Global Thermonuclear War. As the plot unfolds, David discovers that the game of Global Thermonuclear War he chose to play on the mysterious computer was a nuclear war simulation actually capable of enacting its titular form of devastation.

WarGames also contained important messages that are still relevant today about artificial intelligence, and the futility of nuclear warfare. But what was especially poignant to viewers was how easily David managed to get access to nuclear-connected computers. Some in the *WarGames* audience likely knew that this story was plausible after seeing David use many of the same techniques shown on Geraldo Rivera's "Electronic Delinquents" *20/20* report from the previous year.

One viewer who was particularly struck by the movie's plot was President Ronald Reagan, a man who spent time in Hollywood himself. Reagan watched *WarGames* at Camp David the day after its release and had apparently been so influenced by the film that he asked his advisors the following day if any of them had seen it. He then asked the chairman of the Joint Chiefs of Staff, General John W. Vessey Jr., "Could something like this really happen?" General Vessey replied that he would investigate. When Vessey returned to the White House the following week, he delivered a sobering message to the president, ". . .the problem is much worse than you think."[4]

Bureaucratic secrecy kept the extent of contemporary state-sponsored hacking a secret, but the reality of the shortcomings of American cybersecurity was more alarming. Truthfully, the espionage angle of cybercrime in the 1980's wasn't well understood by American leaders. Some leaders inside government scientific organizations and spy agencies had concerns about the growing threat of computer-based espionage, but none of these concerns had yet made their way into the public eye before *WarGames* was released.

Reagan's question about the plausibility of U.S. government networks being hacked led to the creation of the National Security Decision Directive 145 (NSDD-145). This directive tasked the NSA with the responsibility of protecting U.S. government networks from foreign espionage efforts and set the agency up for its current-day role as the nation's foremost computer security agency.

Three years after *WarGames*, Matthew Broderick starred in the 1980s fan favorite *Ferris Bueller's Day Off*. This movie was much more lighthearted than *WarGames* had been but continued the trope of the young male hacker from *WarGames*. A young man with some hacking skills, this time named Ferris Bueller, uses those skills to break into his school's computerized attendance system to reduce his number of school absences. In the next scene, Ferris looks at the camera and declares, "I asked for a car, I got a computer. How's that for being born under a bad sign?"

This time, Broderick's on-screen hacking was for comic relief. We might even look at a character like Ferris Bueller and recognize the self-serving use of his natural charisma as more in

---

[4] https://www.nytimes.com/2016/02/21/movies/WarGames-and-cybersecuritys-debt-to-a-hollywood-hack.html

line with a social engineer than of David Lightman's technical hacking skill. In any case, it's undeniable that both of Broderick's roles influenced the public image of hackers.

1990's Movie Hackers

In 1992, the movie *Sneakers* starring Sidney Poitier, Robert Redford, and Dan Aykroyd explored Cold War anxieties about the use of spy technologies. In the movie, a mysterious black box is brought to a team of hackers by NSA representatives under the pretense of being a tool used by Soviet spies with some unknown purpose. After some investigation, the team of hackers realizes that the box they were given is a tool that can break the encryption on any computer in the world. Although the idea of a one-size-fits-all decryption device is far-fetched for many reasons, the idea played well for an audience concerned with the state of the ongoing Cold War with the Soviet Union.

While *Sneakers* was considered a box-office success, its release coincided with the fall of the Soviet Union, which meant that it was the last film of the Cold War era with hacking at its core. One important concept *Sneakers* brought to audiences was the idea of encryption and the role it played in everyday life in the 1990s. Encryption wasn't something most average people were concerned with, but *Sneakers* helped explain to audiences why it should be taken seriously.

Another hallmark of *Sneakers* was its role in showing American perspectives and fears triggered by the fall of the Soviet Union. The immediate post-Soviet era was packed with the fear that unknown, possibly dangerous technologies would no longer be protected by Soviet leadership. As one government fell and another took its place, would nuclear weapons suddenly be available to the highest bidder? Hollywood was uncertain, but so were Western governments.

In 1993, the old model of the young male hacker was bucked by the hit movie *Jurassic Park*. In *Jurassic Park*, the young protagonist and granddaughter of the park's founder was a hacker named Lex. Throughout the movie, Lex insists that other characters refer to her as a hacker despite any of them taking her self-given title of "hacker" seriously. Lex famously undoes the work of the antagonist hacker Dennis Nedry, saving her friends just as the frighteningly intelligent raptors learn how to use door handles. In one tense moment, Lex excitedly proclaims, "It's a Linux system! I know this!" as if she herself is surprised at her own hacking abilities.

Lex's heroic arc gave girls interested in hacking their first look at media representation proving that young men weren't the only ones who could save the day with their technical abilities. Despite that women and girls have always been deeply involved in the hacking community, *Jurassic Park* was the first mainstream movie to rightfully represent their place in the hacking community.

Hackers.   Perhaps the most important movie of the 1990s for the hacking community, *Hackers* put a spotlight directly on real-life hackers, giving several nods to the culture and history hackers had built by the time the movie was released. *Hackers* opens on the young protagonist, Dade Murphy (who goes by his handle "Zero Cool"), being raided by federal agents. After young Dade's sentencing, the movie rejoins Murphy as a high schooler, just after having the legal ban on his use of computers lifted. After a high-tech duel over control of a local TV station's automated programming system, Murphy realizes that he isn't the only hacker at his new school. His rival turns out to be a fellow teenage hacker, Kate Libby (played by Angelina Jolie), who also becomes the film's romantic interest. The two protagonists engage in a series of tit-for-tat pranks, which calls back to the true-life history of phreakers like Susy Thunder, Kevin Poulsen, and Kevin Mitnick.

The plot thickens when their friend is framed for capsizing a ship with a piece of malware named the Da Vinci Virus. The young hackers then join forces and fight back against an evil corporate hacker trying to extort money from his company by framing other innocent hackers.

Hackers was an axiomatic change in the way that hackers were represented. The movie didn't just change the way that the public saw the hacking community; it changed the way that hackers saw *themselves*. *Hackers* completely reset the archetype of the young white male hacker. This time, the group of teenage hackers came from an array of diverse backgrounds. Each of the teenage protagonists brought a different style and skill, and it took all of them working together to finally defeat the corrupt corporate hacker antagonist.

What made *Hackers* special was that it didn't just borrow from hacker culture the way that movies and TV had in the past. *Hackers* gave back to its namesake culture. Popular catch phrases coined by *Hackers* like, "Hack the planet!" and references to a nonexistent pool on the roof of Dade's high school are still heard regularly around any given hacking conference today. *Hackers* was the coming-of-age tale that the generation of young 1990s hackers desperately needed, and it celebrated a group of hackers in a way that they hadn't seen before.

Hackers reimagined what the hacker aesthetic could be. The movie's characters proved hackers could be stylish and cool, but they could also be attractive. The main characters were smart and capable, but they were also socially aware. The aesthetic *Hackers* cultivated was also remarkably queer. Although the main love interest is heterosexual, *Hackers* managed to expertly employ queer-coded characters, which gave an additional layer of representation to hackers who hadn't yet been acknowledged before in pop culture.

Throughout the remainder of the 1990s, big-budget Hollywood movies continued to show a fascination for hackers. The year 1995 was a banner year for hackers with the release of *Johnny Mnemonic, The Net, James Bond: Goldeneye,* and the classic anime *Ghost in the Shell.* All of these films prominently featured hacker protagonists and drew their inspiration from the exploits and culture of real-life hackers. These movies also touched on issues of surveillance and privacy, two growing anxieties among Americans.

The presentation of hackers in media helped to elevate the niche community of hackers from an oddball collection of outsiders to an important and increasingly powerful subculture. The media was in awe of what hackers could do, and the portrayal of youthful fun-loving hacking culture encouraged new generations of hackers to get involved themselves. The power of the American TV and movie industry provided a tailwind for hackers to coast into the American mainstream.

10

The DEF CON Effect

I n 1995, the Federal Bureau of Investigation (FBI) opened their first case file on the annual DEF CON conference hosted in Las Vegas, Nevada. The FBI file on DEF CON begins with a brief introduction:

> *DEF CON is a conference that has taken place in the Las Vegas area for the past three years. It is a gathering of "hackers" from throughout the country. . . .Inasmuch as this conference appears to be a yearly gathering and in an attempt to maintain all information regarding DEF CON III in one file it is recommended that this matter be opened. . . .*

The file only contains a single news article about the conference.

First held in 1993, DEF CON had become *the* yearly social event to hobnob with hackers from around the world by the time FBI wrote its first file on the event. The founder of the conference, Jeff "The Dark Tangent" Moss described the first DEF

CON as a lemons-to-lemonade story that started with an open invitation to hackers in the various Internet Relay Chats (IRCs) of which Moss was a member. The invitation was so open that he even faxed cheeky invitations to U.S. government agencies including the Secret Service and FBI letting them know the time and location of the first conference. Freedom of Information Act (FOIA) requests to the FBI asking for information about the conference suggest that the FBI rudely did not even keep a copy of the invitation for their records.

The subculture hackers had built online was crossing the boundary between online spaces and the real world. But before that subculture could be fully integrated by mainstream society, it needed more exposure to everyday Americans.

An Internet for Everyone

The pre-1990s history of the Internet was defined by a limited group of users who had the technical knowledge of how to access it. The result of this sharp technical learning curve was a culture built by the system administrators, programmers, and hackers who populated the early Internet. Simply knowing enough about how to connect a computer to a Bulletin Board System (BBS) was even enough in many circles to earn enough credibility to become a respected member, but this basic challenge did not necessarily constitute *hacking*.

When America Online (AOL) began offering a relatively easy dial-up Internet service to its customers in the early 1990s, a whole new group of Internet users was born. These new users were bound to change the makeup of online culture. In September 1993, AOL proved just how naive the online nativist hope of keeping the Internet a pristine space catering to their interests was when they gave their subscribers access to Usenet.

Usenet was a later alternative to BBS networks, which had been a favored communication tool used by many hackers of the previous generation. This event was called "Eternal September" by the online nativists who didn't appreciate the influx of new users to spaces they felt were rightfully theirs. So-called "lamers" or "newbies" were hated by the online nativists who felt that they were diluting the online experience.

These new users were often on the receiving end of the same sort of mean-spirited comments and pranks that had been deployed by users in the old BBS days. At times, the edgy antics of this particular group went too far and made the jump to offline spaces. In a 1993 Phrack entry titled "Pump Con 94: The Legacy Continues," the prolific Phrack contributor Erik Bloodaxe lamented the fact that one attendee named "GrayAreas" had become the target of some of harassment saying,

> GreyAreas got up next and talked a bit about her magazine and then in a heartfelt plea, asked whoever was bothering her to stop. Many in the audience seemed indifferent to her cause, which upset her greatly. She had to leave immediately afterwards. I hope I wasn't the only person who felt kind of sorry for her.

Erik Bloodaxe goes on to hedge his comment, to some extent defending the abrasive attitude with which some in the community displayed toward outsiders,

> To be fair, people who decide that they want to get on the net need to be reminded that THE NET IS NOT REAL! THE NET IS NOT REAL LIFE. IF THE NET SCARES YOU OR WORRIES YOU, TURN OFF THE F- COMPUTER! GO HANG OUT ON ANOTHER CHANNEL! GO PLAY ON A MUD! GO READ NEWS! If that doesn't placate you, go to AOL.

What nativist hackers of the time didn't realize was that the Internet they knew and loved could still exist, just not in the same way it had before. The Internet was always bound to be tamed in the same way all frontiers are, through a combination of economic interests and government regulation. By the end of the 1990s, the Internet would be a place of business. It was up to hackers to maintain a place for themselves in their changing world.

A Great Migration

Known as Eternal September, this period marked the beginning of a mass migration of people from exclusively offline modes of communication, telephones, fax machines, and even in-person meetings with others to a form of hybrid communication used by phreakers in the 1980s. *Cyberspace*, as many began calling it, was growing, and it was changing the way Americans communicated in a big way. The Bulletin Board Systems (BBSs) of the past, many of which were still in use, were being replaced by newer forum software and "listservs," which connected groups of people in a way they hadn't been before. Those who began using the Internet were sending fewer letters in the mail and sent more emails instead.

Not only were people spending more time online, but they were also starting to spend real money there, too. The success of websites like eBay proved that there was money to be made in online retail sales, and search engines like Yahoo and Google were creating new business models to monetize user data. New investment swept onto the Internet like the Gilded Age oil barons did in the Southwest at the turn of the 20th century.

Despite its growth, cyberspace was still a place of vast possibilities particularly for hackers but also for investors. The Internet gave people with a message from politicians to salespeople, a new means of mass communication with a presence on the Web. Websites simplified the delivery of information to a wide audience and could also function as modern storefronts.

They may not have realized it at first, but soon those placing heavy bets on the future of the Internet would need people who could protect their investments.

Web Defacements

Websites were becoming both the roadside billboards and storefronts of the Internet and were soon an indispensable asset for brand promotion. By the end of the 1990s, everyone from for-profit companies to government agencies were planting their flag on the Internet with a website, but the cyberspace frontier hadn't yet been conquered. Throughout the 1990s, hacktivists were becoming more skilled with their ability to hack for a purpose, and websites were their perfect target.

Breaching a government agency in the same way the WANK worm hackers had done wasn't as easy in the late 1990s as it had been a decade earlier. With law enforcement finally proving their competency in catching and prosecuting cybercrime, the stakes were higher than they had ever been for hacktivists. It was easier for hackers to hide their location with quick and easy website defacements, which made them even more attractive activities for hackers to engage in, compared to longer attacks that forced hackers to run the risk of leaving more evidence behind during longer, more intensive breaches. To hackers of the 1990s, there was no better way to express political disagreements than by directly hacking the website of a government agency.

Hackers began using *web defacement*, which involved breaking into a vulnerable webhost and replacing the legitimate webpage with one made by the attacker, as a way of sending a message to the site's owner. Web defacement was a natural evolution of more labor-intensive hacktivism of the past. The rapid growth of websites and the relative ease hackers seemed to have compromising them, made web defacements a quick and easy way for hackers to send a message. In the mid-1990s, federal agencies including various branches of the Department of Defense (DoD) and even the Central Intelligence Agency (CIA) were hit by web defacements, proving just how ubiquitous defacements had become.

Y2K

As the New Years Eve ball in Times Square dropped in the final moments of December 31, 1999, the end of society as we know it was mere moments away. . .at least that's what cracks holding signs on nearby streetcorners believed for the better part of the last year. Concerns had been brewing about the turn of the millennium and whether computers would still function on January 1, 2000, due to an error in the way that computers understood date values.

To save on valuable computer memory, programmers in the 1970s decided to provide only two-date year values. This meant that most computers before 1999 understood the date to be 99 rather than 1999. It was expected that systems from complex medical and banking systems all the way down to industrial systems and elevators could be impacted by the issue.

Something so simple yet fundamental to the ongoing operation of computerized systems created a very real concern that virtually any device using a microchip would simply stop working on January 1, 2000. This issue became known as the "Y2K crisis" and sent the government and major corporations scrambling to correct the underlying problem.

In 1998, the Clinton administration ordered the U.S. government to direct a massive effort to address the Y2K bug ahead of the century changeover. In less than two years, the lion's share of the work had been done to correct the bug, costing the U.S. government $100 billion and averting the crisis.

The Y2K crisis exposed just how much the world depended on computers, and proved that the American government was capable not only of understanding serious issues in technology but also addressing those problems. The subtext of the Y2K crisis was that problems of the future could be created by hackers, and it would take hackers working together for the common good to solve them.

Hacker Conferences

Over the years, offline hacker meetups have become an important part of the subculture and gave hackers an opportunity to meet each other and greet newcomers to the community. Meeting other hackers face-to-face was a way of building trust, making plans, and partying together as far back as the 1970s, but it wasn't until the early 1990s, that the government began to take an interest in these meetups. Perhaps the most well-known conference, both inside and outside of the hacking community is called DEF CON.

The first year of DEF CON was the sort of improvised moonshot for which major tech companies would come to be known. Originally planned as a going-away party for a colleague, the event had to be quickly reimagined when the guest of honor couldn't attend. Even so, DEF CON ended up being exactly the type of event that spoke to an underground community of passionate tech hobbyists.

Moss chose Las Vegas as the home for DEF CON concluding,

I'd never been to Vegas and if the show was a total failure, I wanted to at least be bankrupt and sitting by the pool with a foofie pina colada drink with an umbrella in it.

Although they may not have realized it at the time, the 1990s generation of hackers was building cybersecurity into an industry. The rapid expansion of the Internet and e-commerce had blossomed into a golden age of online entrepreneurship starting in the mid-1990s and was attracting investment opportunities. As the economic engine of the dot-com era began to warm up, it drew hackers directly into its economic gears, which was a new and unusual position for hackers who never had an opportunity to turn their hobby into a career. Forward-thinking companies began to see the need to better protect their customers and themselves by hiring many of the same people who were hacking in the first place.

Moss told the story of DEF CON's early years to Help Net Security in 2007:

> *The first three years everybody was at the show because they cared. You couldn't get a job in security; you did this because you loved it. Then all of a sudden, you could start getting jobs, then all of a sudden, money entered the equation. You could feel the underground change around DEF CON 4. . . .[1]*

As the U.S. government caught onto the recurring presence of DEF CON, some concern was brewing about exactly what kind of mayhem the ever-growing gathering of hackers would cause each year. Over the years, DEF CON cultivated a reputation for inviting mischievous hackers to Las Vegas, which often resulted in mostly harmless pranks and harassment in and around the Las Vegas conference halls. Although the presence of hackers in Las Vegas didn't often create complete chaos in the already chaotic Vegas strip, federal law enforcement, which wouldn't otherwise have had much interest in the yearly events, weren't quite sure how to react to the information being discussed at DEF CON.

In addition to their social offerings, hacking conferences like DEF CON also gave hackers of all expertise levels a chance to practice public speaking. These events were often used to

[1] https://youtu.be/1g6bQMTjHCE?si=N9EX_265y2KomDbt

showcase new research the speaker had done, which sometimes included demonstrations of new hacking tools, or even information about new, so-called "zero-day" vulnerabilities that could have worldwide implications. Zero-day vulnerabilities are weaknesses in a computer program's code, which the producer of the code does not yet know about. Vulnerabilities of this sort can leave the vulnerable code users in a precarious position, and have often left vendors scrambling to release a fix for the code to stop the potential for hackers to exploit them.

While the types of information available at these conferences typically ranges from new lockpicking tools and techniques to mental health support for hackers, zero-day research was the most relevant to government officials. Knowing about the existence of a zero-day vulnerability could give conference attendees the earliest possible chance to either plan defenses against it or find ways to exploit it. One of the most popular places for hackers to make a spectacle of their new research was at the annual DEF CON conference.

Hackers from the Cult of the Dead Cow (cDc) had made a splash at DEF CON 7 in 1999, when they released a new backdoor program for attacking Windows systems called "Back Orifice 2000." Written by a member of the cDc team who went by the name "Dildog," Back Orifice 2000 was immediately criticized by Microsoft and condemned as "a very malicious, destructive program."[2] Back Orifice 2000 was just one of many tools and techniques, which first saw the light of day on DEF CON's famous stages. Before long, FBI agents began to see the value of attending DEF CON so that they could get a preview of threats they might see in the future.

DEF CON still celebrates the social rejects and outsiders who care about technology and embrace the oddballs that mainstream

---

[2] https://www.cnet.com/tech/tech-industry/back-orifice-2000-makes-its-debut

society doesn't always appreciate. It managed to bring out a unique crowd of hackers with interests ranging from radio frequencies to lockpicking, all of which were of interest not only to hackers but also to spies who also made the yearly pilgrimage to Las Vegas to rub elbows, albeit secretly, with hacker royalty.

The Business of Hacking

The information that hackers shared between them behind closed doors was beginning to show a value to both the security-conscious public and private organizations. As the Internet became a serious policy concern, a new term was desperately needed to communicate the complex technical concepts of computer and network security to policymakers. For inspiration, security practitioners reached deep into the bag of historic terms and found that the term *cyber* was a reasonable fit. Its origins went all the way back to the old familiar mid-century technological principles of *cybernetics*, the same discipline practiced by Stafford Beer in the 1970s.[3]

After being coined by technologist Norbert Weiner, the term *"cyber"* took on a life of its own in science fiction. Cyber was adopted by various influential science-fiction authors like William Gibson and Pat Cadigan, who used the term in their writing. Their popular stories solidified the term for the hacking community and pop culture. It was the perfect prefix to update already familiar concepts for decision-makers. It sounded sufficiently futuristic and gave its users a feeling that they, too, had the technical chops to talk the talk, and before long, *cyber* was being used everywhere.

---

[3] https://gizmodo.com/today-cyber-means-war-but-back-in-the-1990s-it-mean-1325671487

By the mid-2000s, cybersecurity had become big business. In an online interview with Help Net Security posted in 2007, Jeff Moss described the rapidly changing subculture[4]:

We went from say, 100 people the first year to 200 people the next, 300 the next, and it grew, and it grew, and it grew. And as it grew, the internet security space changed around us. The dot-com bubble started forming. It's really funny, the first three years everybody at the show was there because they cared. You couldn't get a job in security; you did this because you loved it. Then all of a sudden, you could start getting jobs, and then all of a sudden, money entered the equation and the feel of the underground changed.

If cybersecurity was poised to be an industry, then hackers would be a highly valued commodity. It was around this time that the terms *white hat* and *black hat* took on new relevance for hackers. As "ethical" hacking became a viable and even profitable career path, there were small but growing business opportunities for hackers who operated outside of the law as well.

White-hat hackers also formalized a code of ethics to distinguish themselves from hackers who made their living extralegally. It was done to legitimize hacking as an essential piece of the collection of technical services necessary to make the future's online economy possible. A side effect of the growth of hacking as a service was that it drew the interest of a whole new generation of hackers. In the same way that major innovations like ubiquitous home computers and the Internet had created their own generations of hackers, the viability of turning hacking into a career was an attractive prospect for many young hackers in the early 2000s. This was reflected in the evolving feel of the underground that Moss described in his 2007 interview.

---

[4] https://youtu.be/lg6bQMTjHCE?si=9POmq49iTa2W3MMS

Hackers seeking a promising career path sometimes were regarded as "less legitimate" for their interest than hackers who participated in the community simply because they were interested in learning. This bias was also present in hiring managers seeking hackers with a "passion" for hacking and who spent substantial amounts of their free time on independent research and tinkering. This bias persists at times even today, despite the ubiquity of hackers and security professionals in office settings.

Through a combination of public visibility, interest from industries looking to hire hackers, and government agencies becoming more involved, the hacking community was enjoying a surge of mainstream interest in the late 1990s that translated into institutional legitimacy by the end of the 1990s.

Spot the Fed

The introduction of federal agents into the social community of hackers happened slowly. In the first few years of DEF CON, the government painted hackers with a broad brush. Hackers were considered criminals, and law enforcement pursued them using many of the same methods they used against any other group they considered criminal. As attitudes changed, law enforcement both locally and federally began to self-integrate into the social networks of the hacking community. However, American law enforcement was working against significant headwinds that they themselves had created.

Operation Sundevil had been a high-profile failure for law enforcement, but it wasn't the only example of law enforcement burning their own bridges with the hacking community. Only a few short months after Operation Sundevil began, the Secret Service raided the homes of members of a hacking group called the *Masters of Deception (MOD)*, including a particularly popular and skilled hacker who went by the name "Phiber Optik." The Secret Service raid was based on the flawed belief that the group was responsible for an AT&T service interruption before the company admitted that the crash in their network was due to their own human error.

Instead of being humbled by the mistake, the Secret Service doubled down on their investigation of MOD, pulling out all the stops in their pursuit of the members of the group. The Secret Service even went so far as using wiretaps on several members of the MOD to justify charging them. At the time, Phiber Optik (whose legal name was Mark Abene) was still a minor, but that didn't stop prosecutors from pursuing charges against him. Abene ultimately pled guilty to the charges and spent a year in jail. When he was finally released in 1994, he became an overnight celebrity in the hacking community.

Abene's treatment was emblematic of the sort of overly aggressive policing federal law enforcement brought to bear against hackers in the early 1990s. With few legal or financial resources to defend themselves, hackers had to find other ways of coping with the unfair legal strategies being used against them. One of the ways this frustration manifested was with the creation of DEF CON's famous *Spot the Fed* game. The goal of Spot the Fed was simple; any conference attendee could point out a person they thought might be a member of a federal agency, and they would win a free T-shirt.

Despite its playful name, Spot the Fed became a fun yearly event that was generally enjoyed by everyone who participated, even the Feds. Spot the Fed went a long way in helping relax tensions between hackers and federal officials who attended the events, which, over time, led to something resembling mutual respect. It became well understood that Feds would be present at DEF CON, and as long as both groups maintained their mutual understanding of how the other operated, unpleasant interactions could be avoided. But this didn't mean that there still wasn't a power dynamic at play.

Between 1993 and 2007, the hacker/government relationship was in an awkward position. Hackers understood that they were locked in a perpetual game of cat and mouse with law enforcement, who'd taken many opportunities over the years to remind them who played the role of the cat. In 1998, the Digital Millennium Copyright Act (DMCA) was passed, giving new legal authority to intellectual property holders. Provisions within the DMCA included Section 1201, which legally prohibits the circumvention of Digital Rights Management (DRM) and encryption used to protect digital products. Section 1201 became yet another tool for law enforcement to use against hackers.

In 2001, the FBI shocked conference goers by publicly arresting Russian Cryptographer, Dmitry Sklyarov, after he gave a talk at the conference titled "eBooks Security—Theory and Practice." Dmitry's talk covered methods of defeating basic DRM used on Adobe PDFs and eBooks, which technically ran afoul of Section 1201 of the DMCA. Ironically, a day before he was arrested at the same conference, another hacker named Dario Diaz spoke, warning hackers of how overbroad and indiscriminate use of the DMCA could be used by law enforcement against them. The charges against Skylarov were later dropped, but his public arrest at DEF CON left a bad impression on the hacking community. The understanding struck by hackers and the government in the late 1990s led to a working relationship of sorts between the two groups. After Sklyarov's arrest, the tone changed toward the FBI. Some DEF CON attendees felt that the FBI was trying to send a message by unduly exercising their power. This wasn't the last time outsiders overstepped with hackers on their own turf, and in 2007, the conference and its attendees took matters into their own hands.

At the closing ceremonies for DEF CON 15, a frustrated Moss took to the stage and addressed the crowd,

We all understand that trust is a very critical component of the underground of the real-life computer security scene. Sure, we all have secrets, sure we all hide stuff from each other, but I kind of like to have things out in the open. It came to our attention that there may be people here under a false identity, or pretending to be something they're not.

It came to our attention that a reporter might be here with a hidden pinhole camera, not as press recording people for a piece on hiring hackers. I'm not cool with that, especially when they turn down the offer to be given a press badge. So, I need a show of hands for a new contest, "spot the undercover reporter."[5]

The audience booed the prospect of a reporter breaching the trust of conference attendees with a hidden camera. Reporter Michelle Madigan from the investigative reporting outfit, *Dateline*, sat nervously in the audience as Moss spoke. As his speech ended, Madigan quickly got out of her seat and left the hotel, flanked by her cameramen as conference attendees jeered at her.

Madigan had reportedly been trying to secretly film federal officials attempting to hire hackers at the conference,[6] but Madigan didn't accept multiple offers from DEF CON organizers to be recognized at the conference as a member of the press. A retrospective read of Madigan's removal from the conference suggests that the organizers had taken action to protect federal officials at the conference, but this wasn't an accurate reflection of where the relationship between hackers and the government was at the time.

---

[5] https://youtu.be/zQcmWHwsYUU?si=D2g1HFpEZbD8w9Nu
[6] https://www.wired.com/2007/08/media-mole-at-d

By 2012, it was clear that the relationship between the government and the DEF CON community had softened somewhat when National Security Agency (NSA) Director Keith Alexander was given a keynote-speaking slot that year. Normally seen in his U.S. Army dress uniform, Alexander instead chose to appear on stage in a black T-shirt and jeans, blending into the regular DEF CON crowd.[7] It was the first time that a director-level official of the U.S. intelligence community spoke before the crowd of Las Vegas hackers. General Alexander's keynote was an effort to set a new tone with the hacking community and promote partnerships between government entities and private entities in a new form of engagement that the NSA had never done before.

For an agency so dedicated to secrecy, Alexander's presence was a tremendous gesture of goodwill and marked a high point in the relationship between hackers both inside and outside of government service. Alexander's message for a positive government relationship with hackers didn't sit for long with listeners before a new controversy created yet another major setback for that relationship. In May 2013, a former government contractor named Edward Snowden appeared alongside reporter Glenn Greenwald inside a Hong Kong hotel room with a hard drive full of evidence he claimed was evidence of civil rights abuses by the NSA.

Snowden and Greenwald claimed that the information showed the extent of U.S. government surveillance against the American public. The programs Snowden exposed gave a window into a secret world built by hackers with the blessing of the American government. After the Snowden leaks in 2013, DEF CON organizers explicitly announced that federal agents were not welcome at that summer's conference.

---

[7] https://www.theverge.com/2012/8/1/3199153/nsa-recruitment-controversy-defcon-hacker-conference

Behind the scenes, federal officials who regularly attended DEF CON kept in contact with conference organizers in an effort to salvage the long-term relationships they had built. Rather than damaging the relationship permanently, the Snowden leaks were a return to form for most regular DEF CON attendees, who'd always been skeptical of the federal government's activities. However, at an increasing rate, DEF CON attendees had also been becoming federal employees at an increasing rate over the years.

This slow and steady integration of hackers coming to and going from government service helped build long-term bridges between hackers and the American government. While DEF CON managed to maintain a mooring to a truly organic community for and by hackers, companies looking to raise their profile among hackers by sponsoring their own corporate conferences became popular in the 2000s.

II

The Post-Broadband Era

The wide availability of broadband Internet subsumed the online world of the past, but the road to a newer, faster online experience came with rules that changed the way hackers could legally interact with the space of which they had always been a part. The Internet became a ubiquitous, always-connected space that unified the online and offline worlds, which merged the realities of both. For average Americans who found themselves with access to the Internet for the first time, seeing the familiar faces of their friends and family through social media websites eased the merging of worlds. With the addition of Internet-connected consumer electronics and smartphones, the ability for ordinary people to disconnect became more and more difficult. Over time, the lines between online and offline life became blurred beyond recognition.

11

In from the Cold

May 19, 1998. In a stuffy, dimly lit room with wood-paneled walls and window blinds drawn shut, seven hackers sat in the front row of a chamber in the U.S. Senate building. They are representatives of the L0pht hacking collective, and their purpose is to testify before the Senate on questions relevant to the security of American government computers. The droning voice of the chair of the Governmental Affairs Committee, Republican Senator Fred Thompson, introduces the young men: "Due to the sensitivity of their work, we will be using their hacker names of Mudge, Weld, Brian Oblivion, Kingpin, Space Rogue, Tan, and Stefan."

American lawmakers had finally seen the importance of addressing decades-long concerns expressed by hackers about the way America's legal system dealt with technology and the hackers that work with it. To that end, hackers had been invited by the Senate to represent those concerns. It may not have been the first time hackers testified to Congress, but it was the wide scope of cyber-security related issues Senators sought answers for that made this hearing important.

Hackers Meet Congress

L0pht Heavy Industries (or L0pht as they're more commonly known) was a Massachusetts-based hacking collective that had set up one of the first continuous "hackerspaces" in the country. When L0pht started, it was originally called "The Loft," and was intended as a place to store the various electronic components bought by its early members. As more and more hackers from the Cambridge area were invited to the space, the purpose of the hackerspace changed. The Loft became a dual-use space both for storage and tinkering away on technical projects using the items stored in the space.

L0pht took on a community feel, becoming a shared knowledge space where participants could draw on the knowledge of other members to grow collective understanding. The inside of L0pht's hacking lair looked more like an overcrowded storage closet of esoteric flea-market sourced electronics stacked on top of each other than a mad scientist laboratory, but the research the hackers of L0pht did inside its walls was important, nonetheless.

Inside L0pht's workshop, hackers could share tools, software, and any other equipment needed for ongoing hardware and software hacking projects, which could also be stored inside the hackerspace. They were a well-qualified group of hackers to speak on the state of hacking laws in the United States, and had earned their representative status for the hacking community of the mid-1990s.

The quickening pace of news stories highlighting the activities of hackers since the late-1980s paired with a 1990 Government Accountability Office (GAO) report detailing hacks against the government prompted Senators to take the cybersecurity issues more seriously. Although stories abound of how L0pht came to be invited to testify before the Senate Government Affairs Committee, the invite likely came through a connection between L0pht member, Peiter "Mudge" Zatko, and White House advisor Richard Clarke.[1]

The members of L0pht recognized that much of their hacking activity was viewed as a legal gray area—perhaps not illegal per se but certainly not endorsed by the government or the companies who produced the equipment they hacked. The hackers of L0pht feared the legal reprisal of large companies as much as government imposed jail time; a single successful lawsuit could have ended L0pht in one fell swoop as certainly as a prison sentence could. The members of L0pht knew they were in the lion's den.

L0pht's Congressional testimony came just as the dot-com boom was ramping up. In previous decades, lawmakers had notoriously been behind the curve on updating legal statutes to meet the technology of the time. L0pht's appearance before lawmakers had major implications, not just for hackers and the members of L0pht specifically, but for all Americans. Computer technology in the 1990s wasn't a novelty in the way it had been two decades before. Personal computers and telecommunications were quickly becoming a part of daily life for most Americans. With the internet poised to make or break billions of dollars in the dot-com era, lawmakers didn't have the luxury of delaying their understanding of cybersecurity.

During the L0pht testimony, one of the main issues they raised was the lack of action on the part of hardware and software manufacturers to respond to security problems raised by hackers.

---

[1] Space Rogue How the hackers known as L0pht Changed The World, Thomas, Cris 2023

From the hackers' point of view, if they told a company about a vulnerability they had discovered, then the manufacturer should be expected to fix it. This wasn't always the case in practice, however. L0pht urged Congress to set regulatory expectations and standards and to create guidelines for security products and vendors. One result that came much later was the concept of responsible disclosure and safe harbor policies that provided hackers with a safe legal basis for submitting vulnerabilities to manufacturers.

Although L0pht's Senate testimony had given hackers a proverbial place at the table, it couldn't completely undo the complicated relationship between hackers and the government. However, the testimony of L0pht members to the Senate represented a chance for a new start. The success of the Congressional hearings proved that hackers could be strong partners to the government, as long as they were treated with respect. The economic changes promised by the internet were enough for Congress to take interest in computer security, but the year before L0pht testified on Capitol Hill, lawmakers had a hacking scandal of their very own, which added to the urgency.

In April, 1997, the *New York Times* reported that Florida couple, John and Alice Martin, faced wiretapping charges in a politically charged hack against members of Congress. The couple described by the Times as "political junkies," was ordered to pay a fine of $500 each for using a simple radio scanner to intercept and record a private phone call made by Speaker of the House, Newt Gingrich.

The intercepted discussion between Gingrich, Representatives Bill Paxton, Dick Armey, and future Speaker of the House, John Boehner involved Gingrich's announcement of a settlement in his House Ethics committee investigation. The investigation focused on accusations that Gingrich had received illegal donations in exchange for teaching biased course material to his classes during his time on staff at Reinhardt College in Georgia. After intercepting the call, the Martins gave the recording to a House Democrat. The recording ignited a political fury in Washington, and forced politicians who may not have had much interest in their personal communications security to take the matter more seriously.[2]

Now that the American public was becoming more familiar with cybersecurity, they were also beginning to learn what it would take to maintain.

Development of the Red Team

Amateur hackers found success in attention to growing cybersecurity problem both for government agencies and private companies, organizations were forced to embrace cybersecurity programs it hadn't considered before. One such option was *red teaming* (also called *penetration testing*), a form of preventative security auditing that the government itself had developed decades before.

In the 1950s, teams of physical penetration testers audited the security of nuclear launch sites belonging to Strategic Air Command (SAC), the agency that held the keys to America's nuclear arsenal. As part of its mandate, the SAC operated black-hat teams tasked with ensuring that nuclear weapons security policies were being followed. These teams were tasked with testing facilities and personnel of SAC's nuclear command-and-control network to discover weaknesses in the security of their operations and processes. If any were found, those vulnerabilities were reported to the SAC's leadership, who would use the information to improve their policies.

---

[2] https://www.nytimes.com/1997/04/26/us/couple-fined-1000-on-gingrich-phone-call.html

Black-hatting teams were a means to an end for the SAC's leadership. They had needed a response to questions about a handful of mishaps involving nuclear weapons, which called into question just how secure our weapons really were. The theory was that if the SAC could break into its own secure sites and preemptively fix their own security, they could reduce the possibility of uncontrolled security incidents happening.

Black-hat operations within SAC were granted permission to engage in a range of activities, including simulated bomb placement and physical security breaches, aimed at both understanding the gaps in nuclear site security and educating on-site personnel on the importance of adhering to security standards. Some black-hat activities even used social engineering as a means to gain access to protected information.

In Eric Schlosser's history of America's nuclear weapons, *Command and Control: Nuclear Weapons, the Damascus Accident, and the Illusion of Safety,* Schlosser recounts a black-hat operation where an operator demanded technical diagrams of a nuclear system from a crew commander using the pseudonym "General Wyatt." Before the short interaction was over, the fictitious General Wyatt was able to convince the unsuspecting officer to send the diagrams for which he had asked. These 1950s black-hat operations had clear similarities in terms of goals and operational planning to modern red teaming activities and even share many of the same methods.

Operation Cybersnare

Using their authority over fraud cases, the Secret Service once again took the lead in a sting aimed at disrupting the multimillion-dollar network of fraudulent mobile phone and credit card information. In January 1995, the Secret Service began an eight-month "undercover" sting called *Operation Cybersnare.* As was the case with Operation Sundevil, they set up a central office from which to conduct the operation, this time in Bergen County, New Jersey.

The Secret Service had to prove that they were competent to run an operation to enforce fraud statutes in a new online environment. To this point, their attempts had resulted in middling controversial arrests and had attracted heavy criticism of the agency and its activities. For the sake of the Secret Service's credibility, Operation Cybersnare had to be different.

Planning for it was considerably more complex than the Secret Service's previous raids against online fraud had been. The Secret Service tapped Special Agent Stacey Bauerschmidt to lead the investigation, who had new ideas about how to run an online fraud investigation. Secret Service agents were no strangers to pushing the envelope while investigating cybercrime, as they had proven during Operation Sundevil and the investigation of the Masters of Deception hackers. For this investigation, Secret Service agents decided to collaborate with a confidential informant and together set up a forum advertising fraudulent credit and mobile phone card numbers they called *Celco 51*. Within hours of going live, the Celco 51 had their first customer.[3]

Agent Bauershmidt went undercover as the owner and operator of the Celco 51 forum named "Carder One." The forum's purpose wasn't just to sell fraudulently obtained credit card information but also to facilitate the sale of stolen information to Carder One. Within a month, the Secret Service had their first arrest. In total, Operation Cybersnare ran for eight months, and this time they had something to show for it.

When Cybersnare ended, six hackers had been charged with mobile- and computer fraud–related charges, including two men who conspired to breach the computer network of a small

---

[3] https://web.archive.org/web/20230609210258/https://www.latimes.com/archives/la-xpm-1995-09-13-me-45480-story.html

Oregonian mobile phone company called McCaw Cellular.[4] The material taken in as evidence from the 12 raids conducted by the Secret Service proved that the suspects had been involved in the thefts of which they were accused.

Thinking About the Future

Despite some forward-thinking military leaders who understood the threats posed by hackers in the 1970s and 1980s, there were many more who were only beginning to understand just how behind the eight-ball they were on cybersecurity by the 1990s. As the list of U.S. government agencies that had fallen victim to network breaches grew, the need for action to protect American defense systems was clear.

After being prompted by President Reagan to investigate the true danger posed by the David Lightmans of the world, military higher-ups found that *WarGames* was, indeed, a serious problem. But how exactly were generals with little real technical knowledge supposed to turn the untamed wilderness of cyberspace into a new domain of combat? The digital frontier was explored by young rebels who, generally speaking, weren't a great fit for the rigid rules and hierarchies of the American military.

One clear problem that needed to be solved was the language barrier. The term *hacking* was too simple to describe the array of disciplines necessary to attack and defend cyberspace. After Ronald Reagan passed the presidential torch to his successor George H. W. Bush in 1989, the Pentagon issued DoD Directive TS-3600.1, which began formalizing a new domain they called *information warfare (IW)*. Terms like *IW* and *information operations (IO)* gained currency in official military vernacular through

---

[4] https://www.chicagotribune.com/1995/09/12/on-line-swag-shop-sting-yields-6-arrests

memos and briefings in the mid-1990s. Formalizing language went a long way in legitimizing cyberspace as a military domain of combat, but it was only a small part of the puzzle.

The government needed to improve their outreach to hackers, who were being seen as a valuable resource by the end of the Clinton administration. They needed to find a way to recruit, train, and maintain their own contingent of hackers, but they had an uphill battle ahead of them.

Agencies like the Secret Service and Federal Bureau of Investigations (FBI) had spent the last half-century arresting hackers stemming from legally questionable raids. Even before the crackdowns of hackers in the early 1990s, the FBI earned a reputation for being dismissive of cybercrime. As Cliff Stoll points out in *The Cuckoo's Egg*, the FBI agent he tried to contact for help with his own investigation, FBI Special Agent Fred Wyniken, was particularly disinterested.

As Stoll recounts, Wyniken rudely interrupted Lawrence Berkeley Laboratory's (LBL) attorney, Aletha Owens, telling her, "If you can demonstrate a loss of more than a million dollars or that someone's prying through classified data, then we'll open an investigation. Until then, leave us alone."

Embarrassingly, the Bureau hadn't taken any interest at all in the LBL hack Stoll had reported until after they'd received a tip from Interpol two years later.[5] Stoll handed the agency a counterintelligence coup with a bow on it, and the FBI dismissed him out of hand. This dismissiveness was thanks in part to an FBI policy to cross-train their special agents into cybersecurity. This meant the majority of the Bureau's computer-based investigative needs were met by special agents who had little-to-no formal

---

[5] Federal Bureau of Investigation. (1988). Interpol—Foreign Police Cooperation Unit; Financial Crimes Unit. Chaos Computer Club.

training, experience, or, in some cases, even personal interest in the subject of cybercrime or computers in general.

The Bureau's reputation for being the luddites of the national security establishment had become the subject of abject mockery and turf battles when the FBI was selected to take charge of a newly established agency overseeing the protection of critical computerized infrastructure. Established in 1998, the creation of the National Infrastructure Protection Center (NIPC) caused a fiasco within the DoD when they were told that they would be reporting to the FBI on matters related to the NIPC. Surprised DoD officials expressed concern that the FBI didn't have the cybersecurity chops to lead such an important organization, and they were right.

According to former U.S. Attorney General Michael Vatis, the Bureau didn't take the threat of cybercrime seriously enough. Grizzled FBI agents who had built careers on high-profile mafia cases and traditional counterintelligence cases considered cybersecurity a distraction more than a legitimate investigative domain.[6] Given this attitude, it's easy to see how the FBI managed to repeatedly fumble a potentially fruitful partnership with the strong culture of hackers who'd become prevalent in the United States.

The FBI's interest in cybercrime didn't truly begin until 2001 under the FBI leadership of then-director Robert Mueller. But even then, it would take one of the most devastating terror attacks in U.S. history to force the FBI to take the investigation of cybercrime seriously. After September 11, Director Mueller ordered the establishment of cybercrime investigative resources to be available in every field office across the country. This is when the FBI began deliberately training and hiring special agents to do the work of cybersecurity investigation.

---

[6] https://www.propublica.org/article/fbi-ransomware-hunting-team-cybercrime

Mueller's decision was a step in the right direction, but despite this effort, leadership at the Bureau continued treating their own hackers as second-class citizens. This treatment continued to stymie the FBI's cybersecurity talent retention for years to come. In particular, there was a contradictory mandate in law enforcement agencies that needed to both enforce the law and hire technical talent from the same candidate pool they were arresting. The solution became obvious—the government would need to recruit hackers in the communities *before* they ran afoul of the law.

It was with this difficult history in mind that the national security establishment began forming relationships with hackers directly by partnering with hacking conferences across the country. By respecting the space and expertise hackers built for themselves, the FBI was able to build inroads with hackers over land many thought had been permanently spoiled. With a lot of hard work and humility, the FBI began to see the benefits of treating hackers as partners, rather than adversaries.

For the sake of national security, these inroads weren't a moment too soon. By the end of the 1990s, an eye-opening series of military exercises once again opened the eyes of national leadership, shining a spotlight on the state of American cybersecurity.

Evident Surprise and Eligible Receiver

In 1997, the Pentagon ordered a series of exercises that served as a ground truth for just how prepared the U.S. military was for the next generation of warfare. These tests were organized into two main exercises called *Evident Surprise* and *Eligible Receiver*. The first of the two exercises was Evident Surprise-97 (ES-97) in March, followed by Eligible Receiver-97 (ER-97) in June. ES-97 and ER-97 were the first large-scale exercises that integrated both offensive and defensive cyberoperations. Isolated cases of cyber integration for operational planning had happened in the past, but these hadn't been well-coordinated with other agencies or military divisions.

Evident Surprise's aim was to test the U.S. military and intelligence community on their competence to coordinate IO attacks against other nations. Responsibility for this exercise was given to United States Atlantic Command (USAC). One system targeted by USAC during Evident Surprise was a medical record system to track blood supplies for use by military medical staff.[7]

On the other hand, ER-97 was a two-week no-notice exercise to evaluate America's resilience to a nationwide cyberthreat against both military and civilian assets. No notice meant that the participants in the exercise didn't have the benefit of knowing ahead of time that an exercise was taking place. This element gave military leaders an idea of the true capabilities of the American defenders to respond when an attack was unexpected.

The series of attacks outlined by the ER-97 operational plan specified that the simulated enemy in the exercise would be the Democratic People's Republic of Korea (DPRK) military. Within this context, the NSA's red team played the role of DPRK attackers and used commercial, off-the-Shelf (COTS) tools and techniques in their attack simulations.

One of the findings of these exercises was the need to establish working groups to refine IO policy and address technology shortcomings for critical infrastructure protection. ER-97 was a full-spectrum simulation aimed at all of America's critical infrastructure, not just military assets. The NSA's red team was wildly successful in their efforts to exploit the American military and civilian systems.

---

[7] *Cyber Warfare and Cyber Terrorism*, Lech J. Janczewski and Andrew M. Colarik, 2007.

Several lessons were also learned by the U.S. government about what a large-scale attack would look like. What leadership learned is that it would be difficult to discern whether an attack was part of a larger state-sponsored offensive effort or if it was simply a one-off attack by organized crime or individual hackers. Part of the attack focused on surveillance and telecommunication disruption, which involved the theft of an STU-III secure telephone.

When the dust cleared, the chief targeting officer of NSA's red team, Keith Abernathy, believed that his team had utilized only about 30% of their capabilities. In a handful of cases, defenders realized an attack was happening and independently reacted to it by doing things like limiting firewall rules. This stopped the red team from progressing to their intended targets, but their decisive actions weren't driven by existing policy. The military had plenty of technology; what they were clearly lacking was the proper know-how and expertise to create the playbooks.

By the mid-1990s, the American military understood that the future of armed conflict would involve weaponized computers. As military leaders digested the lessons learned from ER-97 and ES-97, a clear set of terminology was necessary to communicate new concepts. Past breaches in prominent government organizations exposed essential weaknesses in America's cyber defense. The DoD expected that some of the same vulnerabilities that had been used as leverage in breaches in the past could be used to compromise U.S. military assets.

The introduction of IO and IW marked the beginning of a paradigm shift in the way that hackers would be treated by the government. It was a change that came with its fair share of caveats but was undoubtedly a major step forward for legitimizing an industry that would soon come to be called *cybersecurity*. U.S. military leadership had placed the country on a pathway to a future with greater computer security. Yet, there was one nagging question in the back of everyone's mind: were they already too late?

CHAPTER

12

Anonymous

In May 2011, an Alphabet City resident named Hector Monsegur left his apartment in the Jacob Riis housing project for the day. The building he left was a worn-down tenement in New York City, but it had views overlooking the East River on the lower-east side of Manhattan. The area contained plenty of parks for him to take his young cousins, who he was raising while his aunt served a prison sentence for drug distribution, a career he himself had been forced into by circumstance. He kept a well-groomed goatee and tight edges on his buzz-cut hair and sideburns and maintained a fashionable style that contributed to his reputation as the "party boy of the projects."

Something seemed off to Monsegur that day in May. Traffic was moving as normal, neighbors made their way to work, and the mail was out for delivery. Still, something didn't seem right. Monsegur noticed a Con-Edison van parked across the street from his apartment building, and the Con Ed employee was talking to a mailman. Monsegur didn't recognize either of them, but then again, why would he? New York was a big city, and it wasn't unusual for new faces to come and go.

Less than a month after this morning, Monsegur heard a knock on the door. He had been planning for that moment for weeks, so when he opened the door to find a team of FBI agents outside, he wasn't surprised to see them. He wasn't just Hector Monsegur; he was also an internationally known hacker who went by the name "Sabu." When he was asked many years later about when he knew he was under surveillance by the FBI in May, Monsegur told Charlie Rose of CBS, *I knew something was up.*

By the time FBI agents took Monsegur in for questioning, they had been hot on his trail for several weeks. The hacker they were after, Sabu, had built a reputation in previous months for high-profile hacks he had conducted with his crew of hackers calling themselves *LulzSec*. A short time after his questioning, FBI agents handling Monsegur had secured an agreement to become a confidential informant working for the Bureau. As a part of the agreement, Monsegur would turn over any information he had on his LulzSec cohorts in exchange for a lighter sentence in his own trial.

As agents walked Monsegur out of his apartment building to a waiting car, he wondered, how did it come to this?

Since 2000, the rules for Americans had completely changed due in no small part to the amount Americans relied on an array of technologies in their daily lives. After the testimony of L0pht, Congress was finally addressing technology issues in their legislation, but the solutions they came up with did not always have the best interest of the American public at heart.

USA PATRIOT Act

After the September 11 attacks, the U.S. government kicked into high gear, turning the entirety of the American national defense apparatus toward conducting the *"war on terror."* This included the National Security Agency (NSA), the Federal Bureau of Investigation (FBI), and the Central Intelligence Agency (CIA) working in tandem on worldwide counterintelligence operations. September 11th had been seen by many in government as an intelligence failure that demanded a legislative remedy.

The remedy contrived by Congress was a piece of controversial legislation called the *Uniting and Strengthening America by Providing Appropriate Tools Required to Intercept and Obstruct Terrorism Act*, recognized by most by its abbreviation: the USA PATRIOT Act (or just *the Patriot Act*).

The stated goal of the Patriot Act was to prevent future terrorist attacks in the United States, using the September 11 attacks as justification. From a practical perspective, the Patriot Act created a whole host of new legal surveillance options for the federal government to use to collect electronic communications. The collection of government programs created by the Patriot Act presented a fundamental question about the erosion of American rights in exchange for security. To many Americans, this tradeoff was unacceptable, particularly for how invasive the law's impacts would be on American citizens.

Among those who felt that the Patriot Act went too far were hackers who'd been warning about the dangers of federal surveillance for decades. As the Patriot Act evolved over the years, members of the hacking community continued to watch and act to counter surveillance with encryption strategies meant to frustrate it.

In 2008, the Patriot Act was amended. It was amended a second time for the purpose of squaring the application of the law to restore the civil rights of Americans. Americans, however, had already digested the reality that the government would position itself in opposition to civil rights if there were ever to be a concern about the nation's security. The effects of this reality were yet another catalyst that urged hacktivists to organize.

Project Chanology

In January 2008, a video was posted to YouTube featuring an interview with legendary action movie star, Tom Cruise. Cruise was a notoriously private celebrity who rarely gave interviews, which would have been leading news on its own, but what made the video remarkable was the subject matter of the interview. In the video, Cruise was being interviewed exclusively about his membership in the notoriously secretive and obscure Church of Scientology. The Church of Scientology claimed a handful of recognizable movie and television celebrities among its membership, including actor, John Travolta, musical artist, Isaac Hayes, and voice actor for popular television show, The Simpsons, Nancy Cartwright.

The interview with Cruise was promotional for the Church of Scientology, but it hadn't been made with the intent of being released to the public. Described by the now-defunct muckraking website Gawker as "the Tom Cruise indoctrination video Scientology tried to suppress," the interview had somehow been leaked, but by whom?

A few days after the Cruise interview was released, another video was posted to YouTube, with a much more ominous tone than the recording of the Tom Cruise interview had. Opening with a B-roll of dark rolling clouds, the video dramatically declared that "Anonymous" was responsible for the leaked interview and promised that more attacks against the famously litigious organization would follow. Unbeknownst to the Church of Scientology, the video's release was part of a new project being organized on a niche-interest online image forum called 4Chan.

4Chan dubbed their campaign against the Church of Scientology *"Project Chanology"* and had more activities against the Church of Scientology planned for the future. Thanks to their attention-grabbing headlines, Anonymous became the first hacking group that most average people could name.

Coming together around 2003, Anonymous took their name from the default user account given to users on 4Chan. Anonymous was assigned to users of the image board who did not have registered accounts. Often referred to by other posters on the board as "Anons," Anonymous drew a membership, which by all appearances, was an organic online movement.

4Chan was part of the pervasive culture of edgy, teenage angst found on other image, and text-focused online forums like Something Awful, Newgrounds, and 9gag. These forums were known for their ability to crowdsource the creation of new content that each site's membership excitedly consumed. In its own way, the foundation of Anonymous was just another manifestation of crowdsourced content.

On 4Chan, the creation of Anonymous came together on a sub-forum called "/b/" which was created to host "random" or uncategorized content. Anonymous organically came together on the /b/ board after a plurality of active members of the forum agreed that the Church of Scientology represented a problem that needed to be dealt with. The so-called *"hivemind"* (a term describing the general consensus of /b/ users on any given issue) had distinct overlaps in terms of values with the traditional ethos of hackers. The hivemind of 4chan shared anti-censorship ideals and supported the free flow of information with hackers. It was in this way that 4Chan became a refuge for a new generation of hackers and became a natural evolution of the culture that had existed on past BBS networks.

Even before Project Chanology, Anonymous took part in online trolling, (which they called *"raids"*) against websites, including one popular with 4Chan users chronicling petty disagreements between Internet users called *Encyclopedia Dramatica*. Encyclopedia Dramatica also held a special place among late-2000s hackers as a place to air grievances and carry-on the time-honored tradition of flame wars, which had been enjoyed by hackers of the 1980s on Bulletin Board Systems in decades past. Project Chanology was Anonymous's big break into hacktivism and capable of capturing the public's attention.

As Anonymous built a name for itself through the news, they also cultivated an aesthetic that they used to further capture the attention of offline observers. Outsiders began to recognize their symbolism, including the smiling mustached Guy Fawkes masks made famous by the 2006 film *V for Vendetta*. Guy Fawkes masks popped up during protests and demonstrations around the world becoming popular even among supportive non-members of Anonymous to represent a sort of populism that wearers felt added credibility to their participation. In a way, the appearance of a Guy Fawkes mask implied the approval of Anonymous as a force behind any popular movement where they appeared. The aesthetics of Anonymous even inspired future portrayals of hackers in media, including the "F-Society" masks used by the underground hacking group of the same name in the popular TV drama, *Mr. Robot*.

Unlike hacking crews who came before it, Anonymous described itself as "decentralized," meaning that the group was loosely affiliated and didn't have a single leader. At various times, several people have claimed the title of "leader" or "founder" of

Anonymous, but these titles were fundamentally at odds with the idea that the group was directed by anyone. The decentralized organization of Anonymous also allowed hackers who were interested in the group to freely associate with Anonymous at their leisure. This free association model also gave hackers who had no real affiliation with the group a cover for their actions. This cover could be used as a convenient disguise for state-backed influence operations online.

Inspired by hacktivists of the past, Anonymous made headlines by targeting individuals and organizations who were perceived to be powerful at the time. In one attack, Anonymous claimed responsibility for hacking the email account of American conservative politician Sarah Palin, who was running for vice president with Senator John McCain in 2008. Again in 2010, Anonymous launched a politically motivated denial-of-service (DOS) attack against the Australian government in opposition to a government proposal to censor Internet pornography.

While it was easy for Anonymous to claim the moral high ground against powerful governments and secretive organizations accused of abusive practices, its lack of organized leadership led to muddled messaging. In 2009, Anonymous claimed victory over the organizer of a small activist organization called the "No Cussing Club," which sincerely advocated for the abolition of profane language. The campaign against McKay Hatch—the teenage California-based organizer of the No Cussing Club—included doxing Hatch's telephone number and home address, to which deliveries of pizza and pornography were sent. The campaign amounted to little more than common cyberbullying, not the high-minded crusade against the rich and powerful that many in Anonymous felt was their cause. This element didn't reflect well on Anonymous and eventually caused some former participants to view the group and its activities with skepticism.

HBGary

Project Chanology had briefly captured the media's attention, but it wasn't until February 2011 that Anonymous conducted a truly impactful raid. That month, four Anonymous members launched a cyberattack against the chief executive of a U.S. government contractor called HBGary Federal. Aaron Barr had drawn the attention of Anonymous after claiming that his company, HBGary Federal, could collect information about hacktivists, including Anonymous, and sell intelligence products based on that information to the U.S. government.[1]

The products Barr claimed he could provide were built on techniques that amounted to little more than social engineering and an open-source intelligence collection, but his arrogant claims only made him a target for the same groups that he claimed to be targeting. The ensuing attack on HBGary resulted in the release of internal emails and sensitive company documents and a compromise of HBGary's website.

The U.S. government had come to rely on government contractors so heavily in the post-Reagan era that sensitive information related to government operations and planning could be found on contractor networks. This fact led to concerns by government officials that the hack of HBGary Federal may have resulted in a leak of information that the government would consider sensitive. This placed HBGary Federal in a difficult position, as its financial success depended on the government's trust to win the lucrative contracts it provided.

Desperate to stop hackers from continuing their attacks, the president of HBGary Federal's parent company joined the

---

[1] As of the writing of this book, collecting information through social media on intelligence targets has been a common practice for many years, but at the time Barr's comments were considered a serious threat to hacktivists.

Internet Relay Chat (IRC) the attackers used to coordinate their attack, in a confusing attempt to resolve the situation diplomatically. Unfortunately for HBGary, the damage had already been done. In less than a month, the entire HBGary brand had become radioactive and sent company stakeholders scrambling to distance themselves from it and cut ties with the company. For his part, the man who started the firestorm, Barr, resigned from his position at the company, but it wasn't enough to stem the political hemorrhage. Less than a year later, HBGary was bought out by a competitor, and the controversy quietly went away.

HBGary Federal wasn't the only target that Anonymous had their sights set on in February 2011. Near the month's end, one of the core members responsible for the HBGary Federal raid named Topiary joined an online "debate" with Shirley Phelps, the notorious pastor of a hate organization located in Topeka, Kansas, called the Westborough Baptist Church.

The debate was hosted by Internet personality David Pakman and showcased much of the same loud bigoted rhetoric that the church had become known for over the past decade. Westborough Baptist Church was often seen picketing the funerals of American military members and primarily focused their hatred against the LGBT community. Although he did the interview without showing an image of himself, Topiary used his unaltered speaking voice during the interview and announced live during the debate that he'd defaced the church's website, which declared that the site had been hacked by Anonymous.

Topiary's antics on the air with Phelps were representative of a more technically talented group within Anonymous. The distributed denial-of-service (DDoS) attacks Anonymous relied heavily on to keep up appearances in the media were more akin to an annoying flash mob than a professional attack. In most of the pre-2011 attacks, Anonymous would simply make an announcement to their followers to "fire your cannons," including the time

and who their target would be. Followers would then use a popular DoS tool called *low-orbit ion cannon* (LOIC), lending their
computers to a massive flood of requests meant to exhaust the
target's resources. Even in the most effective attacks, the most
damage they could cause was a temporary website outage.

Digital populism could be powerful in expressing general
displeasure, but the HBGary Federal hackers had shown much
more prowess at hacking than boilerplate Anonymous attacks of
the past. In April 2011, another member of anonymous named
TFlow found vulnerabilities in several servers belonging to the
right-wing media giant Fox News. After successfully gaining
access to their servers, TFlow, working with another hacker,
managed to steal login credentials for Fox News radio personali-
ties. This information, along with UK ATM transaction logs stolen by Topiary, would become foundational for a new hacking
group that would outshine Anonymous.

In May 2011, Topiary registered a new Twitter (now known
as X) account meant for publishing hacks done by the new as yet
nameless group. After checking the availability of a few possible
names for the group's account name, Topiary found one that was
perfect: @LulzSec. There were seven core LulzSec members,
which included Topiary himself, TFlow, Palladium (of the Fox
News hacks), a well-known botnet owner who went by the name
Kayla, and a key participant in the HBGary Federal hacks who
went by the name Sabu.

That same month, the core members of LulzSec came
together for the first time and announced themselves to a private
Anonymous chatroom as an independent group. Right away,
excitement abounded over the possibilities of the new group
founded by the hackers behind the HBGary breach.

LulzSec fashioned themselves as something different than
what had been seen with Anonymous. Although the members of
LulzSec had come from the same center-left populist roots

within Anonymous, Anonymous had become known for the communication style that they'd used over the years. Their overly preachy press releases had earned Anonymous a reputation among young hackers for taking themselves too seriously and overvaluing their contributions to the public discourse through their hacks.

LulzSec had learned that publishing information stolen from their victims had the potential to hold the media's attention for a longer time period, which maximized the public relations pain that their victims would experience. This also meant that it was more valuable to publish large amounts of raw information that journalists could then spend days or weeks sifting through, writing stories based on the leaked information for days, weeks, or even months on end. This ensured that the original hack would remain relevant far into the future, as new information periodically trickled out.

LulzSec also gave themselves the opportunity to control the messaging of their own hacks, which they did on a popular text-sharing service called *Pastebin*. Pastebin was favored by hackers for its ability to quickly and anonymously post blocks of text that could be shared with others with little to no moderation or censorship. Pastebins, which had often been left in the wake of hacks, often included blocks of sensitive information like usernames and passwords and may have also included statements by the hackers themselves. Pre- and post-hacking statements were popular among Anonymous hackers, who often used these statements extoling their own virtue over their targets.

That air of self-righteousness had been one of the reasons for LulzSec to break away from Anonymous in the first place. In some ways, the core members of LulzSec wanted their group to be a playful rebuke to Anonymous—one that took itself less seriously but was still capable of being taken seriously by others. They wanted their hacks to speak for themselves.

Despite their playful demeanor, victims of LulzSec didn't consider them harmless. Among the first releases by LulzSec was the material they'd stolen from their Fox News hack in prior weeks. The reason given for their hack was that Fox News had called Common, a popular rapper of the time, "vile" following his visit to the White House in May 2011. A few days later, LulzSec released the ATM logs stolen by Topiary around the same timeframe, before conducting a new attack against the Public Broadcasting System (PBS) website.

LulzSec's attack on PBS included a web deface of a news story declaring that Biggie Smalls and Tupac Shakur—two rappers who had famously been murdered at the height of their careers— were alive and well in New Zealand. In a moment of seriousness, LulzSec claimed that its attack on PBS had been politically motivated by the revelations the year before of U.S. military massacres in Iraq and Afghanistan. This wasn't the last time that the U.S. government would find itself in the sights of LulzSec.

In late May of 2011, the Pentagon announced a policy change that declared that cyberattacks on U.S. infrastructure could be interpreted by the U.S. government as an act of war.[2] There had been significant concern among the hacking community for years about the so-called "militarism of cyberspace," but the 2011 Pentagon announcement was a clear sign of the times. Speaking on the record, Pentagon Spokesman Colonel David Lapan told the press that *attacks in cyber would be viewed the same way that attacks in a kinetic form are now.* If there was any confusion about what this meant, another unnamed Pentagon staffer clarified to the media, "If you shut down our power grid, maybe we will put a missile down one of your smokestacks." This announcement

---

[2] https://web.archive.org/web/20110821192455/https://www.nytimes.com/2011/06/01/us/politics/01cyber.html

upped the ante for hackers worldwide and brought a new significance to the world of hacking.

LulzSec responded to the Pentagon's provocative statements over a two-day period, beginning on June 13, 2011, by dumping user credentials of accounts on the U.S. Senate official website. LulzSec followed up its attacks on the U.S. government with an attack on the FBI's Detroit call center and a takedown of the CIA's public website.

Occasionally, LulzSec would participate in similar tit-for-tat hacks, which would raise the group's profile. However, drawing attention to themselves would ultimately be the group's undoing. Ultimately, LulzSec's existence was short-lived. Fans and observers of LulzSec were treated to two glorious months of seemingly nonstop leaks from the group throughout May and June of 2011. The whole vibe of LulzSec was different from Anonymous, from their hacking techniques to their way of communicating.

Even the crudely drawn "rage face" comic logo they used to represent their group, featuring a stick figure wearing a top hat, monocle, and twirly mustache, with one hand tucked into a suit pocket and the other raising a glass of wine, was endearing to a public who'd become accustomed to a preachy breed of hacktivists coming out of the ranks of Anonymous. Comparatively, LulzSec didn't take themselves as seriously, which attracted a whole new group of fans who may not have paid much attention to Anonymous hacks before.

The populist Robin Hood aesthetic that had drawn followers to Anonymous was still intact for LulzSec, but it had taken on a new feeling. LulzSec was both insincere and serious at the same time, making them entertaining for their fans to watch but a serious threat to those they put in their crosshairs. However, LulzSec's hacking streak was short-lived.

LulzSec's activity had been politically motivated, especially given the target types they selected. In all, LulzSec left a long record of hacks in the wake of its two-month operation, which had quickly drawn an intense amount of attention to their group. The final nail in LulzSec's coffin was their hack of InfraGard, a professional cybersecurity organization that partners with law enforcement including the FBI.

The appearance of Anonymous and LulzSec forced world governments to respond to the threats they posed. The government's response proved that law enforcement was taking the threat posed by hacking much more seriously than it had in the past. It also demonstrated that law enforcement and intelligence were learning how to counter cyberthreats in a way they hadn't been able to in decades past.

Both Anonymous and LulzSec represented different evolutions in the way that hacktivists engaged with political issues. LulzSec, in particular, was much more reactionary and quicker to respond to political events, often targeting organizations within days or even hours of a related event taking place. The high visibility responses to current events turned the members of LulzSec into folk heroes, and the pageantry of Anonymous releases made the group into a constant spectacle that raised their profile in the eyes of both the public and the government.

Both groups managed to fuse an online brand of populist politics into their activities and demonstrated that releasing hacked documents could be an effective catalyst for public controversy. This influenced other hackers as well as a new generation of whistleblowers to follow a similar model, especially if the hackers wanted to benefit from the protection of public support. Moreover, the reactionary nature of both groups reflected a trend in the way hacktivism responded to current events. In the near future, this reactionary approach to politics became common even in the mainstream. With online culture increasingly escaping the containment of the Internet, the distinctions between life online and life offline began to blur. It was only a matter of time before online reactionary politics expressed itself offline.

CHAPTER

13

Spy vs. Spy

On April 4, 2010, a video began hitting news stations across the world. It was a high-aspect grainy black-and-white recording from a helicopter flying over Iraq. The video was instantly recognizable to military observers as being taken by an onboard video-recording device on an attack helicopter, common in the skies over Iraq after the March 2003 invasion. A helicopter pilot's voice could be heard over the gunship's loud rotor blades, narrating the scene in real time via the pilot's radio headset.

As the recording continued, the pilot's attention was drawn to a small crowd on a city street corner. The shot lingered on the group of apparently unarmed men for a moment, before a man's voice broke in on the radio frequency with a command *"Light 'em up!"* Another moment passed before a second command was given, *"Come on, shoot 'em...."* The M230 Bushmaster chain gun attached to the helicopter's fuselage then let loose a barrage of 30mm rounds, each as big as a grown man's forearm. The shots could be heard in the recording—a rhythmic series of popping that ripped through the men who disappeared in a cloud of dust. One man escaped the initial volley, but the crosshairs of the gunship's camera followed him. It was only a few more seconds before the dust from more 30mm rounds engulfed him.

"Collateral Murder"

This video in its entirety is nearly 40 minutes long, but the press only played clips from it, adding context. Two of the men in the group shot down by American forces were members of the Reuters news agency, who were preparing to record material for a story in the war-torn nation. The recording was taken during an airstrike that occurred in July, three years before its release to the press by an organization called WikiLeaks. WikiLeaks announced the video with great fanfare in 2010, giving it the provocative name, *"Collateral Murder."*

To make matters worse for the government, more than 200,000 private diplomatic cables had been leaked along with the videos. These leaks came as a surprise to leaders at the Pentagon and Department of State, which had never seen a public leak of this size before. One month after the *Collateral Murder* video was released, the source of the leaks was identified as a 22-year-old U.S. Army intelligence analyst, Private Manning (who has since changed her name to Chelsea Manning).

The revelation that the source of the leaks was Private Manning came from a friend of hers who was a regular in the hacking community named Adrian Lamo. Lamo, who was also known as "The Homeless Hacker," had long conversations with Manning prior to her arrest. According to reporting in the aftermath of the leaks, conversations between the two covered various topics including details about the information Manning had intended to leak. In their conversations, Manning admitted to collecting classified information off sensitive government networks with the intention of passing it to WikiLeaks. Lamo felt conflicted about Manning's admissions, so he passed a tip on to authorities who arrested Manning shortly after. Manning's leak of classified information was one of the largest leaks of classified information in US history. Manning pled guilty to charges of espionage and spent years in prison until her sentence was commuted by outgoing president Obama in 2017.

At the time of Manning's leaks, the name *WikiLeaks* didn't mean anything to most people. Most Americans didn't know anything about the mysterious white-haired founder, Julian Assange, with the gentle Australian accent. The prospect of WikiLeaks itself represented a dramatic shift to many observers. What exactly was WikiLeaks after all? It billed itself as a journalistic organization, but its methods didn't exactly fit the traditional description. Readers of the *New York Times* weren't used to having the sort of raw information provided through WikiLeaks given to them in the pages of their daily paper. This level of transparency to information gave readers a sense of control over their own interpretation of news stories. They no longer needed to have a trusted writer parse the information for them to pass along "the narrative."

WikiLeaks claimed the likes of Daniel Ellsberg as their pedigree, drawing on the Pentagon Papers leaks of the 1970s as foundational to the spirit of their new organization. In the 1970s, the Pentagon Papers had changed the public's perception of the Vietnam War. This leak had been the catalyst for a growing frustration about the war's handling and became a flashpoint for the Nixon administration. Nixon and his team were furious about the leak of classified wartime information, but the leaks provided a much-needed light source for a public who'd been largely kept in the dark about just how badly things had been going in Vietnam. The Pentagon Papers leak also kicked off a chain of events leading to the Watergate scandal, which eventually led to Nixon's resignation. This was the legacy Assange sought to invoke and re-create for WikiLeaks.

When Assange first began his hacking career, he went by the name "Mendax" and proven himself to be one of the most enthusiastic willing-to-do-anything-for-the-hack affiliates of the International Subversives. Assange's background as a member of one of the original hacking crews had preceded him, as had suspicions that he might have been directly involved in the WANK hack of NASA in 1989. For his part, Assange admits to knowing that WANK had come from the International Subversives, but was ambiguous about who exactly wrote the code for the worm itself.[1]

By all appearances, WikiLeaks was an organization founded and supported by a new hacker generation. Not only had Assange himself had an established history on the Melbourne hacking scene, but he had also appointed his long-time friend Suelette Dreyfus to the WikiLeaks board. Using their shared knowledge of the detailed history of Australian hacking, Assange and Dreyfus had written a book together, titled "*Underground: Tales of Hacking, Madness and Obsession on the Electronic Frontier*" published in 1997. This book had rubbed some of their contacts in the hacking community the wrong way, but it did inform the direction that Assange and Dreyfus would take together in publishing.

Manning's 2010 whistleblowing catapulted WikiLeaks and Assange into the spotlight, while Manning herself went to trial and was eventually convicted for her leaks. But popular support from the hacking community was behind both Manning and WikiLeaks. Even before the 2010 leaks, WikiLeaks was earning awards and critical praise for its new approach to breaking news.

---

[1] *The Most Dangerous Man In The World Julian Assange and WikiLeaks' Fight For Freedom*, Fowler Andrew, updated publication, 2020.

After publishing Manning's material in 2010, public opinion was split. An August 2010 poll by Pew Research found that 42% of Americans asked believed that the leaks served public interest, while 47% believed the opposite. Recognizing the threat posed by WikiLeaks, the American government wasted no time opening an investigation into the organization after the Afghanistan and Iraq leaks went public. Inside the Pentagon's Office of the Inspector General (OIG), bios on Assange were emailed to senior officials in July 2010, who were clearly surprised by the leaks.

In the years that followed, WikiLeaks positioned themselves as a clearing house for stolen information and encouraged hackers to leave their findings in a secure drop box operated by their organization. WikiLeaks' pre-2010 publications weren't aimed at any particular target, which lent credibility to the idea that they didn't reserve any particular bias. At one point in 2009, WikiLeaks even published a list of their own confidential donor information, which had apparently been leaked by the organization itself due to an email oversight.

WikiLeaks was a party to a changing body of politics in America that had been accelerating since the September 11 attacks. This trend was deeply distrustful of established media and government and favored conspiracy theories over established narratives. The backdrop of this change was a growing landscape of unreliable information, which could easily be found on every corner of the Internet. Establishment politicians and their media allies had begun to take criticism from the anti-war public over America's involvement in Iraq and Afghanistan, which was becoming a significant strain on American resources by the time WikiLeaks was founded in 2006.

After the 2010 leaks, WikiLeaks and Assange successfully attracted the attention of the American government and their allies. In November 2010, prosecutors in Sweden began pursuing Assange on multiple sexual assault allegations stemming from people he had visited with earlier that year while he was in the country. The charges prompted an arrest warrant for Assange in Britain, and after a legal battle to avoid extradition to Sweden on rape charges, Assange was eventually granted political asylum in the Ecuadoran embassy in London in 2012. Despite his mounting legal challenges, Assange was still involved in the operations of WikiLeaks.

While the case against Assange was building in multiple North American and European countries, in 2011 Assange took interest in a hacking group with a growing reputation. That group was LulzSec, who had hacked PBS earlier that year, claiming they were done in support of WikiLeaks. WikiLeaks had relied on hackers in the past to leak information to them, but they hadn't crossed the line into working directly with hackers in target designation or further coordination. The recruitment of LulzSec was the brainchild of an ambitious young volunteer who had come to WikiLeaks less than a year earlier, known online by the name "Siggi Hakkari" or "Siggi the Hacker."

Siggi Hakkari was a young Icelandic hacker named Sigurdur Thordarson who'd been arrested in 2010 when he was 17 years old for his own set of informational leaks, which he'd stolen from his employer while working at an Icelandic financial firm Milestone ehf. Thordarson's story became international news, and shortly after, Thordarson was arrested for the leaks. Siggi's decision to leak this sensitive financial information set him on a path that intersected with a global movement, which was inspired by the old hacker ethos of freedom of information at all costs.

After his arrest, Thordarson found support from members of the media who believed that Siggi's leaks had global significance. A Reykjavik reporter named Kristinn Hrafnsson saw Thordarson's potential use to his friend, Assange. Assange agreed with Hrafnsson's assessment of Siggi and took the teenage hacker under his wing. By all accounts, Siggi earned Assange's trust quickly. But even from the beginning, other WikiLeaks volunteers recognized that Siggi had a loose relationship with the truth, and his wild ideas made him unpredictable. At one point when Assange let Siggi in on the fact that he expected to be arrested, Siggi even intimated that he would help bust Assange out of police custody.

Siggi's grand plan for WikiLeaks (with the tacit approval of Assange himself) was to transform the organization's role from the agnostic clearinghouse and publisher of hacked information it had received to being a director of who was to be hacked. Although the change seems subtle, the plan crossed a legal line. WikiLeaks would occupy strange territory, as both the exclusive publisher of hacks and also the target designator for who would be the next victim.

Outside of WikiLeaks, supporters defended the organization by comparing their activities to a journalistic enterprise, which deserved the same hallowed "free press" designation given to legacy media organizations. This had always been a somewhat awkward classification for an organization that seemed to selectively publish complete information with little attention paid to the outcomes this might have. This recklessness cost WikiLeaks many of their earliest core members post-2010 and elevated Siggi into positions of importance within the organization to which few other hackers his age has ever had access.

The loss of core members of WikiLeaks, coupled with deepening investigations worldwide against him, forced Assange into a paranoid state of mind. This led to internal investigations of his own organization and its members, which sounds like a page out of a history of the famously paranoid Cold War CIA Chief of Counterintelligence James Angleton. While Assange chased ghosts and his paranoia grew, he withdrew deeper and deeper into his friendship with the one person he felt he could trust more than anyone else: Siggi Thordarson.

Siggi had first become aware of LulzSec through news of the HBGary breach. Siggi maintained contact with hackers throughout the world, including a hacker by the name of Gnosis. Gnosis suggested that Siggi seek out Kayla, one of the core members of LulzSec. Siggi's pitch to Kayla was, as it had been with other hacks in the past, to allow WikiLeaks to take the lead on the hacked material stolen by LulzSec. When LulzSec decided to leak the database themselves, Assange expressed his anger at being deprived of the privilege to publish it in an entitled outburst to Siggi.

Despite being told by his Gnosis contact that a targeting arrangement of the kind Siggi had in mind wouldn't be possible, he tried again anyway. His next attempt to coax the unpredictable hackers into bending to his will was more successful. Siggi asked Kayla directly to conduct an attack on an Icelandic power company in retaliation for the loss of contracts WikiLeaks' hosting company experienced for their support of the leak organization. Kayla obliged and within minutes launched a denial-of-service (DOS) attack against the power company's website landsnet.is. A few moments later, Kayla offered to do a similar takedown of an Icelandic government ministry. Siggi urged Kayla to attack, and again moments later, an Icelandic ministry website went down.

After forming an alliance with Kayla, Siggi contacted the mysterious person who had proclaimed himself the leader of LulzSec: Sabu. Sabu had been involved with Anonymous, and later LulzSec for many years, and had personally taken part in hacks against large multinational corporations and government websites. He had made such a name for himself by the time Lulzec's activities went full tilt that he was practically considered royalty among the Anonymous set. Through Kayla, Siggi had built enough credibility with LulzSec and Sabu that he could continue to coordinate who LulzSec's next targets would be.

The arrangement that Siggi offered to LulzSec wasn't particularly advantageous to LulzSec. LulzSec would gain the benefit of raising their profile through material published to WikiLeaks, but the main beneficiary of LulzSec's hacks would be WikiLeaks themselves. The proposed agreement was that LulzSec would be tasked with a list of targets of interest by WikiLeaks, LulzSec would attack those targets, and WikiLeaks would publish the information LulzSec stole. WikiLeaks would then go on to collect donations from observers eager to support what many in the public saw as legitimate journalism. In this way, Wikieaks was able to shift a significant burden of the risk associated with stealing sensitive information away from themselves and onto ideologically motivated hackers. For WikiLeaks, the agreement was a nearly risk-free win.

Of course, the fact that WikiLeaks was participating in the questionable act of selecting LulzSec's targets wasn't intended to be shared with the public. Any arrangement involving WikiLeaks as the target designator would've raised questions about conflict of interest and impartiality, which had never been a real issue for WikiLeaks in the past. Before the WikiLeaks-LulzSec agreement between Siggi and Kayla, WikiLeaks acted only as the impartial handler of stolen information, which to some extent absolved them of the responsibility of having to explain how and why certain sensitive documents were placed into their hands. To some, this would have made WikiLeaks look more like the spies they were so determined to expose.

With his partnership with LulzSec firmly established, Siggi managed to take WikiLeaks to a place that no other organization of its kind or scale had gone before. WikiLeaks, an organization born and supported by hackers, had become, at least in part, a hacking collaborator itself. In 2017, CIA Director Mike Pompeo publicly proclaimed that WikiLeaks had become a "hostile intelligence service." Pompeo recognized a reflection in WikiLeaks of his own agency, as it had become an independent spy agency unto itself.[2] But how independent was it in reality?

Behind WikiLeaks' collaboration with a collection of seemingly radical and notoriously difficult-to-control hacktivists was a secret that many individuals involved in the recruitment had been keeping from the others: many of them had already been recruited to be confidential informants for the FBI.

Gnosis, the hacker who had originally suggested that Siggi contact Kayla, was in fact an FBI informant by the name of Laurelai Bailey. Bailey's home had been raided by the FBI in June 2011, and she had been offered leniency in exchange for becoming a confidential informant. Sabu, the famous LulzSec leader, would also go on to sell out the rest of his hacking crew by turning them in to the FBI, leading to the capture and arrest of all the LulzSec members in 2012. But the FBI's penetration of the WikiLeaks partnership with Anonymous hackers didn't end there. As it would turn out, Sigurdur "Siggi" Thordarson himself was an FBI confidential informant.

Siggi's time as an FBI informant culminated in a February 2012 trip to a Washington, D.C. Marriott, where he was debriefed by his FBI handlers and also held discussions with representatives of various four-letter agencies, including the CIA and DoD who were working to build a case against Assange. However, his time as a volunteer with WikiLeaks ended a few months before in spectacular fashion, when he was accused by the then spokesman for WikiLeaks, Kristinn Hrafnsson, of embezzlement of around $50,000 of income due to WikiLeaks.

Although it still operates today, questions about the operations of Wikileaks have been raised in recent years, thanks in no small part to Thordarson's exposure as an FBI informant.

---

[2] WikiLeaks' response to Pompeo's claim was to prepare what would become the infamous Vault 7 leaks, comprised of information related to CIA and its operations.

The degree to which the FBI managed to infiltrate both WikiLeaks and a prominent active hacking group was a feather in the FBI's cap. The FBI had come a long way since the days of giving Cliff Stoll the cold shoulder, and their human-enabled operation against these two groups shows just how effective their updated law enforcement strategy was.

Siggi's saga proved that the FBI had managed to play to its own historic strengths of investigation and asset recruitment against organizations that were deemed a threat to the U.S. government. The lessons the agency learned in the 1990s proved to be important steppingstones to combatting global information operation threats against the government, and in the early 2010s, the FBI had shown that they were now a force with which to be reckoned.

14

Cybernetting Society

In February 2014, a helicopter idled on a landing pad in Kyiv, Ukraine, in the dark of night, its heavy rotors ripped through the chilly winter air, waiting for its passengers to arrive. The helicopter, an AugustaWestland Model 139, had a spacious interior and enough room to comfortably seat six passengers and two pilots. When the passengers finally arrived, the pilots wasted no time getting airborne, knowing that time was critical and that one of their passengers was the most wanted man in Ukraine, the recently declared former president, Viktor Yanukovych. Unverified recordings published by international media outlets show passengers boarding the helicopter with wheeled travel bags in tow. Shortly after the president and his aids boarded the helicopter, it lifted off into the night sky, ultimately bound for the safety of the Russian Federation.

The events of February 2014 had been the direct result of a popular political movement called the *Euromaidan Protests* (or more commonly referred to as simply "Euromaidan.") Euromaidan was the culmination not just of political uprisings in Ukraine itself, but across the regions of the Middle East and Eastern Europe. Much of the coordination for these demonstrations was done online, which drew the attention of world leaders to the way the Internet was being used to shape popular politics in their nations.

In the days after Yanukovych fled, a warrant was issued for his arrest by Ukrainian authorities on charges of treason. As Russian leadership scrambled to arrange for the arrival of Yanukovych, the implications of his ouster were clear. The geopolitical trajectory of Ukraine was moving beyond the non-violent control of Russian leadership. In their view, they had lost their influence over Ukraine due to the actions of Western Nations. The loss of Urakine from the Russian sphere of influence was a threat that Russian leadership would not soon forget.

Consumer Electronics

Telecommunications technology that had been maturing since the 1980s had bloomed into a major industry by the late-2000s, paving the way for yet another cybernetics revolution. The promise of Star Trek–style portable communication devices was finally being delivered with the right set of features and price point for the average American consumer.

In 1999, the Blackberry was released by the Research in Motion (RIM) company. With a small keyboard and track ball for reproducing the experience of a mouse, the Blackberry gave consumers a look at what mobile, Internet connected devices of the future would look like. The Blackberry got its biggest exposure to the public when President Barack Obama adopted the device for his daily work, becoming an indispensable technology for the White House. But Blackberry's time at the top of the pile would only live for a few years before a more substantial change would come.

Once again, Apple Computers ushered in a new era of society-changing technology with the release of the iPhone in 2007. Like the Apple II before it, the iPhone combined modern technology with an attractive form factor, which made it approachable and easy for consumers to use. Smart phones expanded the online space originally created by the convergence of internet connected personal computers, offering users a persistent online world.

Some of the social changes the iPhone brought to American culture were evident right away. News stories about pedestrians preoccupied with their phones began to find themselves in dangerous situations as a result. Stafford Beer's promise of a cybernetic future was, in some ways, being realized, but the effects of closer human interactions with technology were complex and difficult to predict.

According to the Pew Research Center, the percentage of American adults who owned smartphones jumped from 20% of the population in 2010 to 68% by 2015.[1] This meant that more information than ever was getting into the hands of more Americans faster than it ever had before. This also meant that more Americans than ever were exposed to online culture, and for longer periods of time than they ever had been before.

In 2010, Pew also found that 26% of Americans used their phones to learn about or participate in the election that year. With more than a quarter of the population of American adults now engaging with politics through their phones, the statistic

---

[1] https://web.archive.org/web/20231209053329/https://www.pewresearch.org/internet/2015/10/29/technology-device-ownership-2015/pi_2015-10-29_device-ownership_0-01

reflected a fundamental change in the way that Internet-connected consumer electronics impacted the public's understanding of politics.

The online culture these Americans were spending so much time immersed in was transferring to their lives offline as well. Terms that were first used online like "LOL" and even later phrases like "for the lulz" (which had been adopted by the hacking group LulzSec) made their way into everyday use by millions of Americans. Thanks to the popularity of the Internet, an entire career path opened up for some prominent Internet users as product "influencers," which took advantage of the impressionable effect that the Internet had on consumers.

With few tools to evaluate the reliability of information found online, the Internet had become a powerful tool for those interested in spreading questionable information. In the early 2010s, the dubious reliability of information sourced online led researchers to be concerned about the Internet's effect on the political system. It didn't take long for their concerns to be realized.

A Politicized Internet

The Internet of the 2010s had grown far beyond the comparatively close-knit bulletin board system (BBS) networks of the 1980s, but much of the culture remained the same. After the burst of the dot-com bubble in late 2002, a new manifestation of the Internet was built from what remained of the ruins of e-commerce empires: web 2.0. The term *web 2.0* was coined in 1999, and was eventually given to the next evolution of the Internet. Web 2.0 was defined by the emergence of social media and user-generated content. Web 2.0 promoted a user-friendly experience that would give users more opportunities to interact with others.

At the beginning, web 2.0 promoted content creation around communities of interest. Social media websites like Twitter, Facebook, Reddit, and Digg cultivated massive userbases, and became important sources of news. The Internet wasn't just a place for average users to work as many did in the 1990s, it had become a public forum for regular people to chat about everyday matters from mundane life issues to breaking political news. With new information constantly becoming available, it was easy for users to be constantly focused on their screens to get the most up to date stories.

In the past, Internet users could escape the Internet by simply walking away from it. Before smartphones and broadband Internet, much of the average American's life existed offline. This meant that at some point, even the most avid Internet users would be forced to log off. However, in the age of the smartphone, disconnecting became nearly impossible. For many Internet users, the online world had become one with the offline world.

Ironically, while the Internet was expected to bring the world closer together, it also began dividing users ideologically. A 2017 Harvard study suggested that digital technologies might account for some amount of the political polarization happening since the beginning of the 2010s. The study went on to say that technology would likely continue to intensify political polarization in the future.[2] Another study, published in 2015 by the Midwest Political Science Association, cited the increased average amount of time users spent online with persistent broadband Internet access. More time spent online also increased users' time-consuming slanted political information.[3] The online culture that can be accessed through our always-connected mobile

[2] https://scholar.harvard.edu/files/shapiro/files/age-polars.pdf
[3] https://pcl.sites.stanford.edu/sites/g/files/sbiybj22066/files/media/file/lelkes-ajps-hostile-audience.pdf

devices has created a persistent reality that users effectively cannot easily escape.

This conclusion follows a long-term downward trend of how well average news consumers could discern properly sourced true information from the alternative. The term researchers gave to this question was *media literacy*, and several attempts to gauge media literacy have been made over the years. Social media tools have also helped create so-called "echo chambers" where political information can be shared exclusively among those with likeminded political opinions, thus deepening pre-existing partisan divides.

Through the various incarnations from the creation of the modern Internet in the early-1990s to the foundation of web 2.0 in the early-2000s to the introduction of persistent Internet access via mobile devices in the early-2010s, each new decade built new layers of abstraction, each distorting human communication in its own ways. Hackers were native to their own spaces and had long since learned to navigate the Internet and all of the things that made it treacherous for civil engagement to nontechnical users.

As the offline world became a more polarized place, hackers developed their own unique and far-reaching way of playing a role in world events. In 2011, hackers would show the true extent of their reach.

Global Instability

The consequences of the rapid growth of the Internet as a tool for political communication and organization were evident almost as soon as smartphones became available. In the early-2010s, those consequences were exposing political rifts throughout the world, and giving activists a new method for quickly and cheaply organizing public demonstrations. The parts of the world where these technologies were having the biggest impact were in countries that diplomats least expected to see mass demonstrations.

Arab Spring

Even before Euromaidan protests began, regional instability was growing worldwide. In 2011, the size and scope of the Internet had grown globally, bringing web and social media services to even the most remote areas of the planet. Internet connectivity had reached towns and cities in nearly every country on Earth, and was taking an ever-increasing role in the everyday lives of millions of people. In particular, social media became a tool to find others with overlapping political interests and organize against corrupt national leaders in hopes of forcing political change. Nowhere was this effect more direct than in the Middle East, which had become a haven for dictatorships in several countries since the beginning of the Cold War. The movement to reform these governments in the early-2010s was dubbed "*The Arab Spring.*"

The first of the Arab Spring demonstrations began in December 2010, when Tunisian authorities shut down a produce cart belonging to an impoverished street vendor named Mohamed Bouazizi. Bouazizi struggled to survive on the streets of the Tunisian city of Sidi Bouzid and was under constant harassment from city officials who often demanded bribes from him so he could continue operating.

On the morning of December 17, 2010, police visited Bouazizi's cart and impounded the scales he used for operating as an illegal vendor. After the police forced the closure of his only income source, Bouazizi was turned away when province authorities refused to hear his complaint against the police. Out of sheer desperation, Bouazizi walked across the street and bought a small can of petrol from a gas station. He went back to the office of the provincial authority, doused himself with the gasoline, and set himself on fire on the street outside.

News of Bouazizi's shocking suicide traveled quickly, instantly triggering more than a week of demonstrations across the country of Tunisia. Tunisian President Zine El Abidine Ben Ali, who had ruled Tunisia for 24 years, warned that protestors would be subject to severe crackdowns if they took to the streets, but this only exacerbated the anger of the crowds.

Operation Tunisia   A month after Bouazizi's self-immolation, tensions were at a fever pitch with regular protests in the streets throughout the month of December. Recognizing that the protests were largely being organized online, Tunisian authorities turned to government hackers to help control the protests. Hackers working for the Tunisian Internet Agency (TIA) began targeting popular bloggers with phishing attacks aimed at stealing their passwords and ultimately disrupting their ability to both report on the protests and organize them.[4]

The strategy the government took to quell protest organization online was to block access to any website mentioning the protests or Bouazizi in any way. This paired with efforts to break into the email accounts of targeted individuals who were helping organize the protests were the first shots in an online conflict that was quickly getting out of control.

The efforts of online actors defending the Tunisian government grabbed the attention of Anonymous after censoring access to Wikileaks inside of Tunisia, which was outrageous to many Anonymous members. Their response was to join the conflict themselves on the side of the protesters. Tunisia had become a

---

[4] https://www.aljazeera.com/features/2011/1/6/tunisias-bitter-cyberwar

catalyst for hackers around the world to become involved in what many within groups like Anonymous saw as a righteous conflict to free the average citizens of the Arab-speaking world from the tyranny subjected on them by their dictators. Even Hector "Sabu" Monsegur of LulzSec recalled his participation in the conflict during Operation Tunisia in an interview with the online publication CNET in 2017.[5]

During Operation Tunisia, Anonymous-affiliated hackers claimed responsibility for hacktivist attacks against the Tunisian government, which included a denial-of-service (DoS) attack and provided Tunisian revolutionaries with stolen Tunisian government documentation that hackers had managed to obtain. Western hackers also urged Tunisian protesters to use an anti-censorship tool that had been developed independently by Western hackers called *The Onion Router (TOR)* to help circumvent strict crackdowns and Internet blackouts aimed at frustrating protest organizers.

The Tunisian revolution ended less than a month after Bouazizi's death, when President Ben Ali fled Tunisia for Sudi Arabia and acted as a role model for other modern political revolutions that followed. Even though it had been successful, the revolution ultimately cost 300 lives yet was seen as a worthwhile cause when Tunisians turned out to vote in their first election in decades in October 2011.

The embers of revolution spread from one Arab-speaking dictatorship to another as other mid-Eastern revolutions began in Libya, Egypt, Bahrain, Saudi Arabia, and Yemen. Demonstrators in each of these revolutions found spaces online to organize, and events on the ground inspired memes that found traction online. But not all of these revolutions would have the same level

---

[5] https://youtu.be/gaLxSpwcAUw?si=rf8Ixasag6yndunf

of success and relatively small number of casualties as Tunisia. When the Arab Spring eventually came to Syria, it resulted in a bloody civil war that continues to this day.

The Syrian Electronic Army   The Syrian revolution started in March 2011, only a few months short months after President Ben Ali fled Tunisia. Syrian protesters demanding reforms and the release of prisoners from President Bashar al-Assad took to the streets in the cities of Damascus and Aleppo. One group significantly involved in the Arab Spring uprisings was a group calling itself the Syrian Electronic Army (SEA). Beginning in July, 2011, SEA attacks used the tried-and-true hacktivist technique of web defacement to first spread its message by attacking the University of California Los Angeles (UCLA) website.

The SEA replaced the UCLA webpage with a black-and-white page of text declaring love for Syrian patriotism and the long-time dictator Bashar al-Assad. They continued their attacks in 2011 and 2012 against American universities and widened the scope of their victims to include other American organizations like popular social media sites X and LinkedIn.

In 2013, the SEA's activities picked up in frequency. SEA began targeting major Western news organizations with the intent to spread misinformation in order to create confusion and chaos. In their campaign, the Twitter (known now as X) account of the Associated Press (AP) was breached, giving the attackers access to post on the AP's main Twitter account. After getting access to the AP account, the attackers posted that President Barack Obama had been injured in an explosion at the White House. Despite the information being untrue, the attack still created enough fear that the S&P 500 stock index suffered a $136 billion loss.[6]

---

[6] https://www.cnn.com/2013/04/24/tech/syrian-electronic-army/index.html

In attacks between 2011 and 2012, SEA continued posting pro-Assad messages. They broke an unspoken standard in the minds of many public observers who grew to believe that hacktivism trended toward "grassroots" popular movements. Web defacement was generally considered to be a low-skill and low-impact result of hacking. In their messages, SEA hackers appeared to be true believers. It seemed that nothing would shake their pro-Assad beliefs.

On August 21, 2013, rockets containing canisters of weaponized sarin gas landed in a suburb of Damascus called Ghouta. Low international estimates placed the attack's death toll at hundreds, while U.S. estimates claimed more than 1,700 attack victims, including many children.

In an interview with *Wired* magazine a few days later, SEA's de facto leader, a hacker (using an old form of Internet slang called *leetspeak*) calling themselves "Th3Pr0," was asked directly about the attacks. In the interview, Th3Pr0 continued spreading many of the same pro-Assad talking points they had during their earlier attacks. Th3Pr0 was even speaking about the Ghouta massacre claiming, as Assad's press office did, that the gas attacks had been conducted by American-controlled terrorist organization Al Nusra and the rebel Free Syrian Army (FSA).[7] Was the SEA affiliated with the Assad government?

SEA had deep ties to the Assad family, tracing its establishment back to the creation of the Syrian Computer Society (SCS), which was founded and led by President Bashar al-Assad's older brother Bassel in 1989. The SCS was dedicated to promoting future generations of Syrian IT workers, and at least originally didn't maintain a charter to teach young Syrians how to hack.

SEA's attacks weren't considered highly technical, but where they fell short in terms of technical complexity they made up for

---

[7] https://www.vice.com/en/article/4w7g8q/the-syrian-electronic-army-talks-about-yesterdays-hacks

in effectiveness. SEA had become a participant in a 2013 hacking scene that had a constant flow of new hacks. LulzSec's attacks, which emphasized the release of information to hold sway over extended news cycles, had convinced some that the face of hacktivism had permanently changed. But SEA's attacks had proven that there was still propaganda value in simpler hacks like web defacements.

The American response to SEA was to task the FBI with investigating the hackers involved with SEA themselves and to target them with indictments. This strategy became a common response for the FBI through the mid-2010s. The theory behind this strategy was to intimidate hackers by messaging through indictments in the same terms that hackers themselves used. By publishing personal information about a hacker and including a clear picture of their face on one of FBI's famous "Most Wanted" posters, it was believed that it would eliminate the anonymity that hackers enjoyed in their offensive activities.

The reality of this strategy was that many of the hackers that the FBI indicted weren't subject to U.S. law and were living abroad in nations without U.S. extradition treaties. In the case of Th3Pr0, the FBI indictment against him in 2016 didn't result in an arrest, and he is believed to still live in Damascus. This FBI strategy was controversial among members of the intelligence community. In many cases, hackers like Th3Pr0 had been under intense surveillance by Western intelligence.

Indictments from FBI's legal division sometimes meant that intelligence collection against these individuals was lost as hackers, now knowing that authorities were onto them, would change their attack signatures, creating a blind spot in intelligence collection. As a result, it forced the FBI to go back to the drawing board on collection and to relearn an entirely new set of attack fingerprints, which often took months or even years to gather and learn.[8] This was seen by intelligence officers as a waste of valuable intelligence collection because the indictments rarely resulted in the arrest of a hacker. An added concern to this situation was the unintended consequence of exposing valuable "sources and methods" used by the intelligence community in the process of pursuing international indictments with little chance of a hacker's arrest.

In recent years, the virtue of the symbolic indictment approach has been scrutinized by FBI leadership who has been considering ways of improving its relationship with inter-agency partners.[9]

After the collapse of the Soviet state, several color revolutions became waypoints on the national journey from post-Soviet satellite to ally of the West. In some cases, such as Serbia and Georgia, these nations went so far as to seek North American Treaty Organization (NATO) membership, which Russian leadership interpreted as Western hostility. In the mid-2010s, Ukraine became the most recent example of this trend.

NATO was formed as a global counterbalance to Soviet-aligned Warsaw Pact nations, but even after the fall of the Soviet state and the dissolution of the Warsaw Pact, NATO continued to increase its influence in Eastern Europe. Situated between Russian interests on Ukraine's Eastern border, and European interests to the West, Ukraine has been a long-term area of concern for Russian leaders. The shifting geopolitical interests in Ukraine became the pretext for accusations by Eastern governments that their rival nations in the West were waging information warfare with the help of hackers to promote unrest on the Asian continent.

---

[8] https://www.federaltimes.com/management/2022/01/19/fbi-us-agencies-look-beyond-indictments-in-cybercrime-fight
[9] https://apnews.com/article/technology-indictments-crime-europe-hacking-8e97ebd22a64a28bfc4ea83c123ee1dc

The leadup to the collapse of the Yanukovych presidency had been building in the decade before he fled Ukraine. The 2004 Ukrainian presidential election had major implications for the future of Ukrainian sovereignty both in terms of foreign, and domestic policy. During the election, the pro-Western candidate, Viktor Yushchenko, survived an assassination attempt after he was exposed to a concentrated dose of a toxic biproduct of herbicide production called dioxin. The attempt left Yushchenko's face discolored and scarred but the assassin was never caught. The assassination attempt drew attention to the election, but Yushchenko's pro-Russian opponent, Viktor Yanukovych, was declared the winner of the election.

Yanukovych's victory in the 2004 election was short-lived. The results were immediately called into question under suspicions that the election had been corrupt. The corruption allegations resulted in a series of protests referred to as the "Orange Revolution" in Ukraine, which forced the Ukrainian court system to declare a new election. In the second runoff, Viktor Yushchenko was declared the winner, and became the third president of Ukraine. When Yanukovych won the 2010 presidential election, the issue of Ukrainian sovereignty was back on the table.

After the 2010 presidential election, Ukraine's political proximity to Russia was a festering wound, which was represented by the presence of Yanukovych himself. A growing number of Ukrainian citizens urged their leaders to pursue NATO membership as several other post-Soviet nations had, but Yanukovych had other plans. After Yanukovych failed to sign a popular diplomatic pact with the European Union (EU), which would have drawn Ukraine closer to their Western European neighbors in NATO, the stage was set for a political showdown.

During Euromaidan, tens-of-thousands of protesters poured into the streets in November of 2013, demanding the resignation of Viktor Yanukovych. The demonstrations were organized with the help of social media websites and the telecommunications technology. The scale of the demonstrations prompted leaders in Russia to accuse the United States and its allies of promoting unrest in post-Soviet nations with the help of hackers, although evidence for this was never provided.

In the West, leaders saw the Euromaidan protests as a popular uprising among the Ukrainian people, who wanted to move away from Russian influence and form closer ties to its European neighbors. Having a NATO ally sharing a border with Russia had been a major Cold War diplomatic strategy for American leaders since the end of WWII. For Russian Federation leaders including President Vladimir Putin, the prospect of a NATO-aligned Ukraine was a nightmare scenario.

The Euromaidan Protests

Taking its cues from the Arab Spring protests, Euromaidan kicked off in November 2013. With the help of social media, mass protests were organized around the Ukrainian capital city of Kyiv, drawing thousands of demonstrators out into the streets. Calls by the political opposition of President Yanukovych on Twitter (now X) helped draw out crowds of protesters angry about rampant government corruption and human rights violations within the country. Public fury at the Ukrainian government built throughout the cold Eastern European winter and culminated in President Viktor Yanukovych's voluntary exile.

As had been the case with the Arab Spring uprisings, broadband Internet and mobile phones played a major role in the spread and organization of the Euromaidan Protests. In addition to text-based social media, services like Ustream and Periscope were used by the protesters and helped draw attention to events on the ground. Periscope, an early livestreaming service, gave users the ability to operate their own video broadcasts, which were often used to promote live events as they unfolded.

Images have always been seen as a powerful medium for communicating with the public, and livestreams were poised to capture more images from more perspectives of an active revolution and then broadcast them to more people throughout the world. Encouragement for the protests poured in from the Western world and accused Yanukovych and those in his government of violence and censorship. In addition to the livestreams used by protesters, bloggers documenting the events unfolding in Ukraine became an important segment in the pipeline of preparing news for consumption by larger world media outlets, by aggregating various informational threads and making public posts containing the most up-to-date information.

East of Ukraine, Russian Federation President Vladimir Putin saw the hand of the U.S. government controlling the Euromaidan crowds. Resentment toward the West had been building in Russia since the fall of the Soviet Union and grew with each successful color revolution, and in the view of Russian leadership, including Vladimir Putin, something needed to be done.[10]

The reason for Putin's perspective on the Euromaidan protests was rooted in NATO's Cold War politics. From the Russian perspective, NATO's encroachment was a threat to Russian sovereignty, and Ukraine was seen as a buffer between Russia's western border and NATO's eastern front. When Ukrainian politics moved to favor closer relations with the West, this was a bridge too far for Russian leadership. Viktor Yanukovych was seen by Russian leadership as friendly to their geopolitical interests, and when he was unseated, the stage was set for a Russian military incursion into Ukraine within the next decade.

---

[10] https://ca.news.yahoo.com/vladimir-putin-never-understood-why-162432512
.html

CHAPTER

15

Hackers Unleashed

In the mid-2000s, an unknown employee working on a U.S. military base in the Middle East noticed an unsupervised USB drive laying outside of their classified office building. The unsuspecting employee took the drive inside with them and did what most people would do in the same situation—they plugged the drive into their classified office computer to see what was on the drive

Sometime later, in 2008, Department of Defense (DoD) network security analysts noticed the patterns in computer and network logs that pointed to the presence of computer worm moving through multiple DoD networks. The analysts were surprised by the presence of a widespread malware infection, because it had somehow made its way onto a highly protected classified network called SIPRnet.[1] This network was specifically designed with an *air-gap*, meaning that it wasn't permitted to have

---

[1] https://www.wired.com/2010/08/insiders-doubt-2008-pentagon-hack-was-foreign-spy-attack

connections to untrusted networks. Theoretically, this type of network architecture would minimize the possibility of encountering the sort of routine network attacks seen on networks without an air-gap.

Network security personnel at the National Security Agency (NSA) within a group called Advanced Network Operations (ANO) were the first to discover signatures of the worm's behaviors. According to government reporting, their subsequent investigation, codenamed Operation Buckshot Yankee,[2] moved quickly to investigate the malware while beginning the process of mitigating its spread. Operation Buckshot Yankee took 14 months in total, and by the time it was complete the DoD had learned several important lessons.

The malware used in the incident had been specially designed to operate on the type of air-gapped network on which SIPRnet was built. The revelation was startling to network analysts who realized that the multiple layers of defense used to protect DoD's secret classified network had failed, and it raised concerns that a new paradigm shift was underway. So much work had been done in the late 1990s and early 2000s to safeguard those secrets, but the work wasn't over yet.

Solar Sunrise

In February 1998, the Pentagon was still digesting the ER-97 test results as related to the preparedness of the American military to counter a cyberthreat at scale against American defense networks. Government leaders were just beginning to understand how seriously unprepared they were to ward off a computerized attack when network analysts within the DoD began noticing the markers of a network attack within their logs. Someone was

[2] https://www.govinfo.gov/content/pkg/CHRG-111hhrg62397/html/CHRG-111hhrg62397.htm

trying to exploit their way onto a server owned by the U.S. Air Force just as a force of U.S. Marines was being deployed to Iraq to support site inspections on Saddam Hussein's weapons programs.

The attacks targeted a Linux-based operating system called Sun Solaris, popular in server administration. ER-97's test results were helpful in advising government leaders on what the remedy for this attack type needed to include, and network defenders were more prepared to mount an investigation.

When analysts began to investigate the breach, they discovered that the DoD wasn't the only organization that had fallen victim to the same hackers. Several other U.S. government agencies and universities had also been breached along the way. The initial concern on the part of U.S. government investigators was that, under Saddam Hussein, the Iraqi government had launched attacks in response to the recent weapons inspections. This concern was, in part, due to the findings that some of those attacks traced back to a commercial network named Emirnet used in the Middle East.

Investigators discovered that the attackers responsible were two young American hackers named Mak (short for Makaveli) and Stimpy. But this wasn't the open-and-shut case that investigators first thought it was. When interviewed, the two hackers mentioned a third hacker who'd acted as a mentor of sorts, teaching them everything they needed to know about working offensively against computers. They'd been taught by a mysterious third hacker named Analyzer in chats with the teens. A further investigation of Analyzer found that he was an Israeli citizen named Ehud Tenenbaum.

When Tenenbaum was arrested and questioned about his reasons for participating in the attacks, he clarified that he wasn't trying to steal U.S. government secrets but was instead trying to highlight how vulnerable American institutions really were.

This was a common refrain used by hackers to defend their actions, but it didn't change the way the law applied to hackers. After pleading guilty to the charges against him, Tenenbaum served eight months in prison, but the cadre of hackers had proven their point.

Great strides had been made to protect American government computer systems, but despite being more organized, they were still vulnerable to the young and capable hackers they always had been. Military leaders realized that they had dodged a bullet when they found out their attackers were seemingly disinterested in the intelligence value of their targets. After the Solar Sunrise breach and the results of ER-97, one question lingered in the back of the minds of some policymakers: if U.S. military systems could still be breached by a small group of teenagers, what damage could a geopolitical peer do?

Advanced Persistent Threat

In 2016, a computer security researcher and college professor named Thomas Rid found his holy grail. Rid's work had painted him to be something close to a "digital Indiana Jones" as he followed clues left behind in computer logs and code, sometimes squinting at data in hopes of finding a critical piece of information to link one breach to another. The holy grail Rid was after was a 20-year-old server held by a retiree in London who had once worked as an IT consultant. When Rid contacted David Hedges and asked him about the missing computer, Hedges promptly responded that the computer Rid was looking for was indeed still in his possession. In fact, it was gathering dust under an unused desk in Hedges's home office.[3] When Hedges generously allowed Rid to take a look at the server, what Rid found was astounding.

---

[3] Thomas, Rid. (2020). *Active Measures: The Secret History of Disinformation and Political Warfare*. Farrar, Straus, and Giroux.

For Rid, getting a peek at the contents of Hedges's server was like opening an ancient tomb—a space that had been untouched for almost two decades. Hedges's server had been provided to him by the U.S. DoD, who had reported that the server had been part of a September 1998 breach used as a midpoint host to launch attacks on other U.S. government networks. The DoD asked Hedges to turn the server into a *honeypot*—a computer kept in isolation and used to secretly surveil hackers—and to send anything he collected from the server back to them.

Twice a week, Hedges would transfer the server's contents to physical disks, which he would then take to the London Metropolitan Police. From there, the London Police would pass Hedges' information on to London's American embassy where it would then be sent back to the Unites States via a diplomatic pouch. This convoluted delivery system was seen as a more secure method of transmission in 1998 than transferring the information over more convenient computer networks.

Working with researcher Juan Guerrero-Saade from Kaspersky, Rid and Guerrero-Saade analyzed the clues they found on the server provided by David Hedges and found a treasure trove of untouched evidence. As the details from the evidence they found came together, they began to realize that the story of one of the first documented attacks by a foreign government against the United States still had secrets to reveal. In fact, evidence on Hedges's server suggested that the operation began a full two years earlier than anyone previously believed.[4]

The breach that Rid and Guerrero-Saade were investigating was called "Moonlight Maze" by the DoD and differed from other government breaches in a few key areas. First, the attack was well-coordinated and methodical to a degree that hadn't

---

[4] https://www.vice.com/en/article/vvk83b/moonlight-maze-turla-link

been seen before. The actors had continued their attacks for years and were tenacious in their efforts to obtain and maintain their access. If one technique to get into a target system didn't succeed, they continued their attempts to regain access until they were successful. In other words, the networks the Moonlight Maze actors targeted could never truly be considered fully secure as long as they were on the prowl.

The attackers were also exceedingly aware of their own presence and exercised an abundance of caution to minimize any clues they left behind in the process of breaching their targets. This level of care was uncommon for hackers of the past who had often attacked U.S. government systems with little regard for how much evidence their activities left behind.

These hackers had used specialized backdoor programs, giving the attackers on-demand access to compromised computer systems. These backdoors maintained a connection back to the server that the DoD had placed under the sharp eye of David Hedges in London. Unwittingly, every move the attackers made was recorded on Hedges' server, including their comings and goings in an electronic log file. When the logs were analyzed, they indicated that the attackers were using Internet Protocol (IP) addresses assigned by Russian Internet service providers (ISPs), leading analysts to conclude that the attacks had originated from Russia. Had this been the real-life high-tech spy scenario that had kept American government leaders awake at night since the 1980s? All the available evidence suggested it was.

The tools and techniques used by the Moonlight Maze hackers were some of the most sophisticated that the world had ever seen. As Rid and Guerrero-Saade continued their investigation of Hedges' server, they found a program used by the attackers that had been missed during the initial server investigation. The program was a backdoor called Loki2 and dated back to 1996.

That same year, a write-up on the code for Loki2 was submitted to the popular hacking publication *Phrack* and detailed the backdoor's unique features.

In addition to giving attackers access to computer systems they had previously compromised, it also utilized special methods of routing its communications to help it stay undetected. This method, called a *covert channel*, was designed to disguise its communications as a common seemingly innocuous protocol that wouldn't stand out if seen by a skilled analyst. Even to investigators in the late 1990s, Moonlight Maze appeared to be a true spy operation, stealing as many secrets as the hackers could and spiriting them away to the Russian intelligence services as quietly as possible. The hackers were patient, opting to loiter inside of victim networks for as long as possible before being caught.

The investigation into Moonlight Maze continued beyond the government's original discovery of the breach in 1998 and is believed to have links to Russia's Federal Security Service (FSB), their equivalent of the American FBI. The FSB's attacks on the American government infrastructure continue to the present day. They now bear different names from Turla to Uroburos and still demonstrate some of the most deviously effective offensive security techniques.

Moonlight Maze was only the first instance of what was becoming known as the *advanced persistent threat* (APT) among computer security professionals, but it wouldn't be the last. In 2003, years after the Moonlight Maze discovery, another group of hackers using similar techniques appeared to be attacking the American government computing infrastructure. The investigation of this second group, called Titan Rain, who appeared to have Chinese government origins, proved that threats to American computer networks were evolving rapidly in the new millennium.

Emergence of Chinese Hacking

Internet development in China began in earnest in the mid-1990s, and within a few short years, the nation began laying the groundwork for a national force dedicated to offensive cybersecurity. In 1997, the same year that the United States was conducting its own formalization of offensive Computer Network Exploitation (CNE), China carried out its own military exercises with the goal of exploring the use of media disruption using online attacks. That April, the Chinese military tasked a 100-member team to research offensive cyber methods for disabling Western defense networks.[5]

The incursion of the North Atlantic Treaty Organization (NATO) into Kosovo had been one of the first large-scale modern conflicts that attracted both military and freelance nationalist hacking from all sides. The online battlefield forming around the conflict in Serbia was an awkward middle ground between hacktivism and being officially sanctioned. By all appearances, the freelance hackers on either side of the conflict weren't operating explicitly on behalf of any government but nevertheless were aligned with pro- or anti-Milošević positions.

Among the first targets for Chinese hackers were the websites of the U.S. Department of Energy, Interior, and National Park Service.[6] Chinese hackers replaced the Department of Interior's website with images of the journalists killed in the bombing and left a message on the website operated by the U.S. Department of Energy, condemning NATO and the United States. The online conflict between American and Chinese hackers continued, even after the United States left Kosovo in June 1999.

---

[5] https://www.jstor.org/stable/26461991
[6] https://www.washingtonpost.com/wp-srv/inatl/longterm/balkans/stories/hackers051299.htm

As it turned out, in the late 1990s, Russia and China weren't the only countries developing an elite force of government hackers. Since the late 1990s, the United States had been creating the foundation for a dedicated organization of hackers just as formidable as the Titan Rain and Moonlight Maze hackers were.

American Elite

In 1985, the NSA initially began developing its capabilities in the "cyber" realm, with the establishment of two offices: P04 and B03. B03 focused on the development of packet switching and computer networking, while P04 conducted a study of computer technologies that led to the creation of a new NSA office named G08. The following year, G08 began focusing on computer exploitation and their joint efforts with the Central Intelligence Agency (CIA) on the exploitation of telephonic voice networks in Southeast Asia and China. After several of NSA's popular and frequent reorganizations, G08's computer exploitation capability was merged with the packet-switching capabilities being explored by G08 into a group named K7.

For decades, hackers existed on the periphery of world events, only occasionally becoming participants independently. In the late 1990s, the American government began to seriously formalize and hire hackers for intelligence collection targets abroad. In the 1990s, the NSA had been in a transitory phase. By the late 1990s, however, the NSA had become an agency split by two missions fundamentally at odds with each other. One mission, the Information Assurance Directorate (IAD) mission, was defensive in nature. IAD's job was to protect American national defense communication devices and networks. They accomplished this mission through research that supported best practices in the 1970s and 1980s and by developing advanced cryptographic technologies.

The second of NSA's missions, the Signals Intelligence Directorate (SID), was focused on collecting and analyzing intelligence. In contrast to IAD, SID's mission was offensively focused and benefitted from tracking and stockpiling computer vulnerabilities that supported its mission, which was in direct contradiction to IAD's mission. Hackers recruited by NSA could be found throughout the NSA in an array of both offensively and defensively focused roles.

America's ability to focus on training and recruiting hackers came at a crucial time of reorganization for the NSA, which had historically been focused on the collection of traditional signals. After the fall of the Soviet Union, Western leaders celebrated their victory in the decades long Cold War. After the celebrations were over, however, Western leaders were left to imagine the post-Soviet world, but this world came with caveats.

One of the trade-offs for Western intelligence officials was now that the main geopolitical foe of Western-style capitalism had been defeated, there was no longer the same pressing need for the oversized budgets for defense organizations like the DoD, CIA, and NSA. American defense spending for the 1991 fiscal year dropped by the most substantial margin of the past 30 years, amounting to a dip of more than $150 billion.[7]

The drawdown in post–Cold War defense spending between 1985 to 1997 constituted a 33% decline from its height from 1979 to 1985. Without the Soviet threat, American intelligence agencies needed to re-imagine their role in a post–Cold War era. With spending shifting away from national defense, the intelligence community needed to find more cost-effective ways of conducting its foreign intelligence missions. The most sensible place to shift this spending in the late-1990s was toward building America's computer-based signals intelligence (SIGINT) capability.

---

[7] https://www.defensedaily.com/wp-content/uploads/post_attachment/148400.pdf

The NSA wasn't always destined to become America's preeminent computer hacking agency. In 1997, a Senate intelligence subcommittee, called the Technology Advisory Group (TAG), was created to investigate the NSA and to deliver a report on the agency's effectiveness. In their report, TAG raised concerns that the agency was at risk of falling behind in its ability to conduct its technical missions. In 1999, the DoD appointed General Michael Hayden to be the next NSA director. With TAG's report in hand, Hayden had a mandate to take a forward-looking position on the technologies that NSA's core missions would encounter over the ensuing 30 years. Under Hayden's leadership, the NSA's mission would rely less on traditional passive intelligence collection by intercepting radio signals as it had done during the Cold War. Instead, the NSA needed to invest in computer network technology for its long-term viability as an agency. In his memoir titled *Playing to the Edge: American Intelligence in the Age of Terror*, General Hayden recalled the dilemma at the time:

> . . .*with little debate, we went from a world of letting radio waves serendipitously hit our antennas to what became a digital form of breaking and entering.*

The direction proposed by General Hayden was to bolster America's CNE activities, but this direction wasn't immediately accepted by the NSA's rank and file. Many in NSA's contingent of aging cold warriors were inimical to the agency's new direction, but Hayden's plan eventually prevailed. At the end of 2000, General Hayden reorganized all of the preexisting efforts on the edges of CNE into a new organization focused exclusively on Hayden's plan for a CNE mission called the Tailored Access Operations (TAO).

According to Hayden, the NSA's reorganization was perfectly timed. Pulling together pockets of expertise from divisions throughout the agency, the NSA had an opportunity to bring together some of the best experts on assorted topics related to network exploitation and defense. The NSA was also in a position to benefit from external factors. The September 11, 2001, terrorist attacks, coupled with the end of the dot-com bubble, made a new generation of technical talent available to the agency. Taking advantage, the NSA managed to do the impossible—it folded third-generation hackers into government service. Hayden recognized the value of establishing a dedicated team of top-tier hacking talent and managed to realize his vision for an elite corps of American hackers by hiring thousands of hackers during his time leading the agency.

As the NSA formally added offensively focused hackers into its ranks, their organizational objective was to meet so-called U.S. Code Title 50 requirements for the collection of intelligence for national defense purposes. Title 50 collections were the bread-and-butter authority used to conduct signals intelligence in the United States, and with the addition of CNE to the existing portfolio of NSA collections, the agency's responsibilities were poised to grow significantly into the 2010s, keeping pace with the growth of computer technology.

A New Domain

Noting the success shown by the NSA's technical experts by the end of the 2000s, America's "cyber" mission was expanding enough to merit consideration of becoming its own "combatant command." After all the decades-long handwringing of hackers about the militarization of cyberspace, a new cybersecurity-focused combatant command was formalized under the name of the United States Cyber Command (USCC), under the recommendation of President Obama's First Secretary of Defense Robert Gates.

In the same way that the advent of the airplane necessitated the addition of air assets and piloting expertise to national defense missions found in the U.S. Air Force in 1947, breaches of American computer systems called for computers to be added to their own mission. The missions of the NSA and USCC were so similar that they shared a director, which meant that the director of the NSA would be responsible for representing the needs of both the NSA and its complementary agency, the USCC. The first person to serve in this role was the man who would go on to speak in front of DEF CON two years later, General Keith Alexander.

A congenial man with a sharp technical mind, there was no doubt that General Alexander shared many traits of those within the agency he led. The USCC was the beneficiary of a decade of outreach to the hacking community, which translated into having a greater pool of technical talent at its disposal at the time of its founding. The USCC aimed to add a new capability to America's growing cyberwarfare capacity in the form of destructive CNE operations to complement the NSA's intelligence collection operations.

By the end of the 2000s, world governments managed to integrate the technical skills of hackers over a 30-year period, effectively domesticating a force of hackers for both offensive and defensive purposes. Hackers had started as an oddball community of proud misfits and introverts skeptical of the world of global politics. In a post-2010 world, however, hackers gained access to a major level of geological power to become a powerful force in determining the course of history.

CHAPTER

16

Cyberwar

In March 1999, the North Atlantic Treaty Organization (NATO), led by the United States, was engaged in an air superiority campaign over the Baltic nation of Yugoslavia. Their mission was to defend the nation of Kosovo from Yugoslavian invaders accused of engaging in a genocide against their neighbors, the Kosovars. Despite being in an active war zone, the Chinese diplomatic mission stayed in Belgrade to support their ally, Yugoslavian President Slobodan Milošević, who had been formally indicted by The Hague that same month for war crimes against humanity for his actions in Kosovo.

Near midnight on May 7, 1999, most of the employees working inside the Chinese embassy had retired to their residences, unaware that silently an American B-2 "stealth" bomber flew high above them. The bomber blended in perfectly with the night sky, and as it passed overhead, it dropped a clutch of five joint direct attack munitions (JDAMs) out of the exposed bomb bay beneath the aircraft. A few moments later, the

261

precision weapons found their targets, spread across the grounds of the Chinese embassy. In the morning light, the remains of the Chinese embassy had been bombed into a cross-section of grotesque broken tile and twisted rebar. The scene looked like a miniature version of the Oklahoma City bombing three years before. The attack killed three Chinese diplomats and immediately became an international incident.

The attack had been planned by the Central Intelligence Agency (CIA), who blamed the attack on outdated maps, claiming that their true target was a short distance up the street. In October 1999, *The Guardian* published an article with the headline: "NATO Bombed Chinese Deliberately," claiming that the Belgrade Chinese embassy bombing wasn't an unfortunate mix-up but rather a purposeful attack. In their article, *The Guardian* stated that electronic intelligence (ELINT) provided by the CIA indicated that the Chinese diplomatic mission had been operating a rebroadcasting station out of their embassy in support of the Yugoslavian military, which *The Guardian* concluded was the reason for being targeted. The American State Department still stands by their statement that the bombing was an accident.

The U.S. interdiction into Kosovo in 1999 was a preview for wars in the coming century. The first generation of intelligence, reconnaissance, and surveillance (ISR) drones were used during the Kosovo conflict and played a critical role in remote-targeting missions to support ground operations. It was also the first armed conflict that the United States engaged in that included an exchange of cyberattacks between major world powers.

In response to the embassy bombing in Belgrade, China placed their own natively trained and untested hacker force to work against the West. Rather than inciting their own online conflict, China's hackers joined an ongoing engagement in which NATO-sponsored hackers were already involved. Even before the embassy bombing, NATO forces had been hitting front-facing Serbian media websites in an effort to shut down pro-Milošević propaganda. Rather than shutting down communications throughout Serbia, NATO's strategy was instead focused on keeping communications lines open.[1]

. Chinese hackers did little to impact the outcomes of the Kosovo conflict, but they had planted a flag in the online space declaring that they could be used to respond to geopolitical events. As it would turn out, Chinese hackers weren't the only newcomers to the online battle happening in Kosovo. On that very same battlefield, the Electronic Frontier Foundation (EFF) was actively playing a role in defending their own organizational interests abroad.

The EFF was in Kosovo supporting a program they called the "Kosovo Privacy Project," with the goal of keeping Internet access open for as long as the conflict was raging. This goal was conveniently aligned with NATO's own objectives, and together they were able to maintain open communications for the conflict's duration. Moreso than a happy coincidence, in 2002, one of EFF's cofounders, Perry Barlow, revealed that he'd been serving in an advisory role to American intelligence agencies since the EFF's founding.[2]

Despite outward appearances, American foreign policy had long since been touched by a select few hackers who had been entrusted to advise leaders. It had taken more time for the message to reach some world governments, but slowly and surely hackers were becoming an accepted part of military establishments worldwide.

---

[1] https://faculty.nps.edu/dedennin/publications/ActivismHacktivismCyberterrorism-NetworksAndNetwars.pdf
[2] https://www.forbes.com/asap/2002/1007/042_2.html

Operation Uphold Democracy

The broadside of cyberattacks exchanged between the United States and China during the Kosovo conflict didn't come out of nowhere. America's use of cyberattacks during the conflict, preceded by the Evident Surprise exercise in 1997, proved that the United States could bring cyber force to the table in an armed conflict, but even Evident Surprise had a basis in proven history.

In 1991, trouble was brewing in the Caribbean when a military coup d'etat led by General Raoul Cédras overthrew Haiti's first democratically elected president, Jean-Bertrand Aristide. Aristide was deposed by Cédras's military junta on September 29, 1991, and a few years later, under domestic pressure from lawmakers in 1994, the Clinton administration was forced to intercede in Haiti's coup. The United States took a stance backing Aristide, reasoning that the drug trade impacting the American war on drugs was out of control in Haiti thanks to the junta government. After years of concerns from U.S. lawmakers, President Clinton was forced to apply a military solution. Plans to remove Cédras from power were drawn up under the name Operation Upholding Democracy.

As was typical of U.S. military planning, threats to U.S. forces were identified, and options to respond to the threats were given to commanders. These options could range anywhere from a diplomatic response all the way up to a full-scale invasion, depending on the threat. In the case of Operation Uphold Democracy, one of the primary threats to American invasion forces were Haitian ground radar sites, which could threaten the operation of American air assets over the island.[3] Operational planners in the Department of Defense (DoD) found that the

---

[3] Kaplan, Fred. (2024). *Dark Territory: The History of Cyber War*. Simon & Schuster.

radar sites were interconnected using commercial telephone lines, which presented an opportunity for a low-cost nonlethal solution for American military commanders.

The plans provided to Operation Uphold Democracy commanders included an option that made use of telephone-jamming attacks for the first time. If the phone lines Haitian radar relied on could be jammed, then they would effectively become unusable, neutralizing them in a possible invasion situation.

The option to jam the phone lines was written by an unnamed staffer who had themselves been a phreaker before they joined the military, which gave them insight into how popular phreaking techniques could be used in this scenario. Instead of being used to win a car as Kevin Poulsen had a few years before, telephonic-jamming techniques could be used for American geopolitical interests. Phreakers had finally been given a spot at the table, and their talents were being noticed.

Despite the idea being a brilliant solution, the plan to jam radar phone lines was never used. Plans for Operation Uphold Democracy were permanently shelved after an American diplomatic delegation met with Cédras, informing him that the American military would be sent into Haiti if he didn't step aside. Fearing that he would be on the losing end of an armed conflict with the United States, Cédras was convinced to flee to Panama.

In later years, lessons learned from Operation Uphold Democracy, including the plan to jam Internet-connected telephone lines, were added to a series of military exercises called Unified Endeavor. The phreaker influence lived on in joint task force (JTF) training, giving military commanders the opportunity to consider how information warfare might be used in future military missions. Even though this cyber-option wasn't used in the conflict, the plan to jam Haitian phone lines took on a post-operational life of its own, foreshadowing the role that computers would play in near-future military operations. With intelligence collection poised to play a critical role in diplomatic negotiations and ISR missions in the 2000s, new possibilities for hackers to make their mark on some of the most highly classified missions developed.

Cyberwarfare in Concept

The idea of cyberwarfare had been the domain of science fiction until the 1990s, and the image of cyberwarfare as presented by fiction has heavily influenced the way the public understands the issue. Although the term *cyberwar* hadn't yet entered the lexicon, after the release of the movie *WarGames*, American fears of a cyber-enabled conflict reflected the very real fears that many Americans had of nuclear proliferation since the beginning of the Cold War. The concept of a computerized war among equals remained a concern underneath the umbrella of nuclear-armed conflict until the mid-1990s, when computers became more integrated with economic development and industrial control. It was at this point that the idea of cyberwarfare changed.

Industrial automation had come a long way since the days of Stafford Beer and his early industry supercomputers by the mid-1990s. In the 1970s, programmable logic controllers (PLCs) were developed and became a popular microtechnology for automating industrial activities. (PLCs control everything from the motion of a robotic arm to the opening and closing of valves and controlling the amount of heat in oil refinery pipelines.)

Concerns about cyberwarfare were no longer exclusively limited to fears that computers would be used to annihilate civilization through nuclear attacks, but that major populations could also face hardship through the manipulation of critical civilian services such as disrupting electricity and water distribution. Seeing this possibility on the horizon, forward-thinking engineers at Idaho National Laboratory (INL), a premier research laboratory operating under the purview of the U.S. Department of Energy, began researching just how much damage a hacker could do using exclusively cyberattacks.

In 2007, INL conducted a test to study the potential impacts hackers could have against the power grid. In a test they called the *Aurora Generator Test*, INL set up an industrial-scale diesel electric generator connected to a computer network. Their objective was to see exactly how far the generator could be pushed by hackers who only had computer-based access to its operation. In the test's recording, the large dark-green generator first appears to be running normally. Suddenly, the generator begins to shake slightly and then more and more violently as the components inside the generator are pushed past their limits. Smoke pours out of the generator, as the moving pistons shred the generator's insides. Depending on the viewers perspective, the test was either a resounding success or an eye-popping failure, though all could agree that the test outcomes were indeed significant.

After the Aurora Generator Test, Internet-connected industrial technology became a major area of interest for American defense officials. It was known that real-world effects could be produced exclusively through computerized access against military targets, but the Aurora Generator Test pointed to the possibility that the same attack types that had been used against information networks in decades past, now applied to civilian critical infrastructure. Fresh on the minds of government leaders was the 2003 Northeast Blackout. This blackout was a cascading failure in the American electric distribution grid, which created an electrical outage lasting days from the Eastern seaboard all the way into mid-Western states.

The Aurora Generator Test, as a small-scale demonstration, suggested to U.S. lawmakers that a hacker could potentially cause a similar electric outage in the future. This fact raised several unsettling questions: if a hacker could hypothetically interrupt electrical service at a larger scale, how many people could potentially be impacted? How long could they be without power? And if an attack did occur, is there anything that anyone could do to stop it?

The Northeast Blackout of 2003 left 50 million Americans effected for days, as the combined effort of multiple states' electrical companies worked around the clock to restore electrical service. It was a frightening glimpse of how society would function in the absence of a critical civilian service. Although the 2004 Eastern Northeast blackout wasn't caused by a cyberattack of any kind, the widespread blackout was the closest approximation to what many Americans believed a cyberattack against the American electric grid might look like.

Stuxnet

In 1968, the Iranian government leadership under Shah Pahlavi began the research and development of nuclear power for the people of Iran. Iranian leadership convened to sign the Nuclear Non-Proliferation Treaty (NPT), which would bring new resources to the Shah's nuclear aspirations.[4] The NPT was created as a carrot-and-stick policy by nuclear signatory nations, which gave incentives to nations that wanted to develop peaceful nuclear projects such as export-controlled nuclear equipment and fissile material in exchange for a promise not to launch nuclear weapons programs. This promise was upheld by certain measures that nations agreeing to the terms would submit to, which included monitoring certain sites used in the enrichment

---

[4] https://iranprimer.usip.org/blog/2020/jan/22/iran-and-npt

of nuclear materials to guarantee that fissile material wouldn't be enriched to "weapons grade."

After the agreement went into effect for Iran in 1970, cameras were installed at several sites throughout Iran identified as relevant to the NPT.[5] It was the cameras, which were installed and monitored by the International Atomic Energy Agency (IAEA) to verify that Iran was meeting its obligations under the NPT, that picked up something unusual in the Iranian Natanz nuclear facility: scientists working in the facility were steadily dismantling IR-1 centrifuges used for the enrichment of nuclear material.

The rate of replacement for these centrifuges was much higher than the IAEA estimated and pointed toward a significant unexpected event happening within the facility.[6] Years later, news broke that the Natanz nuclear facility had come under attack by a highly advanced piece of malware that researchers named Stuxnet based on unique strings found inside the malware.

Based on the malware's sophistication, researchers believed that Stuxnet was the latest volley in an ongoing battle over Iran's nuclear program. It appeared that Stuxnet was designed to create conditions for one specific type of programmable logic controller (PLC) used in the Natanz nuclear facility to spin in an unsafe manner. This uncontrolled spinning would thereby potentially impair the centrifuge's operation, which researchers theorized might have been the reason for the unexpected mass disassembly of the centrifuges that the IAEA observed at Natanz.

Suspicion of who could be behind the attack immediately fell on Israel and their allies because Israel had taken a hardline opposition to Iranian nuclear development, particularly since 2010.

---

[5] https://iranprimer.usip.org/blog/2021/nov/29/explainer-problems-iaea-monitoring-iran
[6] https://isis-online.org/isis-reports/detail/did-stuxnet-take-out-1000-centrifuges-at-the-natanz-enrichment-plant

Israel had proven in previous attacks against its neighbors, including the Osirak nuclear reactor bombing, that it would go to any length to set back Middle Eastern nuclear development.[7] Israeli leadership, which had a long history of military conflict with its Arab neighbors, saw regional nuclear aspirations as a threat to its own national security.

Coming hot on the heels of the Aurora Generator Test, this possibility added urgency to questions about what cyberwarfare meant in the post-2010s world.

Combatant Hackers

As hackers became more integrated into wartime activities, they increasingly became military targets themselves. One such example was the case of Junaid Hussain, better known online by his hacker name, "TriCk," a UK citizen and member of a hacking group from the early 2010s called "TeaMp0isoN." Hussain made a name for himself after serving a prison term for hacking private email accounts belonging to former British Prime Minister Tony Blair, later posting the information online.

TriCk became radicalized during his prison sentence, and after his release, moved to Syria in 2013, where he became an active participant in the ongoing civil war. Hussain aligned himself with the newly declared Islamic State in the Levant (ISIL) and became ISIL's primary online propagandist. He first gained the attention of Western intelligence when he posted a "kill list" of U.S. military personnel, along with claiming responsibility for continued hacks against the U.S. government.

Hussain became involved in the unification of a force of hackers calling themselves the Cyber Caliphate, which claimed

---

[7] https://nsarchive.gwu.edu/briefing-book/iraq-nuclear-vault/2021-06-07/osirak-israels-strike-iraqs-nuclear-reactor-40-years-later

their activity to be in support of the Islamic State. While the hackers in the Cyber Caliphate claimed to be genuinely involved in the support and promotion of the Islamic State, within a year, Western intelligence agencies including the National Security Agency (NSA) and U.S. Cyber Command (USCC) concluded that the Cyber Caliphate was actually a false flag operation run by Russian intelligence.[8]

Ostensibly claiming to be a collection of true "jihadi" hackers, the goals of the Cyber Caliphate had almost exclusively focused their hacking and propaganda efforts against Western governments. This made the group a suitable façade for Russian hackers who shared similar goals. Between the years of 2013 and 2015, Russian government hackers were riding a hot streak of operational successes that showed no signs of stopping, but their activity with the Cyber Caliphate had drawn too much attention. After claiming responsibility for the TV5 Monde hack ahead of the French election cycle, the French government also questioned the legitimacy of Cyber Caliphate's claims as an independent entity from Russian intelligence.[9]

TriCk's role with ISIL wasn't unusual for the time, as other citizens of the United States and UK were known to have traveled to the Middle East to support the growth of ISIS and ISIL and had often taken roles as propagandists such as the English-speaking "Jihadi John." Jihadi John (whose true name was Mohammed Emwazi) was known in the West from his role giving anti-Western diatribes, followed by himself gruesomely murdering captives. Pro-ISIS/ISIL propagandists at this time had a fairly short lifespan, given that they quickly became top targets for Western drone strikes, as was the end for both Jihadi John and TriCk.

---

[8] https://observer.com/2016/06/false-flags-the-kremlins-hidden-cyber-hand
[9] https://www.reuters.com/article/us-france-russia-cybercrime-idUSKBN0OQ2GG201
50610

In August 2015, the U.S. military located Hussain in Raqqa and executed a drone-based operation, which killed him at a gas station. Somewhat ironically, Hussain had originally been located by the U.S. military after clicking a link provided to him by an intelligence asset that transmitted his geographic location to U.S. intelligence. In the end, the same sort of hacking Hussain himself built a reputation through ended up being used to end his life.[10] At the time of the operation, Hussain managed to rise to being the third highest kill-or-capture priority for the U.S. military, just behind Jihadi John and the founder of ISIS, Abu Bakr al-Baghdadi.

The targeting of Junaid Hussain was a foray into the controversial territory of using military force against hackers. Hussain's case had been a soft introduction to the concept because those who left the comforts of Western nations to join ultra-violent Islamic State terror groups were universally despised by average citizens of their nations of origin. Treating hackers as enemy combatants was becoming a more acceptable course of action, as was the case for hackers in Gaza accused of operating on behalf of Hamas. In 2019, the Israeli Defense Force (IDF) dropped a bomb on a building in Gaza it said housed the hackers.[11]

The IDF provided few details about the operation and didn't specify what evidence they had to tie the targeted building to the activities of any specific group, but the attack caused disagreements even among hackers about the legitimacy of treating hackers as enemy combatants in a warzone. A complicating factor for the issue was the fact determining exactly who was responsible for any given hack, and where they were located was a controversial issue in and of itself. To many in the hacking community, the idea of dropping a bomb based on vague attribution was an unimaginable outcome. Others in the community insisted that hackers

---

[10] https://www.birminghammail.co.uk/news/midlands-news/isis-terrorist-junaid-hussain-killed-10069425
[11] https://www.wired.com/story/israel-hamas-cyberattack-air-strike-cyberwar

were indeed legitimate targets of military operations because they themselves were often directly involved in those same conflicts.

As had been shown in the case of Junaid Hussain, hackers had been a critical link in the operation to target and kill him. Regardless of the modern controversy around the legitimacy of targeting hackers, the defense policy of many militarized nations had already advanced the issue of cyberwarfare to the point of defining hacking in the same military language as the rules of engagement had been. As far as these governments were concerned, under the right circumstances, hackers online were the same thing as a soldier with a rifle on a battlefield.

Ukrainian Blackouts

On December 23, 2015, the lights in Kyiv went off in the middle of the afternoon. For the residents of Kyiv and the surrounding areas as well as many densely populated cities around the world, blackouts were (and still are) relatively common. In some areas, the electricity remained off for up to six hours.[12] Two days before the Christmas holiday, many impacted Ukrainians were concerned by the outage but didn't have reason to believe that they were under attack from a foreign power. However, Ukrainian officials working for the power company knew that something significant was taking place. Employees of various electrical companies inside Ukraine reported that a coordinated attack across multiple electric companies in different regions was to blame for the outage.

Network defense professionals from a collection of Western countries responded to the outage and quickly discovered that a piece of malware called BlackEnergy3 had been used to facilitate

---

[12] https://www.wired.com/2016/03/inside-cunning-unprecedented-hack-ukraines-power-grid

Ukraine's energy grid attack. The attack's effects in December 2015 appeared to be fairly limited. Although the attackers had been able to turn off electricity in the middle of winter for hundreds of thousands of customers, proving the theory that hackers could disrupt critical services to civilians, the practice of doing so was somewhat more complex.

According to reports by responders involved in the breach's cleanup, the attackers had indeed managed to open electrical breakers at 30 different substations throughout Ukraine.[13] In addition to opening breakers, the attackers conducted a telephonic denial-of-service (DoS) attack against the central authority coordinating an attack response.[14] This telephone-based attack was an effort to create chaos and confusion among the response staff in an effort to prolong the attack's effects.

However, the effect of disabling automation was tempered by the fact that electrical technicians present during the attack merely reverted their systems to manual operation, which allowed them to regain control of the electric grid in a relatively short period of time. The attacks against Ukraine's energy grid in 2015 pulled out all the stops and had a surprisingly impotent effect. Reports of the incident by security response teams determined that the hackers had originally managed to gain their first access into Ukraine's energy grid six months prior to the blackout incident. It was a substantial investment of time for a relatively small impact.

After a successful attack against the Ukrainian energy grid but with limited long-term impacts, Russian hackers returned to attack Ukraine again the following year. The second attack occurred in the nighttime hours of December 17, 2016, but this

---

[13] https://jsis.washington.edu/news/cyberattack-critical-infrastructure-russia-ukrainian-power-grid-attacks
[14] https://nsarchive.gwu.edu/sites/default/files/documents/3891751/SANS-and-Electricity-Information-Sharing-and.pdf

time, Ukrainian responders were prepared. The 2016 attack focused on Kyiv specifically and only managed to disrupt power for a little over an hour. Later research of the second attack on Ukraine's energy grid indicated that the actors belonged to Russia's Main Intelligence Directorate (GRU) military intelligence unit 74455.[15] Researchers named the group *Sandworm*, based on strings inside malware used by the group that referenced the planet Arrakis from Frank Herbert's hit science-fiction novel *Dune*. Hackers, geeky as ever, were still fans of science fiction.

The pair of attacks became proof of concept for cyberwarfare theories, showing that perhaps fears of cyberattacks permanently turning off the lights in major cities around the world were somewhat overblown. Politicians, who in decades past struggled with the concept of creating policy to govern emerging computer technologies, now had to contend with the foreign policy implications of computer attacks as a declaration of war. While these questions had been answered in terms of the American national defense policy during the earliest days of the USCC, there were open questions about declarations of war with even more precarious and dire consequences.

One question concerned what criteria would need to be met for a cyberattack to trigger an Article 5 reaction from NATO. A provocation of NATO's Article 5 meant that every NATO ally would be bound to provide a military response to the attack. Suppose that a geopolitical adversary to NATO breached a computer network belonging to a NATO partner. Would this constitute an act of war under Article 5 and trigger a response from all NATO signatories? What would this sort of foreign policy stance mean for the United States itself—a nation that had been accused of attacking other countries with similar hacking activity? In

---

[15] Greenberg, Andy. (2019). *Sandworm: A New Era of Cyberwar and the Hunt for the Kremlin's Most Dangerous Hackers*. Doubleday.

2014, NATO answered this question by amending the treaty to accommodate serious cyberattacks as a catalyst for activating Article 5, and the fact that Ukraine wasn't a signatory to the treaty meant that the attacks against their energy grid in 2015 and 2016 were irrelevant to a Western military response, despite that after Euromaidan, Ukraine was moving into NATO's sphere of influence.

The post-Euromaidan landscape of Ukraine was an experiment in future cyberwarfare from the beginning. In 2014 during Russia's original military push into Crimea, Russian hackers took down Ukraine's telecommunications and Internet services in support of the invasion. The telecommunications attack disrupted mobile communications for members of Ukrainian parliament, which frustrated the ability of the Ukrainian government to mount an effective defense of their Eastern border.[16] This imposed a communication blackout designed to create widespread confusion, which allowed the invaders to fight more effectively against a disadvantaged Ukrainian leadership.

This telecom attack against Ukraine was reminiscent of another Russian attack against its southern neighbor, Georgia, during a military incursion in 2008. In the Georgian attacks, Russian military actors used DoS attacks and web defacements to disrupt Georgian Internet resources and spread pro-Russia messages during the military engagement. The 2008 Georgian conflict proved to be a staging ground for Russia to test the integration of its investment in offensive cyber in a real-world conflict, which they used to great effect against Ukraine a few short years later.

The first major shot in this war was the Russian invasion of Crimea in the wake of Yanukovich fleeing to Russia. In addition

---

[16] https://www.cnbc.com/2014/03/04/ukraine-cyberattack-on-communications-mps-phones-blocked.html

to committing on-the-ground military assets to an unfolding invasion of Crimea, Putin turned to his elite hacking unit 74455 within the GRU, Russia's military intelligence agency. When Russia's military campaign concluded with the successful annexation of Crimea, Russia's strategy was to destabilize and discredit the new Ukrainian leadership.

CHAPTER

17

Politics As Usual

Standing on a stage flanked by the Florida state flag on one side and an American flag on the other, U.S. Presidential candidate Donald Trump spoke to an audience of energized voters in July 2016. When Trump spoke to the crowd, he put the extent to which hackers had become a force for global politics on full display saying, *"Russia, if you're listening, I hope you are able to find the 30,000 emails that are missing. I think you'll be rewarded mightily by our press."*

Donald Trump was referring to a collection of emails that had been kept on the private home server of his political opponent, Hillary Clinton. At the time of Trump's run for the presidency, the use of private email addresses and devices for official government communication had become a routinely exploited loophole in U.S. recordkeeping law. These laws, which are designed to promote the retention of official records, mandates that public officials must conduct all of their official communications on devices that are owned and administrated by their home agencies. Many believed that this loophole was exploited for corrupt reasons, and while it's a federal offense for public officials to refuse to turn over official government records, this manner of sidestepping federal law has historically been poorly enforced. Hillary Clinton herself was accused of deleting 30,000 official emails, which Republicans claimed contained evidence of unspecified corruption.

Trump's statement was a recognition that hackers held an outsized influence in American politics, and that he was willing to be a beneficiary of their largess. It was the first time a presidential candidate explicitly called for them to work on his behalf.

Trump's willingness to involve foreign hackers in a presidential election signaled an uncomfortable truth about the American political landscape. If foreign hacking had become an acceptable election-year strategy, many feared that the floodgates would be open for state-sponsored hackers to interfere in any American election. Such an admission shouldn't have been surprising to political observers who knew that Trump actively consulted with Nixon campaign strategist, Roger Stone. Since his time on the Nixon campaign trail, Stone had made a name for himself courting controversy and gleefully engaging in an aggressive form of politicking euphemistically called *opposition research*. Stone, on the other hand, preferred the more honest term, *ratfucking*, for what he did. Stone had proven himself willing to do whatever it took to win a political campaign for the right candidate. Collaborating with hackers was just the newest tool in his bag of dirty tricks.[1]

---

[1] https://www.justice.gov/archives/sco/file/1373816/dl

Memetic Warfare

The user-generated content of Web 2.0 created an environment primed for the spread of inside jokes and the sardonic humor that have become mainstays of the modern online experience. Image boards have made sharing funny pictures and relatable art easier than it has ever been before, and it's taken on a culture all its own. This mix of in-jokes in recognizable formats came to be called *memes* as coined by Richard Dawkins in his book *The Selfish Gene*, published in 1976.[2]

What makes memes particularly effective as modes of communication online are their bite-size form factor of a single image with text overlayed. When memes are shared widely, their reach can seemingly go on forever. Internet memes have become shorthand for communicating messages within online groups, but their cultural reach also has the potential to extend beyond the original intended audience.

During Obama's presidency, the popularity of memes exploded as they were used for the first time to help an American president win a general election. By the end of Obama's second term in 2014, memes had become so commonplace that the president himself both acknowledged and participated in the creation of several memes, sometimes mimicking a popular phrase used online such as "Thanks, Obama," as he did in a promotional video showing the president expressing frustration that he couldn't fit his oversized cookie into a glass of milk.

These factors made memes a perfect conduit for communicating political messages being deployed by campaigns that were seeking ways of increasing their engagement online. Political PR teams are constantly searching for ways to communicate messages to the public, knowing that they have only a few seconds to

---

[2] https://www.nytimes.com/2022/01/26/crosswords/what-is-a-meme.html

meaningfully engage with voters. Internet memes have been a perfect fit for their needs. One popular meme from 2016 tapped directly into the consciousness of massive online communities at the time, including Reddit, Twitter (now known as X), and Facebook, and tore its origin directly out of news headlines from the time.

For many, the frigid combative rhetoric used during the leadup to the 2016 election was strange and alienating. Candidate Trump had already spent the first half of 2016 laying the groundwork for a hyper-nationalistic presidential campaign based on fear of outsiders and skepticism of the political establishment of both parties. The political establishment itself fought back against Trump's candidacy; despite that it was a natural evolution of an increasingly extreme form of right-wing politics that had largely been embraced by mainstream politicians. As a result, many establishment conservatives calling themselves "never Trumpers" mounted an effort to derail Trump's campaign ahead of the Grand Old Party's (GOP) nomination ceremony at their national convention.

As the 2016 election season kicked into full gear, Internet memes were one of the favored mediums of communication by both sides of the political spectrum. Not only were memes being used by legitimate representatives of political campaigns and coordinated with other messaging pushes across different forms of media, but they were also being created and shared independently by voters wanting to express their views and potentially influence others. Political operatives who used meme formats to promote their candidate even had a term they used to aggrandize their efforts that they called, *memetic warfare.*

In the early-2000s, the U.S. Marine Corps (USMC) explored the use of memes for military purposes, calling the effort *memetics*,[3] which later evolved into the term *memetic warfare*. At its core,

---

[3] https://web.archive.org/web/20180219200439/http://www.dtic.mil/dtic/tr/full-text/u2/a507172.pdf

the idea of memetics wasn't much different than any other form of propaganda that had preceded it. Politicians as well as the military and intelligence communities have long been aware of the practical uses for spreading influence through the use of easy-to-share propaganda.

Memes, combined with the ease by which users could share them on social media websites meant that political campaigns had a whole new way of reaching communities of voters. The speed that memes could be shared also played a role in spreading reactionary messages within hours of real-world events. For political campaigns, the Internet was a perfect system of influence, but it wasn't just American political campaigns that were able to use social media influence to its full effect.

Election Interference

In May 2016, Democratic National Committee (DNC) staffers called up representatives of a well-known threat intelligence company CrowdStrike, which provided up-to-date information about trending threats to computer networks to their clients. Another service CrowdStrike provided to its customers was helping to clean up network breaches, kicking hackers out of sensitive networks and helping rebuild impacted systems. CrowdStrike had been brought in to investigate by computer security professionals working for the campaign of Hilary Clinton who suspected that they had been breached by a skilled group of hackers.

In the course of their investigation, CrowdStrike discovered that the attackers responsible for the breach had been meticulous in their efforts to exploit the DNC network and remain undetected. After getting access to the DNC network, the attackers quietly moved from one victim computer to another within DNC's network, cleaning up logs they had left behind and loitering undetected for a long time period. While they sat idle on their victim network, the actors established a network of surveillance across their victims, stealing information on the Clinton campaign and exfiltrating it out of the network.

One of the main breach targets appeared to be the DNC's Microsoft Exchange email server, from which they managed to steal thousands of sensitive emails related to the strategy and execution of the DNC's 2016 election plan. One of the main victims of the attack was Chairman John Podesta, who had been in contact with several people working with the campaign of Democratic candidate Hilary Clinton. Among the revelations from the leaked emails was evidence that the DNC had been selective in deciding the outcome of the Democratic candidate primaries. Some political observers felt that the DNC had stolen the opportunity for the upstart candidacy of Bernie Sanders to be nominated by the DNC in 2016.

The leaked emails raised several questions about the legitimacy of the American electoral process, which until this time had been mostly free from accusations of corruption. However, the emails themselves also didn't come without a hint of public skepticism. Where exactly had these emails come from, and was it possible that the attacks that had released them were part of a larger influence campaign being waged against the United States during an election year?

The attacks against the DNC were actually part of a larger pattern of election-season cyberattacks against Western democracies conducted by the Russian government between 2015 and 2017. In 2015, Russia was accused of hacking both the UK Parliament and the German Bundestag in efforts to influence both elections. A year after the 2016 U.S. presidential election, Russian-controlled hackers turned their attention to the French presidential elections, targeting the Macron campaign in an effort to put their thumb on the scale of the right-wing French candidate Marine Le Pen. The group accused of the French presidential hack was the same group accused of working with the Cyber Caliphate as a front for the TV5Monde hack that nearly took down the broadcasting company permanently.[4]

On June 14, 2016, a *Washington Post* report broke the news that the Russian government had hacked the DNC network. The very next day, a hacker going by the name Guccifer 2.0 took credit for the DNC hack and immediately began a high-profile campaign to publicize the hacked material. Guccifer 2.0 was a throwback to the name from a previously well-known Romanian hacker, Marcel Lehel Lazar, who himself targeted American politicians and their social media accounts.

The Guccifer 2.0 account appeared to be aligned with yet another effort to influence a world election and made efforts to collaborate with the media. In fact, Guccifer 2.0 wasn't shy toward the press and on several occasions interacted directly with press members. From the beginning, the Guccifer 2.0 persona appeared to be an effort to muddy the waters of attribution and make it difficult to pin any particular motive or nationality on Guccifer 2.0. It didn't take long for reporters to notice that the source of emails and chatroom connections used by Guccifer 2.0 were from Russia.

Shortly after the DNC breach became public knowledge, records stolen in the breach were published by WikiLeaks and a second site called DCLeaks.com. The contents of the DNC emails showed that the DNC lent a helping hand to the Clinton campaign, which set off a flurry of accusations that the Democratic selection process for the party's nominee had been corrupt. Unconfirmed rumors pointed to Russian hackers as the likely culprit for the hack. The DNC hack had become one of the most hotly debated scandals in a year dominated by political controversy, and had made the hacking community the unlikeliest kingmakers of the political cycle.

---

[4] https://www.wired.com/2017/05/nsa-director-confirms-russia-hacked-french-election-infrastructure

In addition to working with the press in various capacities, Guccifer 2.0 also collaborated with right-wing politicians who outwardly seemed excited at the prospect of foreign intervention in an American election. Trump's call for Russian hackers to release Clinton's emails came less than a month after news of the DNC hack broke, removing any question of whether the American political establishment would resist the questionable influences of foreign actors. In August, acolytes of the Trump campaign including Roger Stone made direct contact with operators of the Guccifer 2.0 Twitter account. According to direct messages released by Stone himself in 2017, Guccifer 2.0 offered help directly to Stone and, by proxy, the Trump campaign.

Serious questions raised by reporting about foreign influence campaigns, like the one fronted by Guccifer 2.0, prompted answers from the government after the election ended. In 2017, the Department of Justice (DoJ) appointed former FBI Director Robert Mueller as the special counsel to investigate these claims of foreign influence over the 2016 election. The investigation's scope was wide-reaching, and its results were highly detailed in its finding that Russian intelligence had indeed been involved in an orchestrated effort to influence the outcome of the 2016 election in various ways.

Notably, Mueller's final report wasn't able to verifiably establish "collusion" between the Trump campaign and the Russian government. However, the report did find several instances of Trump campaign officials who'd been in contact with elements of Russian intelligence. According to the Mueller Report, the basis of many of these communications had been the solicitation of stolen information, which was seen as valuable to the Trump campaign during the 2016 election.[5]

The Mueller Report also established that the Guccifer 2.0 account was created and used by Russian intelligence as a means

---

[5] https://www.justice.gov/archives/sco/file/1373816/dl

of communication with WikiLeaks in the exchange of information stolen as a result of the DNC hack. After the completion of the special counsel investigation, indictments were issued against a dozen members of Russian Intelligence Services (RIS), specifically from Russian GRU who were involved in the hack of DNC servers. True to form, these indictments didn't lead to any arrests and were instead served as a mechanism to "name and shame" foreign hackers who the DoJ had no sincere expectation would ever be brought to justice.

After decades of development of the culture and technology of the Internet, hackers had finally been recognized for the potential power they held to sway international events. At the time of the alleged influence campaign at play during the 2016 American presidential election, not only had hackers become an accepted and well-funded part of the military establishment of several major nations, but they were also recognized as a relatively low-cost option for international influence.

Hackers could be deployed both to overtly attack, and covertly influence rivals behind the scenes as an extension of preexisting military and geopolitical institutions. By 2016, hackers and their culture had been cultivated by world governments for their skills and knowledge, and their online environment was retooled for the purpose of waging war.

Hacking Elections at DEF CON

The hacking community became a major party to the presidential election and itself had many questions to answer about the involvement of hackers in rapidly evolving global political systems. In 2016, it seemed as though hackers held an outsized influence. Questions about the security of the 2016 election stemmed from concerns that electronic voting machines may have been compromised by foreign actors who had undoubtedly been motivated to influence the election. Those actors had been verifiably involved in public scandals at critical moments during the campaign season including the revelation of DNC emails to WikiLeaks.

These concerns were taken seriously by many inside the hacking community who began looking into technical concerns around these electronic voting machines, with hopes to confirm or debunk public concerns that a compromise of voting systems could sway an election's outcome. Starting in 2017, DEF CON began hosting an event to investigate these technical concerns in an informal, yet structured setting called the Voting Village. Each year, the Voting Village brings hackers together with collections of voting machines meant to be used to probe voting systems for vulnerabilities.

In the years since the Voting Village began, the event has drawn thousands of hackers interested in researching electronic voting systems in a collective effort to improve electoral systems in support of American democracy. Over the years, hackers involved in the Voting Village have identified many startling vulnerabilities in popular voting machines, demonstrating that both physical and remote attacks against the machines can be used to compromise the integrity of the votes they tabulate. These findings are then shared with the companies that produce the hardware and software used in these voting machines in hopes that the issues they find will be addressed.

The existence of the Voting Village reflects the relationship that now exists between hackers and the government. Once a relationship fraught with persecution against a misunderstood subculture by a misguided world, governments have come to realize just how much they need hackers on their side. Fueled by the exponential growth of networked computer technology, the hacking community has carved out a niche for itself against all odds, driven primarily by the human urge to understand. Over 40 years, hackers went from being social outcasts to being placed at the helm of world politics and armed conflict in a way that no other single working-class community has ever been.

On November 9, 2016, Hillary Clinton ended her presidential campaign and conceded to Donald Trump, paving the way for the Trump presidency. President Trump's "American Carnage" inauguration speech portrayed a fire-and-brimstone view of the American system, which had become increasingly alienated from social and political norms. The context for that alienation had been produced in large part by Internet-connected consumer technology that shapes the worldview of modern voters.

The Internet was supposed to be a salve for social isolation—a technology that brought people closer together—and in some ways it worked as advertised. In other ways, the Internet and its often-sarcastic abrasive culture exacerbated an already distressed socio-political fabric.

In an episode of the 1990s kids' television program *Ghostwriter*, a student offers to write a story about a hacker terrorizing their school. A young rebelliously dressed Julia Stiles with an attitude asks the student, "Do you know anything about hackers? Can you jam with the console cowboys in cyberspace?"

Like the cowboys of old, some believed that the online wild west and the hackers who inhabited it had been permanently tamed and put out to pasture. Corporate interests and governments have attempted to subdue and contain hackers as a resource to be used in the advancement of political and financial goals, but the job is incomplete. World powers found that they could train and recruit hackers. Governments had managed to cultivate their spaces, their culture, and to some degree, they were able to cultivate hackers themselves.

Everything that made the hacking community special, from applying their technical skills to military operations and re-appropriating their cultural humor to win political campaigns, has become commodities. Since the 1960s, world governments and politicians have found they could use hackers but that they couldn't subjugate the spirit of exploration that caused the hackers to exist in the first place.

Epilogue

In February 2022, Russia began its offensive into East Ukraine, immediately plunging the nation into chaos. As tanks rolled into strategic Eastern Ukrainian provinces, a major war mirroring the armed conflict broke out online and in the airwaves. Shortwave radio stations, which had long been hiding places for coded government transmissions lit up with activity in a way that had never been seen before. A wave of anti-Russian pirate radio stations began transmitting messages to crowd out Russian military signals meant to coordinate military activity in anticipation of an imminent invasion of Ukraine by the Russian military.

In the early morning hours of February 24, 2022, Russian President Vladimir Putin declared that the Russian military would undertake a "special military operation" in Ukraine. The instant President Putin's speech was finished, Russian cyberattacks against Ukrainian government systems began. The attacks coincided with artillery and missile barrages targeting Eastern Ukrainian military targets meant to pave the way for Russian military ground assets to roll into the country.

As was the case with the 2014 cyberattacks ahead of the Crimean annexation campaign, Russian hackers attacked communications targets belonging to the Ukrainian government with denial-of-service (DOS) attacks. Among the methods used was the deployment of wiper software, capable of damaging computer systems beyond immediate repair and rendering them inoperable.

Cyberattacks capable of imparting long-term damage to computer systems had previously been seen at an increasing rate in years past. Yet, it had rarely been seen as part of a coordinated military campaign to the scale witnessed during the opening hours of the 2022 Ukrainian invasion. Hackers had been directly involved in wartime activities for more than a decade by the time Russia invaded Ukraine, and their presence on the Ukrainian battlefield had become grotesquely routine. Ultimately, the participation of hackers in the opening volley of force leveled by Russia against Ukraine made little difference in the outcomes of a brutal war of attrition that continues to this day.

CISA

After the contentious 2016 presidential election, responsibility for the security of American elections was officially transferred to the Cybersecurity and Infrastructure Security Agency (CISA) in 2017. This change in stewardship was made in recognition of the need for election systems to be treated in the same way as the rest of America's critical infrastructure, such as gas and telecommunications. Threats to industrial systems, which include many categories of critical infrastructure, have also become popular targets of hackers in recent years. The realization that automated industrial systems can be prime targets of opportunity has led to an increase in the number of compromises heavy industry has suffered since 2016. Attacks against these industrial networks highlight the problem posed by opportunistic hackers in a world with an ever-growing reliance on technology.

Of particular interest to cybersecurity researchers has been a form of attack that encrypts files on a victim system called *ransomware*. After a breach occurs, attackers then target important corporate files, encrypting them on the victim's computers and, in some cases, transmitting the files back to the attackers to hold them until payment is received. The attackers then demand a fee for the key used to decrypt the sensitive information and keep the files private. If the victim fails to pay in the allotted timeframe, the attackers may release the files, creating even greater problems for the victim.

Ransomware has become such a problem for corporations that many have sought the FBI's assistance in curbing the ransomware's threat. In the beginning, the FBI had difficulty taking the threat seriously. FBI leadership viewed ransomware as an "ankle-biter crime," hearkening back to their distant history of dismissing objectionable criminal activity just because it took place online.[1]

Ransomware has become a major factor in the evolution of illegal hacking gangs into multimillion-dollar organizations that resemble the same corporate entities they target. Illegal hacking as a big business has created significant problems for modern lawmakers. Despite new technologies designed to help blunt the effect of ransomware worldwide, it continues to pose challenges to cybersecurity practitioners.

Despite (and possibly exacerbated by) the Federal Bureau of Investigation's (FBI's) initial dismissal of ransomware, this criminal activity took on a life of its own and produced a highly profitable global criminal enterprise that seemed nearly impossible to stop. The increase in ransomware attacks through the latter years of the 2010s and into the early 2020s helped create an entirely

---

[1] https://www.propublica.org/article/fbi-ransomware-hunting-team-cybercrime

new industry of cyber-insurance to help companies deal with the effects of being targeted by hackers.

Added to CISA's workload in recent years is the responsibility to protect American elections from cyberattacks and other forms of interference that may compromise the legitimacy of voting systems. CISA, and specifically its director at the time, Chris Krebs came under attack after the 2020 election by Donald Trump and his followers. Trump took issue with Krebs when he countered Trump's accusation that the 2020 election had been compromised to favor his opponent, Joe Biden. As a result, Trump used the final days of his presidency to fire Krebs as the director of CISA.[2]

Pillar II

In the modern landscape of high-value corporate network breaches, new approaches have been imagined for how companies can and should respond to them. One idea that has gained some prominence in the last decade is opening legal pathways for companies to employ their own offensive hackers to "hack back" those that have attacked them.

These so-called hack-back concepts have been viewed as controversial for several reasons, not least of which is that identifying source networks where hackers come from is notoriously fraught with uncertainty. This uncertainty stems from the dramatic improvements to the operational security that hackers use to hide themselves. Therefore, allowing companies to legally engage in what amounts to corporate espionage in any other form is seen by many in the hacking community as a dubious prospect.

---

[2]https://www.cnn.com/2023/07/25/politics/chris-krebs-special-counsel/index.html

However, the underlying concept of hacking the hackers appeared to some in American leadership to have merit under the right circumstances.

After the 2016 election, a significant rise in organized crime driven by ransomware turned cybercrime into a billion-dollar industry unto itself. According to the FBI's Internet Crime Complaint Center (IC3), cybercrime cost companies $1.5 billion in damages in 2016. By 2021, this number ballooned to nearly $7 billion.[3] In response to the growing threat, the Biden administration outlined an ambitious national cybersecurity strategy to combat the worsening state of cybercrime in 2023.[4]

The success of this national cybersecurity strategy relies heavily on relationships built between the government and their counterparts within the hacking community. In particular, Pillar II, called "Disrupt and Dismantle Threat Actors," hinges on the participation of nongovernment affiliated hackers for its success. Pillar II calls for the U.S. government to use "all instruments of national power to disrupt and dismantle threat actors whose actions threaten our interests." Notably, Pillar II specifies that the government may utilize diplomatic and military resources (specifically including both kinetic and cyber) to accomplish the goals of the national strategy.

For many years, computer security experts have debated the best way to respond to cybersecurity threats presented by ransomware gangs and other forms of organized cybercrime, including so-called hack-back schemes, which would have enabled companies to hire their own cyber mercenaries to attack the attackers. Pillar II responds to this concept with the legitimacy and coordination of a government operation.

---

[3]https://www.statista.com/chart/20845/financial-losses-suffered-by-victims-of-internet-crimes/
[4]https://www.whitehouse.gov/wp-content/uploads/2023/03/National-Cybersecurity-Strategy-2023.pdf

Cyberwarfare in the 2020s

As it had been in the late 2010s, cyberwar of the 2020s is being dictated by the ongoing territorial conflict between Ukraine and Russia. Both sides of this armed conflict have produced their own assets dedicated to engaging in online information warfare, keeping the concept of cyberwar alive and well. Counterintuitively, as more cyberwar strategy is seen on the world's battlefields, the less serious the threat seems to have become. In the 1980s, fears of cyberwarfare existed alongside the threat of nuclear war. The idea that a hacker could single-handedly launch or detonate a nuclear weapon has remained firmly in the realm of fantasy, However, the idea of what practically constitutes cyberwar in the modern era seems to involve something more akin to industrial warfare.

This isn't to say that cyberwarfare isn't a serious concept; rather, its consequences are less about life and death than was originally believed. The cyberwarfare threats demonstrated in the past 10 years have much more significant financial consequences than any other outcome. As was the case in the 2017 "NotPetya" attacks (thought to be a part of the ongoing war between Russia and Ukraine), the attacks did, in fact, touch the lives of average Ukrainian citizens by interrupting the availability of monetary transactions, resulting in several downstream effects, including making public transit much more difficult to use during the attack's duration. However, the true risks of cyberwarfare involves the concept of "collateral damage." In recent attacks, including the 2017 ransomware attack involving the NotPetya malware, the effects of the attack spread well beyond the intended target.

During the deployment of the NotPetya malware, a worldwide financial impact occurred as a result of the uncontrolled spread of the malware beyond the Ukrainian borders. The malware's effects were felt in the pocketbooks of global corporations, with losses during the attack globally calculated to be in the hundreds of millions of U.S. dollars. Ongoing business shutdowns and interruptions of the worldwide digital financial system does represent a serious threat to global stability. Nations must take care to reduce the potential for these sorts of outcomes as much as possible to avoid uncontrolled military conflicts in the future. It's possible that as more decision-making is handed off to artificial intelligence (AI) this concept will evolve in the distant future.

The Way from Here

During the 2020 COVID-19 pandemic, the global reliance on the Internet for meeting social needs grew tremendously. The social aspects of hacking communities have always depended on healthy online spaces to facilitate socializing. During the first two to three years of the pandemic, many conferences previously held in person, moved to online streaming. This made attendance at these conferences much more accessible and offered opportunities for new conferences to get started.

One notable example is the online-only PancakesCon, which emphasizes talks that are part technical and part personal interest. The fundamental concept of PancakesCon is an acknowledgment that hackers are people who've developed interests both inside and outside of technical work. PancakesCon is one of the most anticipated conferences of the year for hackers who appreciate the equal passion speakers of the conference bring for *both* computer technology and niche interest hobbies. As the impacts of the pandemic have begun to ease since 2020, many hacking conferences that took place in-person before the pandemic have returned to operation.

Thanks to a successful 40-year campaign from pop culture, media sources, and the government, hackers have gone from being laughed at to being serious power brokers in the 21st century. Through it all, hackers have maintained a sense of humor about themselves and their work that has attracted new generations of both professional and casual hackers.

Overall, the nature of modern hacking culture is more open, accepting, and supportive now than it has ever been before. Although many of the cultural hallmarks of the hacking community remain intact, many obstacles that made entry to a career in hacking difficult have been removed. With a wealth of freely accessible resources to learn and practice technical skills, it's hard to predict what will come in the next century, but what is certain is that hackers will play a decisive role in what's to come.

Acknowledgments

I'd like to thank those who acted as resources for me throughout the production of this book, including the Wiley production team. To mention a few, thanks to my draft editor, Jan Lynn Neal, for reading the roughest of my rough drafts and Pete Gaughan for helping shepherd the project through the publication process. Finally, thanks to Jim Minatel for his patience as the material came together and for giving this project a shot in the first place. Without the team at Wiley, this book would never have been possible.

I want to especially thank my wife, Amanda Crose, for helping proofread various chapters and for keeping home life together during late nights, writing, and rewriting the material for this book. I would also like to thank my mother, Lori Crose, for financially supporting this effort.

I'd also like to thank those who made themselves available to answer questions and clarify historical details. Members of the hacking community have been particularly helpful in writing this book, including Gene Spafford, Kevin Poulsen, and Marc Rogers, all of whom saw the value of a book like this and lent their time to its success. Finally, I'd like to give a special thanks to Emma Best, who helped verify deep lore found exclusively in declassified documents, which can often be difficult to decipher.

About the Author

Emily Crose is a cybersecurity practitioner and researcher of hacking history. Emily has been an avid participant in the hacking scene, speaking at several conferences over the years on topics ranging from computer network defense research to technical ethics and responsibility.

Emily is a former technical intelligence officer in the U.S. intelligence community, working for various agencies, including the National Security Agency (NSA) and Central Intelligence Agency (CIA) and US Army Intelligence and Security Command (INSCOM). She is also featured in several permanent exhibits on network exploitation at the International Spy Museum in Washington, D.C.

Index